365 Prayers

& Activations

FOR ENTERING THE

Courts of Heaven

DESTINY IMAGE BOOKS
BY ROBERT HENDERSON

Unlocking Wealth from the Courts of Heaven

Breaking the Stronghold of Iniquity (with Bill Dennington)

Show Us Your Glory

*Praying for the Prophetic Destiny of the United States and
the Presidency of Donald J. Trump from the Courts of Heaven*

Father, Friend, and Judge

*Issuing Divine Restraining Orders from the Courts of Heaven
(with Dr. Francis Myles)*

Redeeming Your Bloodline (with Hrvoje Sirovina)

The Cloud of Witnesses in the Courts of Heaven

Prayers and Declarations that Open the Courts of Heaven

Receiving Healing from the Courts of Heaven, Curriculum

Accessing the Courts of Heaven

Unlocking Destinies from the Courts of Heaven, Curriculum

Operating in the Courts of Heaven

Daily Revelation for
Supernatural Breakthrough

365 Prayers
& Activations
FOR ENTERING THE
Courts of Heaven

Robert Henderson

DESTINY IMAGE® PUBLISHERS, INC.
P.O. Box 310, Shippensburg, PA 17257-0310
"Promoting Inspired Lives."

This book and all other Destiny Image and Destiny Image Fiction books are available at Christian bookstores and distributors worldwide.

Cover design by Eileen Rockwell.

For more information on foreign distributors, call 717-532-3040.

Reach us on the Internet: www.destinyimage.com.

ISBN 13 TP: 978-0-7684-5591-5

ISBN 13 eBook: 978-0-7684-5568-7

ISBN 13 HC: 978-0-7684-5567-0

ISBN 13 LP: 978-0-7684-5590-8

For Worldwide Distribution, Printed in the U.S.A.

1 2 3 4 5 6 7 8 / 24 23 22 21 20

Contents

May

Introduction

This devotional is designed to help you step into the Courts of Heaven on a daily basis and present your case before the supreme Judge of all. Scripture tell us in Hebrews 12:23 that God is this Judge. He rules the judicial system of Heaven that is referred to as the Courts of Heaven:

> *...to the general assembly and church of the firstborn who are registered in heaven, to God the Judge of all, to the spirits of just men made perfect.*

We know that we shall all stand in the end and give an account for how we have lived before this Judge. However, He is presently sitting as Judge to rule, considering affairs in this life. Especially in things regarding those who belong to Him and are those He has chosen. We have the right to come before Him as Judge and present cases. Isaiah 43:26 encourages us in this.

> *Put Me in remembrance; let us contend together; state your case, that you may be acquitted.*

The purpose of this 365-day devotional is to help us in this process. As you go through this devotional on a daily basis, be encouraged to do several things:

- Read and meditate on the Scripture and thought for the day. Allow the precious Holy Spirit to speak beyond what is written and bring personal revelation.

- Picture yourself standing in the Courts of Heaven before the Judge who desires to render decisions in your behalf. As you stand there presenting your case, allow the Lord to search your heart.

- As you pray the prayer attached to each day's devotion, allow the Holy Spirit to *add* to it. Let it be a jumping off place for you in your contending before the Courts for your breakthrough.

This devotional has been written with thoughts and Scriptures being gathered in themes. In other words, as you walk through this each day, there will be a theme that is bunched together for several days. As you engage yourself in this, believe that new realms will unlock in your spirit and over your life. By the time this has been done over a year's time, operating in the Courts of Heaven should be a much easier process. Plus I believe you will have experienced new dimensions of breakthrough for you, your family, and the assignment you have from God.

Be bold in your God. He is waiting as the Judge to hear your case!

THREE REALMS OF PRAYER

Now it came to pass, as He was praying in a certain place, when
He ceased, that one of His disciples said to Him, "Lord, teach us
*to pray, as John also taught his disciples." —*Luke 11:1

In response to the disciples asking Him to teach them to pray, Jesus put prayer in *three* dimensions in the Book of Luke. He placed it in approaching God as Father, Friend, and Judge. We must allow the Holy Spirit to reveal to us these three realms of prayer, one of which is approaching God as Judge in His judicial system. Understanding these three realms of prayer can change the way we see God and then approach Him. Our perspective of who God is radically affects the way we pray and petition the Lord in His glory. We must ask the Lord for the Spirit of wisdom and revelation to bring us ever-increasing insight to His true nature in all three of these dimensions mentioned (Eph. 1:17). As we grow in the knowledge of who God is, our prayers will be empowered. The result will be changed lives, situations, and breakthroughs.

Lord, as I stand before You, I ask for the revelation and
understanding of who You are. Thank You that because of Your
blood shed for me I can approach You as my Father, as my Friend,
and as my Judge. I take great delight in allowing the Holy Spirit
to teach me how to relate to You in these three realms. Thank
You for the revelation I have and that which I will have and is
to come.

APPROACHING GOD AS FATHER

So He said to them, "When you pray, say: Our Father in heaven, hallowed be Your name. Your kingdom come. Your will be done on earth as it is in heaven." —Luke 11:2

God as our Father is basic to any and all prayer. We will never go any deeper in prayer than our revelation of Him as Father allows. We must have the *spirit of adoption* create in our heart the cry of *"Abba Father"* (Rom. 8:15). This brings revelation of who God truly is. It deals with any religious version of God that the devil would use to pollute our ideas of God and His activities toward us. This will set the platform for our operation in the Courts of Heaven. Most if not all people carry wounds or at least issues in their hearts from insufficient fathering. With the spirit of adoption, the Holy Spirit comes and brings revelation of God as Father. This allows us to come *boldly* before Him without fear and ask abundantly from our covenant position. We are children of the Most High God. First John 3:1–2 speaks of the wonderful love of the Father that has made us His child. Nothing can separate us from Him or His love (Rom. 8:38–39).

> *Lord, I come before You by faith as my loving, benevolent, and caring Father. I thank You that any insufficient fathering I have had in my life that created a wrong perspective of You would now be changed, healed, and removed. I want to see You in the true nature of who You are, that with boldness and reverence I might approach You. Thank You so much.*

APPROACHING GOD AS FRIEND

And He said to them, "Which of you shall have a friend,
and go to him at midnight and say to him, 'Friend,
lend me three loaves...'?" —Luke 11:5

As we approach God in the way Jesus taught us to pray, we are to approach Him as our Friend. As our Friend Jesus said there would be a revelation of secrets that would be shared. He told us we would no longer be servants, but we would be esteemed to be friends with God (John 15:15). As a result of this friendship, Jesus would faithfully reveal the things He was receiving from the Father. The secrets we would know, would empower our prayer life as they empowered Abraham as God's friend (James 2:23). Abraham prayed for Sodom and Gomorrah from the secret God told him. As a result of this revelation, Abraham knew that this wicked place was under judgment and would be destroyed (Gen.18:16–17). Abraham as the friend of God from this secret began to intercede for the future of Sodom and Gomorrah. The purpose of God revealing this secret to Abraham was not so he could prophesy it, but so he could pray from it as God's friend. As the friends of God, we must rightly steward the secrets God revealed to us. The result can be an altering of events that would otherwise devastate life in the earth.

> *Lord, as I approach You as my Friend, I thank You that You desire*
> *to share Your secrets with me. I humbly approach You and ask that*
> *from these secrets You will allow me the grace to pray. As I pray*
> *from the revelation You bring to me as Your friend, things will*
> *change in my life and the life of others. I take my place without fear*
> *with You as a friend of God. From this place I stand and intercede*
> *based on the secrets You reveal to me by Your Holy Spirit.*

APPROACHING GOD AS JUDGE

There was in a certain city a judge who did not fear God nor regard man. Now there was a widow in that city; and she came to him, saying, "Get justice for me from my adversary."
—Luke 18:2–3

The third dimension of prayer that Jesus taught is approaching God as Judge. If this widow could get a decision from an unjust judge, how much more can we come before God as our righteous Judge and see a verdict of justice be rendered in our behalf. He will hear and decree on our behalf righteous decisions that cannot be reversed. As we stand before the Lord as Judge in the judicial system of Heaven, any legal right the adversary, the devil, is claiming, we can see revoked. First Peter 5:8 lets us know that the devil as our adversary, or legal opponent, is seeking a legal right to devour us. From our place before God as Judge we can see any and all legal rights removed because of Jesus and His blood speaking for us (Heb. 12:24). This alone overcomes every accusation satan would seek to use against us. Revelation 12:11 clearly proclaims we overcome every assault against us by the blood of the Lamb.

Lord, as I come before Your throne, I step into the judicial system of Heaven. I thank You that from this place in the Spirit there will be righteous verdicts released that will set justice in place for me and all that concerns me. I thank You that the blood of the Lamb is speaking on my behalf. What the blood is saying grants You, Lord, as Judge what is legally necessary for my forgiveness, redemption, and destiny secured. I thank You that You are the righteous Judge who always does right. Thank You that from the justice of Your throne every evil against me is vindicated. My righteousness is from You (Isa. 54:17). Lord, arise and defend me as Your servant, and set my future for good in order.

WORSHIP AND THE ATMOSPHERE OF THE COURTS

A fiery stream issued and came forth from before Him. A thousand thousands ministered to Him; ten thousand times ten thousand stood before Him. The court was seated, and the books were opened. —Daniel 7:10

There is a very real court that exists in the heavenly realm. This Court is available for us to approach and bring our petitions to for divine judgments. As we come before this Court, we should do so in worship with the myriads that are also there. Worship creates the atmosphere these courts operate from. Revelation 5:8–14 reveals that the worship that begins in Heaven permeates all of God's creation. This worship allows an atmosphere conducive to the functioning of the Courts of Heaven. Real worship originates in Heaven and touches every other part of creation. Worship doesn't start with us. We are touched by the worship that begins in the Courts of Heaven. As we *join* this worship, the atmosphere is created for the operation of the Courts of Heaven. The result will be an entering into a spirit dimension where we can present our case in and see decision rendered on our behalf.

> *Lord, as I come before Your Court, I join the heavenly realm and the worship of the tens of thousands that ascend before Your throne. As I worship, allow me to enter the atmosphere that Your Court operates in. Lord, I love and adore You as the King of all the earth. May Your glory cover the earth as the waters cover the seas (Hab. 2:14). May Your name be known and Your majesty revealed. I come to stand in awe of You as the Judge of all the earth and bring my petitions before this Court. Lord, hear my cry and my petition that I make before You today.*

BOOKS OF DESTINY

A fiery stream issued and came forth from before Him. A
thousand thousands ministered to Him; ten thousand times ten
thousand stood before Him. The court was seated, and the books
were opened. —Daniel 7:10

As we stand before the Courts of Heaven there are books that are opened. These books contain our destiny and purpose for existing (Ps. 139:16). We must discern prophetically what is written about us before time began. This is essential in that any petition we make before the Court must be in agreement with what is in the books. This is why the Court is seated, or comes to session, and the books are then opened. The evidence the Courts will rule on come out of these books. As we discern what is written about us, we then present this as our petition and case before His Courts. We place God in remembrance of what He wrote about us in these books (Isa. 43:26). As we bring this before Him, we ask that He as Judge would render a decision that allows all that is our destiny and future to be ordered and set in place. We ask that everything necessary for us to fulfill what He wrote about us would be granted.

> *Lord, I come before Your Court seeking to agree with what is*
> *written about me in Your books. I ask for spiritual and prophetic*
> *understanding to see what is written about me. Lord, in Your*
> *books are my purpose and future. By faith I present before You*
> *that which You have spoken of in these books. I ask for all that has*
> *been written to become a reality in my life. Allow everything that*
> *is necessary to come to divine arrangement that I might live out*
> *in earth now what was written about me. I ask before You, Lord,*
> *that any hindrances and obstacles would be removed. Lord, I*
> *believe and receive from Your Courts blessings that produce the*
> *fulfillment of my destiny in the earth.*

DESIRES, DESTINY, AND FUTURES

*Your eyes saw my substance, being yet unformed. And in Your
book they all were written, the days fashioned for me, when as
yet there were none of them.* —Psalm 139:16

God imagined and dreamed us up. He saw our substance before it existed. He wrote it in His book. Our substance speaks of our DNA. It is what makes us unique. It is what makes us desire certain things and dislike other things. It is what makes us interested in certain things and not interested in others. It determines our gifting and what we are good at. To discover what is in the books of Heaven about you, pay attention to your desires. Present these before the Courts of Heaven as petitions. Second Timothy 1:9 lets us know that grace and purpose were given to us before time began. This means that before we existed in the earth, grace and purpose were already appointed to us. They have been waiting on us to discover them. As a result of the grace that is attached to our divine purpose, certain desires are created in us. From these desires, we can ascertain the reason for our living in the earth in this age and at this time. We can become aware of the destiny and future we were made for.

> *Lord, as I come before Your Courts, thank You for dreaming me up. Help me to be aware of how You created me and the desires and gifts I have. Lord, I bring these to You and ask that all You have created me for would be realized. Allow me to fulfill the desires You placed in me so that Your will through me might be done. Allow me to be aware of the purpose and grace that has been appointed to me. I desire with passion to live out what You wrote about me before time began.*

NUMBERING MY DAYS

Your eyes saw my substance, being yet unformed. And in Your book they all were written, the days fashioned for me, when as yet there were none of them. —Psalm 139:16

Written in the books of Heaven about us is the number of days assigned to us on the earth. These are the days we have been given to fulfill what is written in His book about us. We must use these days wisely so that all our assigned purpose might be accomplished. Psalm 90:12 tells us to number our days or to be careful with them. In other words, we are to make sure we are using them wisely, investing ourselves in the purposes of God assigned to us. Otherwise the days will pass and become weeks; the weeks, months; the months, years; the years, decades; and the decades, a lifetime. We will have spent our life on something other than the purpose and destiny of God written in our books. May we not squander the time God has granted us in this life. The days were fashioned for us when there was yet none of them. We are here to fulfill all that was assigned to us in the time granted us from the books of Heaven.

Lord, as I stand before Your Courts, I ask for wisdom and discipline to use my days correctly. I want to be faithful with my days that I might accomplish my assigned purpose from You. I ask for strength and grace to be able to fully complete all that was written about me in Your book. Help me not squander my time. Teach me, Lord, wisdom that I might number my days and use them for Your divine purpose belonging to me. I desire to fully complete what is my portion in this life that I might stand before You in the next one without fear, shame, or embarrassment. Lord, help me to be Your servant.

CAUSING GOD TO REMEMBER

*Put Me in remembrance; let us contend together; state your
case, that you may be acquitted.* —Isaiah 43:26

One of the main ways we present cases before the Courts of Heaven is by putting God in remembrance. We should tell Him what He wrote in His book about us. What is our prophetic destiny that has been established before time began? (See Second Timothy 1:9.) We take this purpose of God for our lives and present it as a case before His Courts. When we do this, we are presenting a petition before Him that allows a judicial decision to be rendered. This requires us to have a prophetic awareness of God's intent for our life. With this we begin to ask Him for what He planned for us before the earth was formed. We also should ask that anything that would prevent this from happening to be revoked. As we approach the Courts on this basis, we are presenting our case by putting Him in remembrance and according to His purpose concerning us.

> *Lord, as I come before Your Courts, I ask for clear prophetic understanding of what is written in Your book concerning me. I ask, Lord, that my purpose for existing on the earth would be fulfilled. Would You please cause every resistance to the fulfillment of my destiny to be removed? Lord, I ask that every hindrance is taken out of the way, and let all the things necessary for what is in Your book concerning me be done in Your divine order!*

BOOKS OF REMEMBRANCE

Then those who feared the Lord spoke to one another, and the Lord listened and heard them; so a book of remembrance was written before Him for those who fear the Lord and who meditate on His name. —Malachi 3:16

Books of remembrance in Heaven speak before the Lord and cause Him to *remember* us. These books speak in the Courts of Heaven and testify in our behalf. They cause the Lord to remember our petitions that come before Him. We should be diligent to see these books created and speak before the Lord concerning us! We are told that when we speak often with one another about the Lord, these books are written concerning us. This means our fellowship and communion with one another around the Lord causes these books to be created. As we also walk in the fear of the Lord, these books come into existence. They will speak before the Courts of Heaven and cause God to remember us and our families.

> *Lord, as I come before You, I ask that books of remembrance would be written and speak before You concerning me and my family. I ask that it would be known in Heaven that we fear You and meditate on Your name. Lord, we speak often to others in the Body of Christ in fellowship and communion. May it be recorded in Heaven that we are Your people. May books speak before You that cause us to be remembered and heard before Your Courts. May the case we present be known by You.*

REMEMBERED BY GOD

*Then God remembered Rachel, and God listened to her and
opened her womb. And she conceived and bore a son, and said,
"God has taken away my reproach." —Genesis 30:22–23*

Rachel had been unable to bear children. Through her persistent cry to God, God remembered her. The result of God remembering her was He listened to her and opened her womb. Her deepest desire and longing was fulfilled because God remembered His daughter. When God remembers us, prayers we have been praying for a long time are suddenly answered. Our case presented before His Courts puts Him in remembrance. Decisions are rendered and the passions of our heart are met. When fruitfulness comes, the reproach we carry in our hearts is removed. We were made to be productive and fruitful. The absence of this frustrates and speaks against us, if only in our own minds. When God remembers us and fruitfulness occurs, this reproach is rolled away. The way we see ourselves changes. We have a new sense of worth and satisfaction because the fruitfulness of the Lord is being poured through us.

> *Lord, as I stand before Your Courts, I ask that You remember
> me and listen to my cry. Lord, I pray every place of fruitlessness
> in my life would come to an end. Lord, please remember me
> and take away my barrenness on every level. Hear me, O God,
> as I call and remember Your servant that Your name might be
> glorified and my passion be fulfilled.*

REGARDED AND ESTEEMED BY GOD

*Then God remembered Noah, and every living thing, and all
the animals that were with him in the ark. And God made a
wind to pass over the earth, and the waters subsided.*
—Genesis 8:1

Noah and his family were the only ones yet alive on the earth after the flood. We must ask, if this is so, how could God forget them and not remember them. We see therefore that being remembered by God is not just God being aware of us. Being remembered by God is declaring God is regarding us and ready to move on our behalf. When God remembers us from His Courts, our petition is about to be granted. The word *remember* means to *mark*. It speaks of designating something that belongs to another. When God remembers us, it is because we are *marked* as belonging to Him. The result of God remembering Noah was a wind blowing across the land drying up the waters of the flood. God began to move on behalf of Noah and His creation. That which belonged to God, He moved for. It is a very special thing when God remembers us. It is not that He doesn't know us. He knows all things. It is that He is positioning Himself to now move on behalf of that which is marked as being His. Move, O God, in us and for us!

> *Lord, as I approach Your Courts, I ask that You remember me. According to the Word, I ask that I might be regarded by You and that You would ready Yourself to move on my behalf. Thank You for being mindful of me and remembering me. Thank You, Lord, that what I ask of You now occurs because I am known by God and remembered by You. Your mark is on my life, and I am designated as belonging to You.*

APPROACHING ON THE BASIS OF COVENANT

And I prayed to the Lord my God, and made confession,
and said, "O Lord, great and awesome God, who keeps His
covenant and mercy with those who love Him, and with those
who keep His commandments." —Daniel 9:4

Daniel was beseeching the Lord to bring His people out of captivity at the appointed time Jeremiah had prophesied. According to the prophetic word of Jeremiah, they would be in Babylon for seventy years. Daniel understood the time of their promised deliverance was near. As a result, he began to petition the Lord. His beginning statements in His prayers were to remind God of the covenant He had with His people. Covenant is the basis by which we approach God. We should remind Him of the covenant we have with Him through the body and blood of Jesus. This is the right we have to stand before Him and ask for His deliverance, blessing, life, healing, and all other benefits of belonging to Him. Our covenant with God through Jesus's sacrifice causes God to remember us. Be bold as a covenant person, and request the provisions belonging to you by virtue of what Jesus has done for us and the covenant it has provided!

> *Lord, as I come before Your Courts, I come as one bought by the body and the blood of Jesus Christ. According to Your Word, I am not my own. I belong to You based on Jesus buying me back as His covenant possession. Lord, now based on my covenant position with You, I ask for Your blessings, benefits, and bonuses to come into my life. I ask that all that is rightfully mine through Your sacrifice would now manifest in my life. I thank you that my life, health, family, and provision are abundantly blessed because of the covenant made through Your death, burial, and resurrection.*

GROANING BEFORE GOD

Now it happened in the process of time that the king of Egypt died. Then the children of Israel groaned because of the bondage, and they cried out; and their cry came up to God because of the bondage. So God heard their groaning, and God remembered His covenant with Abraham, with Isaac, and with Jacob. And God looked upon the children of Israel, and God acknowledged them. —Exodus 2:23–25

Not only did God remember the children of Israel because of His covenant with their forefathers, but He also heard their groaning. Groanings are not just the result of hardship and fatigue. They also are birthed by the Spirit of God. Romans 8:26 speaks of "groanings" that come from the intercession of the Holy Spirit in us. As the people of God groaned in their place of trouble, God heard them, looked upon them, and acknowledged or remembered them. There is a groaning born of the Spirit of God that grasps the attention of God. When this occurs, we are remembered before His Court and have the petition we are desiring from Him. As we bring our request before the Lord, we should be yielded in our hearts to the Holy Spirit creating and producing these groanings. They can be powerful before His presence.

Lord, as I come and bring my petitions before Your Courts, I thank You that my groanings and sighs are heard before You. Lord, thank You that I am remembered before You. Not only those groaning that come from my own fatigue and weariness in my situations, but also that born of Your Spirit. I yield myself for this intercession of the Holy Spirit to pour through me on my behalf and also other things needing Your touch. Lord, allow me to be a conduit through which Your passions can be met. I want to join with You through the intercession of the Holy Spirit moving in my life.

BUILDING GOD'S HOUSE—
REMEMBERED BY GOD

Remember me, O my God, concerning this, and do not wipe out my good deeds that I have done for the house of my God, and for its services! —Nehemiah 13:14

Nehemiah in the process of rebuilding the city of Jerusalem and reinstitution of worship did good deeds for the house of God and its services. As he prayed, he presented his case before God and asked that the good he had done for God's house would be remembered and not forgotten. If we have served in the house of God, if we have given finances in the house of God, if we in any way have helped the house of God to prosper, we can ask to be remembered because of this. We can present our case before the Lord and ask for favorable decisions from Him as Judge based on the care we have shown to His house and His people. One of the Lord's greatest passions is His house. This is why it was said of Jesus, *"Zeal for Your house has eaten Me up"* (John 2:17). His passion is His house. Whoever will give themselves to seeing it built up and not diminished will be remembered before God. We can then come before His Courts and ask to be heard because of our heart for His house.

Lord, as I come before Your Courts, I ask that the good I have done for Your house would be remembered. I ask that my good deeds would not be wiped out. Let my passion for Your house stir Your heart toward me. Lord, as I have remembered Your house, now remember me and my house. Let us stand before You and be accepted and received. Lord, from this place I now present my petitions and request. Lord, move on my behalf and hear the cry of my heart that I make before You this day. Move on my behalf, and let Your servant be received before Your Courts.

REPAID WITH GOOD

It may be that the Lord will look on my affliction, and that the
Lord will repay me with good for his cursing this day.
—2 Samuel 16:12

David was running from his own son Absalom, who had taken his throne and rulership from him. David and those with him were leaving Jerusalem in fear of their lives. As Shimei curses David and accuses him of all sort of atrocities, Abishai asks David for permission to take Shimei out. David responds with this verse. David understood that God from His throne can look on unrighteous affliction and repay it with good into our lives. There is justice in God. We can learn how to take our difficulties, afflictions, and things we suffer as believers and present them as a case before God. We can take the criticisms and judgments of others against us and use them to present cases on our behalf. This will cause God to remember us and move on our behalf. Our sufferings can speak for us before His Courts. As we maintain a good heart in the midst of these things and trust in the righteous Judge who judges righteously, God will speak for us and vindicate us.

> *Lord, as I come before Your Court, I would remind You of the injustice done against me. I forgive any and all who have done these things. However, Lord, I ask for vindication in the midst of the suffering, hardship, and assaults I have endured as Your child. Arise, O God, and vindicate Your servant. May I be repaid for any and all affliction I have suffered for Your name's sake. I ask, Lord, that You would be glorified and that I would stand justified in Your sight.*

OUR ACCUSER

Then I heard a loud voice saying in heaven, "Now salvation, and strength, and the kingdom of our God, and the power of His Christ have come, for the accuser of our brethren, who accused them before our God day and night, has been cast down." —Revelation 12:10

The word *accuser* is the Greek word *kategoros*. It means *a complainant at law or in a judicial system*. It is also the word we get *category* from. The accuser of the brethren brings accusation against us by seeking to categorize us and label us. This is designed to place limits on us that God is not placing. This keeps us out of what is written in the books of Heaven about us. We must go before the Lord and present our case to undo every limitation satan as our accuser would bring. As we do this, the limits that so often seem to be on us are removed. We are able to step into the liberty and freedom we were designed for. Our family, our finances, our dreams, and our destinies are then free to come to fulfillment and fullness. One of the main ways the accuser *categorizes* us is in our own thinking. As we deal with his case against us in the Courts of Heaven, our minds become freed to believe and think the right things about ourselves.

> *Lord, as I come before Your Courts, I thank You that I have a destiny written in the books of Heaven. I ask that every accusation that would be against me from the accuser would now be silenced and removed. I ask that the way I think about myself and what I believe would line up with what is written in the books of Heaven concerning me. I ask, Lord, that all efforts of the devil to categorize me would now be revoked. I declare I am now free to be what is written in my book and not be conformed to what the satanic would say. Thank You so much, Lord, for this.*

OVERCOMING THE ACCUSER

Then I heard a loud voice saying in heaven, "Now salvation, and strength, and the kingdom of our God, and the power of His Christ have come, for the accuser of our brethren, who accused them before our God day and night, has been cast down. And they overcame him by the blood of the Lamb and by the word of their testimony, and they did not love their lives to the death." —Revelation 12:10–11

The efforts of the accuser to categorize us are revoked through the power of the blood of Jesus, the word of our testimony, and laying our lives down. These are three ways we overcome the efforts of the accuser against us and our destinies. The blood will undo any and every case against us. The word of our testimony is how we present our own case before the Lord. Not loving our lives to the death is how we gain new realms of authority before His Courts. We must take the blood of Jesus and agree with what it is speaking for us before His Courts (Heb.12:24). It is not enough to undo cases with the blood. We must also present our own case based on what is written in our books. This is the word of our testimony. When we take up our cross and lay our lives down, we gain for ourselves a new place of authority and power before the Lord and His Courts. From this we can present cases that can have great impact.

Lord, as I come before Your Courts, I thank You that every effort of the devil to put me in a box with limits attached is frustrated by You. I thank You that Your blood is speaking for me to undo all accusations against me. They lose the right to define me. I thank You that I present from prophetic understanding my case before Your Courts and receive what is written in the books of heaven for me. I also thank You that I have grace to lay my life down and serve You acceptably with reverence and godly fear (Heb. 12:28). Thank You that every word against me is silent and all of Heaven now speaks on my behalf.

THE BLOOD OF THE LAMB

Then I heard a loud voice saying in heaven, "Now salvation,
and strength, and the kingdom of our God, and the power
of His Christ have come, for the accuser of our brethren, who
accused them before our God day and night, has been cast
down. And they overcame him by the blood of the Lamb and by
the word of their testimony, and they did not love their lives to
the death." —Revelation 12:10–11

As we approach the Courts of Heaven, there are accusations the accuser would use against us. These are to deny us what is written in our books. This is why so many people have an intuitive sense that they were made for more, but they can't seem to get into it. It is because there is a case in the spirit world against you. It can be your own sin; the sin in your generations or bloodline, which is called iniquity in the Scripture; words spoken against you by others in authority; or other activities used by the devil. We must know how by faith to take the blood Jesus shed for us and use it to silence all these words and accusations. We do this primarily through repentance. When we through repentance agree with what the blood is speaking, we are vindicated, justified, and declared innocent. What the blood is saying about us overwhelms every accusation of the devil. Those words assaulting us and our destiny in the spirit world are now denied the right to effect and influence. The blood of Jesus has silenced them and all that would speak against us.

Lord, as I stand before Your Courts, I thank You that the blood
of Jesus is now speaking for me. According to Hebrews 12:24, the
blood of sprinkling is speaking better things than that of Abel.
Abel's blood cried for justice against his brother, Cain. Jesus's

blood, however, is crying for mercy, redemption, and forgiveness. Thank You, Lord, that because of Jesus's blood You now have every legal right to forgive us and silence the accuser against us. By faith I repent and come into agreement with Your Word. I ask that every place I have sinned or my ancestors have rebelled against You, that the legal right of the devil would be revoked to use this against me, because of what Jesus's blood is saying. Thank You so much for the blood!

THE WORD OF OUR TESTIMONY

Then I heard a loud voice saying in heaven, "Now salvation, and strength, and the kingdom of our God, and the power of His Christ have come, for the accuser of our brethren, who accused them before our God day and night, has been cast down. And they overcame him by the blood of the Lamb and by the word of their testimony, and they did not love their lives to the death." —Revelation 12:10–11

We overcome every accusation against us by the blood of the Lamb. However, we then must know how to present our own case before the Lord in His Courts. This is what the "word of our testimony" is. A judge must have a case presented to render verdicts on our behalf. Silencing the accuser is not enough. We must present our own case for judgments and decisions to be rendered for us. We present our case from the opened books before the Court (Dan. 7:10). Out of these books we have prophetic understanding of our destiny and purpose. We then take this that we prophetically sense and offer it as a case in His Courts. We ask for and desire before Him the reason we are in the earth. We request that what we are here to do, we would be allowed to do so His purpose in the earth might be done. His purposes are attached to us getting our destinies fulfilled from the books of Heaven. As we come to awareness of what is in our books, we can then present it before the Judge and ask for it to become reality in the earth.

Lord, as I stand before Your Court, I would present before You that which is in my book. As much revelation as I have concerning what my prophetic destiny is, I ask this Court to render decisions that allow this to occur. Lord, I desire to fulfill my destiny and future so that Your purpose might be done on the earth. Help me, Lord, to properly discern and present before Your Court the "word of my testimony" that You might render decisions on my behalf!

NOT LOVING OUR LIVES

*Then I heard a loud voice saying in heaven, "Now salvation,
and strength, and the kingdom of our God, and the power
of His Christ have come, for the accuser of our brethren, who
accused them before our God day and night, has been cast
down. And they overcame him by the blood of the Lamb and by
the word of their testimony, and they did not love their lives to
the death." —Revelation 12:10–11*

Not loving our lives to the death simply means that we are willing to sacrifice our own desires for God's will. When we lay our lives down to do the will of the Lord, we gain new dimensions and places of authority in the spirit world. Jesus told His disciples they would be *witnesses* (Acts 1:8). This is someone who gives judicial testimony. It also, however, means *martyr* or *those who give their lives for a religious belief or cause.* This does not necessarily mean we die *physically* as a martyr. It does, however, mean we are willing to surrender our own fleshly appetites, dreams for our lives, and our own plans and purposes to His. This gives us a place of great authority and status in the Courts of Heaven. Heaven pays attention to our testimony before the Courts in a new way. The more we surrender and take up our cross and follow Jesus, the more we gain place and position to function from in the Courts of Heaven. This can only be done by and through the grace of God.

*Lord, as I come to stand before Your Courts, I want to lay my life
down. As best as I can through the empowerment of Your grace,
I submit myself to Your will, desires, and purposes. I ask, Lord,
that You would give me the grace out of my love for You to not
love my life to the death. Lord, that I would be willing to wholly*

follow and serve You all the days of my life. Would You please allow this to grant for me a place of authority and status before Your Courts?

THE SPEAKING BLOOD

*...to Jesus the Mediator of the new covenant, and to the blood of
sprinkling that speaks better things than that of Abel.*
—Hebrews 12:24

The blood of Jesus answers every accusation against us and our bloodline. In that the blood speaks, it is declaring and gives judicial testimony for us. When Cain killed Abel, Abel's blood cried from the ground for judgment against Cain (Gen. 4:10–12). As a result of what Abel's blood was saying, God passed a sentence against Cain. We are told however that the sprinkling of the blood of Jesus is saying something much better for us. Jesus's blood cries for mercy, redemption, and forgiveness. His blood is speaking better things. As a result of the testimony of the blood of Jesus, God now has the legal right He needed to forgive us. His heart has always desired to forgive but needed the legal right to do it. We must simply repent and agree with the testimony of Jesus's blood and receive the forgiveness granted us because of what it is speaking.

> *Lord, as I come to stand before Your Courts, I remind You of that which Jesus's blood is speaking on my behalf. I thank You for the forgiveness that is mine as a result of what His blood says about me. I repent of any and every sin and ask for His blood's testimony to speak for me. Thank You, Lord, that Your heart is always to forgive. The blood of Jesus grants You the legal right You needed. I ask, therefore, that every accusation against me because of my sin would now be forgiven and removed. Thank You so much for Your forgiveness, redemption, and mercy.*

ACCESS GRANTED BY THE BLOOD

*Therefore, brethren, having boldness to enter the Holiest
by the blood of Jesus.* —Hebrews 10:19

Our right to come before the throne of God and the Courts of Heaven is granted to us because of what the blood of Jesus is speaking for us. It is His blood that grants us access into the holiest of holies. In the Old Testament only the high priest had access into this place once a year. Now, however, because of what Jesus's blood is saying for us, we have the right to enter this place of the Spirit. Anytime we come on the basis of what the blood of Jesus is saying about us, we can enter this realm. In this place, we find the confirming, accepting, and loving presence of the Lord. This is the place we were made for, and therefore intuitively desire. None of us are righteous enough in ourselves to enter this place. However, because of the cleansing, purifying, and redemptive power of Jesus's blood we have access into this realm. As we come to this place, we can then enter our pleas and petitions before His throne and Courts and find mercy and grace for ourselves and others.

> *Lord, as I come before Your throne and Courts, I enter by the blood of the Lamb. I am only worthy to stand here because of what the blood of Jesus is speaking on my behalf. Thank You for receiving me based on the blood's testimony concerning me and for Jesus's sake. I yield my heart to You as I now stand in Your presence. As I stand in this holy place, Lord, I honor you and bring my pleas and petitions to You. Thank You that You hear me and answer my cry because of what the blood of Jesus is saying over me.*

THE PROTECTION
OF THE BLOOD

Now the blood shall be a sign for you on the houses where you are. And when I see the blood, I will pass over you; and the plague shall not be on you to destroy you when I strike the land of Egypt. —Exodus 12:13

Even in the Old Testament based on the blood of the Passover Lamb, God promised to not allow judgment and harm come to His people. When all other houses were being touched by the destroyer, the blood of the Passover Lamb secured the houses of God's people. Nothing harmful was able to touch them. We as New Testament believers actually have a better promise than they did. If the blood of an animal could keep destruction away from them, then how much more will the blood of the Lamb of God keep it away from us. As we by faith accept what Jesus did for us on the cross and receive His blood that now speaks for us, every destructive thing will not touch us. Though a thousand fall at one side and ten thousand at the other, it will not come near us. We must simply agree with what the blood of the Lamb now speaks for us. As we do, we are secured by the blood of the covenant. The blood is verifying and confirming in the unseen world that we are the people of God. No torment, peril, demon, or power has a right to touch us because of what the blood is saying about us!

> *Lord, as I stand in Your Courts, I thank You that the blood of Jesus is speaking over my life, family, and all I love. Because of what the blood is saying in the spirit realm concerning me, any rights devilish powers might claim to harm me are revoked and*

removed. They are silenced and cannot speak. Therefore, we are secure and safe before You. No evil can come near my dwelling. For You, Lord, are my keeper and my protector. The blood of the Lamb is now speaking for us.

OUR COVENANT-KEEPING GOD

Now may the God of peace who brought up our Lord Jesus from the dead, that great Shepherd of the sheep, through the blood of the everlasting covenant, make you complete in every good work to do His will, working in you what is well pleasing in His sight, through Jesus Christ, to whom be glory forever and ever. Amen.
—Hebrews 13:20–21

We have a covenant with God through the blood of Jesus. As a result of the blood of Jesus and what it is speaking for us, we can be assured that He will never leave nor forsake us (Heb. 13:5). His feelings toward us do not change just because we are weak or even rebellious. Covenant means that He is committed to us and our generations to come. Notice in this Scripture, that because of covenant brought about by the blood, He will complete what He has started. He will bring us to maturity and cause us to be well-pleasing in His sight. He is dedicated to not leaving or forsaking us. He will finish all that He started concerning us and our generations. The blood is speaking for us and causing Him to remember us and His covenant with us.

> *Lord, as I come before Your Courts, I remind You of all that the blood of Jesus is speaking concerning me. Lord, I realize that what the blood is saying reminds You of the covenant I have with You through Jesus. I agree with what the blood is speaking. I take great confidence in belonging to You because of the blood of the covenant that secures me and establishes me as Your child. I stand before You as Your son/daughter because of what the blood has secured for me.*

HIS BLOOD KEEPS ON CLEANSING

But if we walk in the light as He is in the light, we have fellowship with one another, and the blood of Jesus Christ His Son cleanses us from all sin. —1 John 1:7

In the Greek language this verse actually means the blood *keeps on cleansing* us from all sin. The blood of Jesus doesn't just cleanse us at our initial salvation. The blood keeps on cleansing us as we walk with the Lord in His light. This is why the blood "is speaking" and not "has spoken" (Heb. 12:24). As a result of what the blood is saying concerning us, we are progressively sanctified and made holy in our conduct. The blood is continuously removing any remaining sinful thoughts, ways, and practices. We are consistently being transformed into His image and likeness. This is because of what the blood is speaking in our behalf. Anything that would yet cling to us and claim a legal right against us is revoked because of the voice of His blood. Through faith and repentance we agree with this voice and see the powers of the enemy against us broken.

> *Lord, I come to stand before Your Courts. I thank You today for what Your blood is speaking over me. Thank You that Your grace empowers me to walk in the light as You are in the light. I yield my heart and being to You. I agree with the testimony of Your blood in my behalf. Thank You that anything that would seek to cling to me and shape me that is not from You loses its rights. Lord, I ask that these are revoked and removed by the power of the voice of Your blood and my agreement with it. Thank You that I am made in Your likeness and image and I am progressively reflecting Your glory.*

CURSES REVOKED AND REMOVED

Then Noah built an altar to the Lord, and took of every clean animal and of every clean bird, and offered burnt offerings on the altar. And the Lord smelled a soothing aroma. Then the Lord said in His heart, "I will never again curse the ground for man's sake, although the imagination of man's heart is evil from his youth; nor will I again destroy every living thing as I have done." —Genesis 8:20–21

Curses are real. They are spiritual entities that sabotage our futures and destinies. As a result of Noah's offering that was accepted by God, the Lord lifted the curse that was upon the earth. One of the things that allowed this was the whole burnt offering of the animals. In other words, this was a blood sacrifice. The offering of blood is what allowed God to lift the curse. Through the blood of Jesus, the rights of curses are revoked. They lose their legality to function. One of the things the blood is saying concerning us is that curses cannot land (Prov. 26:2). The blood removed the legal rights for them to operate against us. When we repent and come into agreement with the voice of the blood of sprinkling, the right of curses demanding to function is silenced and removed. We become free from their operation and function against us. We are now at liberty to prosper, be blessed, and be successful.

Lord, as I stand before Your Courts, I agree with the testimony of Your blood. I thank You that what Your blood is saying is revoking every legal right of curses to function against me. That which has been working against me in the legal realm is now silenced and can no longer speak. I repent of every agreement with curses or that which allows them to operate. Thank You for Your blood and its voice in my behalf!

FORGIVEN BECAUSE OF THE BLOOD

*...in whom we have redemption through His blood, the
forgiveness of sins.* —Colossians 1:14

The blood of Jesus grants God the legal right to forgive us. No matter what we have done, when we come before Him and repent, the blood's voice is powerful enough in our behalf. We are freed from that which would deny us a future. The future God planned for us is restored, activated, and set in place. Our sin will not be our downfall. The voice of the blood of Jesus in our behalf is silencing every demand of the accuser to destroy us and the destiny God has for us. Our sins are blotted out. They are remembered no more. We are freed from their slander of us before the Courts of Heaven. The blood of Jesus speaking in our behalf requires them to be silent and unable to testify against us. Jesus's blood allows us to be forgiven by the Father. We can walk into the future designed for us by our Father in Heaven.

> *Lord, I come before Your Courts and repent of my sins. I ask that Your blood would speak for me. Let the voice of my sins and the voice of the accuser now be silenced before You. I thank You that because of the voice of Your blood my future planned for me by You is intact. I move forward with full assurance of faith into all that was originally planned for me. Your blood has given the Father the right necessary to forgive me and restore to me all my destiny planned before the beginning of time.*

REDEMPTION THROUGH HIS BLOOD

...in whom we have redemption through His blood, the
forgiveness of sins. —Colossians 1:14

As a result of the blood of sprinkling speaking in our behalf, I am redeemed. To be redeemed means *to be bought back*. In other words, everything that was lost as a result of sin is now re-established. What was lost is now found. What was dead is now alive. What was stolen is now restored. This means that what God originally purposed for my life is still available to me. My sin has not been able to allow me to lose this. I am redeemed or bought back to the original purpose I was created for. All that was written in the books of Heaven concerning me, I can still have. This is a result of that which the blood of Jesus is speaking for me. As I come before His Courts and repent and then remind Him of what is in the books of Heaven about me, the blood takes its place before the Courts in my behalf. I am justified and declared innocent by the Courts of Heaven and freed to come into my original mandate. I am redeemed!

> *Lord, as I come before Your Courts, I repent for all my sins that would seek to deny me my destiny. I surrender myself before You. I ask for the blood of Jesus to speak in my behalf before Your Courts. I agree with what the blood is saying regarding me. I ask this Court to render a decision based on the testimony of the blood in my behalf. Restore to me the purpose and destiny for which I was made. I declare before this Court that I am redeemed and bought back to Your purpose for me. Nothing is lost. Because of the blood, I am restored, found, and alive again to what I was created for.*

AGREEING TESTIMONY

If you confess with your mouth the Lord Jesus and believe in
your heart that God has raised Him from the dead,
you will be saved. —Romans 10:9

Confession is central to the life of the believer. The word *confess* in the Greek is *homologeo*. It means "to speak the same thing." It can also be used legally in a judicial setting to mean *to give a corroborating testimony*. In other words, it is a witness that verifies what has already been testified. God's standard for judicial activity is that only by the mouth of two or three witnesses could a verdict be rendered (Deut. 17:6; 2 Cor. 13:1). When we "confess," we are releasing testimony in agreement with the voices of Heaven. One of these voices is the blood of Jesus. My words must verify and agree with what the blood is speaking. When I agree with what the blood is saying and not my own feelings, justification, or ideas, the Court now has all that is necessary to render decisions in my behalf and Heaven's purposes. My confession must corroborate the testimony of Heaven for the effects of Heaven to be seen in the earth. God as Judge now has the legal right to enter the earth in power, forgiveness, redemption, and fulfillment of His purposes.

> *Lord, as I stand before Your Courts, I agree with the testimony of the blood of Jesus. Through my confession I release agreeing and corroborating testimony before this Court. I ask, Lord, that my testimony might be received here and accepted as true and righteous. May You now have all that is necessary for Your purpose in the earth to be done. May Your will be done on earth even as it is in Heaven (Matt. 6:10). Allow the heavenly realm to now invade the earthly realm. Let there be a demonstration of Heaven's power in earth now today!*

REPENTANCE AND REMISSION OF SIN

...and that repentance and remission of sins should be preached
in His name to all nations, beginning at Jerusalem. And you
are witnesses of these things. —Luke 24:47–48

The word *witness* is the Greek word *martys*. It speaks of someone giving judicial testimony but also of a martyr. The willingness to lay down our life for His purpose grants us great power to testify. Notice that the testimony that is released is a call for repentance that allows the remission or forgiveness of sin. There is no forgiveness of sin without repentance. The blood testifying in our behalf can only do so as we through repentance agree with its voice. When we repent, all that has been made available to us through the death, burial, resurrection, and ascension of Christ can now be ours. Through our repentance we are agreeing with the voices of Heaven and the blood of Jesus. We must allow the witnesses of Heaven to produce in us a repentance that causes our sins to be remitted and removed. May the chief witness, the Holy Spirit, produce in us a repentance not to be repented of. May we come to a place of deep surrender that allows a conforming to His image and likeness. The blood is speaking for us. May we agree and receive all its testimony is securing.

Lord, as I come before Your Courts, I surrender to You and Your
purposes. I respond to the witness of those who represent You and
the power of the Holy Spirit. I repent and yield my life to You as
fully as I know how. I ask, Lord, that today it might be recorded
in the Court that I am Your servant and humbled before You.
May You work in me deep repentance that changes my heart into
Your image and likeness. May I be conformed to who You are in
every aspect of my life. May I reflect Your glory and majesty of
You. May I be a demonstration of You in the earth today.

PRESENTING CASES BEFORE THE COURTS

*And they overcame him by the blood of the Lamb and by
the word of their testimony, and they did not love their
lives to the death.* —Revelation 12:11

It is not enough to silence the arguments against us through the blood. We must also be able to present cases in our behalf. This is the "word of [our] testimony." When we come and petition the Courts of Heaven, we should be able to present our case that allows decision for us to flow from it. In a natural court a judge can render decisions based only on the evidence presented. This is true in the Courts of Heaven as well. We must come before the Courts of Heaven and with understanding and insight make our case before God as the Judge of all the earth. As this is done, God then has the legal right to render to us the verdicts we desire. He is able to answer our prayers and fulfill the passion of His heart. He awaits our presence in His Courts.

> *Lord, as I come to stand before You as the Judge of all the earth,
> I bring my petition. I realize that as Judge You require me to
> present my case. I would put You into remembrance of all that is
> necessary for You to render decisions and verdicts in my behalf.
> Help me, Lord, by Your Holy Spirit to be able to present as I
> ought my case that You might answer my request and fulfill Your
> passion. Thank You for the right to stand before You in this holy
> place.*

PROPHETIC DESTINIES

A fiery stream issued and came forth from before Him. A thousand thousands ministered to Him; ten thousand times ten thousand stood before Him. The court was seated, and the books were opened. —Daniel 7:10

The books are open after the Court is seated because cases are going to be presented from these books of destinies. This requires us to prophetically discern what is in the books of Heaven concerning us. We do not come before the Courts on the basis of need. We petition God as Father and Friend for this. Our cases in the Courts of Heaven must be presented out of God's purposes before Him as Judge. We do this out of what is written in the books of Heaven. We present before Him His passion concerning us and His purpose through us. As we allow the Holy Spirit to develop this prophetic inclination, we begin to get revelation of what is in the books of Heaven. From this revelation we begin to petition the Courts of Heaven.

> *Lord, as I come before Your Courts, I ask for a new realm of prophetic understanding to develop in me. Help me, Lord, to pay attention in the Spirit to what You are revealing to me from the books of Heaven. Allow me, Lord, to discern then present Your passion concerning me before Your Courts as a case. As I do, Lord, I ask for decisions to be rendered that would allow Your will to be done and my destiny to be fulfilled.*

OPENING THE BOOKS OF HEAVEN

For the Lord has poured out on you the spirit of deep sleep, and has closed your eyes, namely, the prophets; and He has covered your heads, namely, the seers. The whole vision has become to you like the words of a book that is sealed, which men deliver to one who is literate, saying, "Read this, please." And he says, "I cannot, for it is sealed." —Isaiah 29:10–11

Notice that the prophets and seers could not receive revelation because books were sealed. When books are closed in the spiritual realm there is no prophetic revelation that can be received. These books need to be opened before prophetic revelation can be understood so cases before the Courts can be offered. It is possible for there to be a book and it is not opened. Prophetic understanding only comes from opened books. We must pray and ask that any books that are shut would be opened. As this happens, we now have prophetic discernment to present cases in the Courts of Heaven. We must also ask that we would be "literate," or have prophetic gifting, that would allow us to discern what is written in the books. When this is in place, we are ready to begin prophetically presenting our cases in the heavenly Court.

Lord, as I come before Your Courts, I thank You for the privilege to stand here. Thanks so much for Your graciousness to allow me entrance into Your Courts. I ask, Lord, that not only would I have access to the books from which I may present my case, but that they would also be opened. I am asking that I might discern from the books Your passion and prophetic desires. I also ask that the gifting of God would operate in my life that I may know and understand what is written in the books of Heaven. I by faith receive of the Holy Spirit the gifting needed to make me literate able to discern Your heart.

TRUE WORSHIP

The whole vision has become to you like the words of a book
that is sealed, which men deliver to one who is literate, saying,
"Read this, please." And he says, "I cannot, for it is sealed."
Then the book is delivered to one who is illiterate, saying,
"Read this, please." And he says, "I am not literate." Therefore
the Lord said: "Inasmuch as these people draw near with their
mouths and honor Me with their lips, but have removed their
hearts far from Me, and their fear toward Me is taught by the
commandment of men." —Isaiah 29:11–13

One of the things that opens closed and sealed books in the spirit realm is true worship. True worship from the heart causes that which is closed to be opened. This is why many of us will recognize that during times of true worship the prophetic realm begins to open. People will start to have prophetic understanding and unctions. In Revelation 19:10 the man who John is encountering declares, *"Worship God! For the testimony of Jesus is the spirit of prophecy."* In other words, worship unlocks the spirit of prophecy to operate. This is because our true, unadulterated worship of Jesus lets books become unsealed. This allows those who are literate, or gifted prophetically, to read what is in the books. It also bring the illiterate, or those who seem to have no gifting, into an ability to perceive what is written in the books of Heaven. This happens because we begin to honor the Lord not just with our lips and mouths, but also from the depth of our hearts. The books in Heaven begin to open, and we are able to present cases before the throne of God and the Courts of Heaven.

Lord, as I come to stand before You and Your Courts, I come
and ask that any sealed book that is related to me would now

be opened. I repent for any and all impure worship. Any place I have drawn near with my lips and mouth while my heart was far removed, I repent. I desire to worship You my God in spirit and in truth. I draw near in full assurance of faith and enter Your presence. Lord, allow the books of Heaven to now open and prophetic understanding to come.

TEARS OF INTERCESSION

And no one in heaven or on the earth or under the earth was able to open the scroll, or to look at it. So I wept much, because no one was found worthy to open and read the scroll, or to look at it. But one of the elders said to me, "Do not weep. Behold, the Lion of the tribe of Judah, the Root of David, has prevailed to open the scroll and to loose its seven seals." —Revelation 5:3–5

The books or scrolls in Heaven were shut and sealed. No one was found worthy to open them. John had a sense of the importance of these books being opened. Without them being opened the devil would win by default. Without them being opened no case could be presented before the throne of God and the Courts of Heaven. Without a case being presented, God's desire and passion would not be seen in the earth. John intuitively knew this and began to weep. His weeping was necessary to opening the books in Heaven. One of the main things that opens books in the heavenly realm are tears of intercession. His weeping actually attached to the sacrifice of Jesus. His tears of intercession were used to bring into reality that which Jesus as the Lion of the tribe of Judah had prevailed in and won. John's tears of intercession were used in the Heavens to allow books to open and cases to be presented. The results were judgments from these books that allowed God's justice and purpose to be fulfilled in the earth. God needs our tears of intercession.

> *Lord, as I come before Your Courts, I ask that I might share in Your passion for Your purposes to be done. I yield myself before You and ask that even tears of intercession might flow from me. Allow me to partner with the Holy Spirit and intercede in such a way that allows the seals on books to be opened. Lord,*

through my intercession I agree with Your work on the cross and resurrection from the grave as the Lion of the tribe of Judah. I partner with You to see every book opened that is necessary for Your judgments to produce Your justice in the earth. Thank You, Lord, for allowing me this privilege.

THE TIMING OF THE LORD

*And he said to me, "Do not seal the words of the prophecy of this book, for the time is at hand." —*Revelation 22:10

Opening books that we might present cases before His Courts can involve the timing of God. In this verse we see the command being made *not* to seal the books because the *time* was at hand. In other words, it was time. There are some books that will not open until God's timing. The fact that revelation is now coming signifies that it is now time. We are to begin to present cases before His Courts based on the revelation we are now receiving. We are to move forward in assurance because the time is now. This will require us stepping into faith and taking risks based on books being opened that are now bringing fresh revelation to us. To delay in these moments can be hazardous to what God desires to be done. Elisha knew it was time for him to receive the mantle of Elijah. Therefore he would not allow anything to distract him or cause him to delay in following Elijah. The result was the receiving of the mantle that allowed him to make history (2 Kings 2:13). As books open in the spirit realm, we must move in agreement with them. These books opening are allowing us to move into the next dimensions of our destiny and purpose. We must not hang back in uncertainty or fear. We must move forward in these moments of revelation and into the purposes of God.

> *Lord, as I come before Your Courts, I thank You for the ability to discern Your timing. I yield to You and move in agreement with the timing I am perceiving as a result of books opening in the spirit realm. By revelation I am sensing that I am stepping into a new realm where breakthrough comes and prayers are answered. Even as Elisha received the mantle from Elijah, I do not become*

distracted in these moments. I move forward in full assurance of faith and believe for the full impartation from You. Because books are opening, I am stepping into the new realm of destiny made and prepared for me.

PROPHETIC WORDS PRAYED INTO PLACE

This charge I commit to you, son Timothy, according to the
prophecies previously made concerning you, that by them you
may wage the good warfare. —1 Timothy 1:18

One of the keys to presenting cases before the Courts of Heaven is using pro-phetic words that have been prophesied concerning you. Paul tells Timothy that he is to take the prophetic words over his life and wage a good warfare to see them come to reality. Any real prophetic word spoken over our life is not automatic. It has to be contended for in the Courts of Heaven. The devil as our legal opponent will resist the fulfillment of the word through judicial activity against us. He will use our sin, transgressions, iniquity in the bloodline, cove-nants, vows, and anything else he can to seek to disqualify us from inheriting the word of God concerning us. We must know how to present the prophetic word we have received and to contend in the Courts of Heaven for its fulfillment. This has two dimensions to it. First, we take the word spoken over our life and present it as our case before the Courts of Heaven. Secondly, we answer by the blood of Jesus anything satan is seeking to legally use to deny us what God has said is ours. When we successfully do this, the prophetic word of destiny over our lives become reality.

> *Lord, I come and stand before the Courts of Heaven. I bring*
> *before You the prophetic word spoken over my life. I remind the*
> *Courts of Heaven that this is what has been spoken by the Holy*
> *Spirit over me though your vessel. I ask, Lord, that what has been*
> *declared would now come to pass. I ask also that any accusation*

satan might bring to deny me the fulfillment of this word would now be silenced by the speaking blood of Jesus my Savior. Thank You so much for allowing my prophetic destiny to occur because of righteous decisions from Your Court.

PARTY TO THE PROCESS

*...in the first year of his reign I, Daniel, understood by the
books the number of the years specified by the word of the Lord
through Jeremiah the prophet, that He would accomplish
seventy years in the desolations of Jerusalem. Then I set my
face toward the Lord God to make request by prayer and
supplications, with fasting, sackcloth, and ashes.*
—Daniel 9:2–3

Notice that Daniel, after realizing from the books of history that Jeremiah had prophesied Israel would be in captivity for seventy years, began to pray, supplicate, and make request for Israel's deliverance. Israel was in captivity because of their sin and disobedience to God. The Lord, however, had specified that they would be there for this seventy-year period. When Daniel realized this he didn't simply think they were going to come out of captivity because the time was up. He realized he had to pray in this significant time or it would pass them by and they would still be in captivity. This is what we must do as well. When the timing of God is upon us, it is not enough to just wait for something to happen. We must engage ourselves in the Courts of Heaven and be a party to the process. We must diligently deal with anything the devil would use to make us miss the timing of God. We must undo with the blood of Jesus anything that satan would contend with. The things he would speak against us must be answered. We must also remind God in His Court that it is time for the prophetic word to be fulfilled and the promise to come to pass. This allows the Courts of Heaven to move in our behalf and our prophetic destiny to be restored.

*Lord, as I come before Your Courts, I thank You that it is time.
The timing is upon me for Your blessings to be manifested. I*

would remind You of the prophetic word that has been spoken over my life. Thank You, Lord, that it is now the moment for this to be reality. I surrender my heart and life to You. I also ask that anything the devil would use to contend I can't have what is mine in this moment that the blood of Jesus would speak for me. I repent for anything and everything he would be speaking against me. I ask that Your blood now silence him and his accusation. Thank You, Lord, that my promises are apprehended and manifested today.

ASKING IN SEASON

Ask the Lord for rain in the time of the latter rain. The Lord will make flashing clouds; He will give them showers of rain, grass in the field for everyone. —Zechariah 10:1

The prophet Zechariah exhorts that we should ask for rain in the time of the latter rain. In other word, prayers are extremely powerful when we pray them in agreement with the seasons we are in. So often we are asking for something from the Lord when it is not the season for it to come. We must be sensitive to the season of God we are in. Our prayers will be increasingly effective when we are agreeing with the season of God. After Elijah called fire down on Mount Carmel, he positioned himself and began to ask for rain. It had not rained for three and a half years. However, Elijah said, *"There is the sound of abundance of rain"* (1 Kings 18:41). Based on what he was hearing in the spirit realm, Elijah began to pray. The result was a torrential rain that broke the drought and famine over Israel (1 Kings 18:45). As we approach the Courts of Heaven, we should seek to discern if it is the season for what we are asking. This will allow the Courts of Heaven to move in agreement with us as we ask and request in season what the Lord has for us.

> *Lord, as I come before Your Courts, I ask that I might discern properly the season I am in. I want to be able to ask in season. Forgive me for the times I have requested of You something that was not in the timing of God. Forgive me for my times of frustration when I thought You weren't hearing me. I realize now it was not in season. Help me to always approach Your Courts in correct season and timing so that You might release to me the fullness of Your promise. Thank You so much, Lord.*

AGREEING WITH JESUS'S SACRIFICE

Surely He has borne our griefs and carried our sorrows; yet we esteemed Him stricken, smitten by God, and afflicted. But He was wounded for our transgressions, He was bruised for our iniquities; the chastisement for our peace was upon Him, and by His stripes we are healed. —Isaiah 53:4–5

When we present cases in the Courts of Heaven, we should remind the Courts that which Jesus has done for us. This carries great weight and significance before the Courts of Heaven. We are presenting testimony based on the finished works of the cross in our behalf. Whatever our need or desire might be, it is met in what Jesus has done for us and the covenant He established in our behalf through His body and blood. As we approach the Courts of Heaven and the righteous Judge of all the earth, our testimony before Him connected to Jesus's work for us, releases faith and stirs the heart of God. On the basis of Jesus's activities and not necessarily our own, we ask that there would be verdicts and decisions rendered in our behalf. The weight of Jesus's work for us will speak before God and cause things to come to divine order. God's passion as Judge will be stirred toward us, and decisions will be set in place for our breakthrough and blessing.

> *Lord, as I come before Your Courts, I come on the basis of who Jesus is and what He has done for me. I come surrendering my heart and life to You. As I stand before You, I ask that this Court would be reminded of Jesus's sacrifice in my behalf. I ask all the body and blood of Jesus purchased for me would now be mine. On the basis of Jesus's work, would You now render a verdict for me that would allow me the breakthrough I need and desire. Thanks You, Lord, that for Jesus's sake this is done from the Courts of Heaven.*

JESUS OUR ADVOCATE

My little children, these things I write to you, so that you may not sin. And if anyone sins, we have an Advocate with the Father, Jesus Christ the righteous. —1 John 2:1

Jesus as our advocate means He is our intercessor and attorney. He stands before the Courts of Heaven in our behalf and pleads our case. Jesus being righteous is of great significance. It is righteousness that grants a place of authority with God and in the Courts of Heaven. Jesus being righteous means that He has standing with God, and He uses it to intercede and speak for us. This righteousness was obtained through His complete and full obedience to the Father. Jesus is therefore deemed to have a right to speak for us because of His righteousness that He gained. This means that whatever He asks of the Father He receives. We must therefore yield and submit to Him. As we do this, we can come into an agreement with all that He, as our intercessor, attorney, and mediator, is presenting before the Lord in our behalf. We get the full benefit of Jesus's obedience and totally yielded life to the Father.

> *Lord, as I stand before Your Courts, I thank You that Jesus is my attorney, intercessor, and mediator. Because of His complete obedience to You, He is Jesus Christ the righteous. From this place Jesus intercedes for me. His intercession grants You, Lord as Judge, the right to render verdicts in my behalf. Thank You for accepting the plea of Jesus for me. Because of Jesus's prayers in my behalf, Lord, now allow my cries to be heard and my desires to be met. Thank You so much for Your graciousness to me because of Jesus.*

PRESENTING THE PROMISES OF GOD'S WORD

For all the promises of God in Him are Yes, and in Him Amen,
to the glory of God through us. —2 Corinthians 1:20

One of the things we can do as we present cases before the Courts of Heaven is to use the promises of God's Word. God's Word is filled with promises. When we take the promise from God's Word and remind Him of it, we are presenting our case in His Courts. Whether it's for breakthrough, protection, healing, prosperity, family harmony, children, or any other thing, the promises of God speak in His Courts. We are literally reminding the Judge of what He has said about a certain thing as His covenant people. When we declare His promises in His Courts in our behalf, we are releasing testimony and allowing it to speak for us. Take the promises of God's Word and speak it in His Courts and ask on the basis of it for verdicts to be rendered. God as Judge will hear and move. He cannot lie. His Word is true.

> *Lord, as I come before Your Court, I remind You of Your Word and its promises. On the basis of that which You have said, I ask that decisions would come from Your Court and into my life. I declare before You that I know You cannot lie. Therefore, I am asking for Your Word and its promises to be fully manifested in me and through me. Thank You, Lord, for being faithful to Your Word.*

FINANCES GIVING TESTIMONY IN THE COURTS

Here mortal men receive tithes, but there he receives them, of whom it is witnessed that he lives. —Hebrews 7:8

The word *witness* here means *to give judicial testimony*. When we bring our offering and our tithe, there is a judicial testimony that is given in our behalf. Our money speaking in the Courts of Heaven causes God to remember us. Our tithe in particular declare in the Courts that we believe He lives. It is a powerful witness for us in the Courts of Heaven and connects us to the Melchizedek priesthood that Jesus operates in for us. As a result of this connection made through our tithes and offerings, we get the full benefit of His present-day ministry in our behalf. His intercession allows us to draw life from the One who lives. Our testimony released through our tithes and offerings speak and allow this to happen.

> *Lord, I thank You that I can stand before Your Courts. I thank You that my tithes and offering are now releasing a witness that You live. Because of this, I am now attached to Your life and all that You are doing for me as my faithful High Priest. I receive fully Your intercession because of this connection. It is my privilege to honor You with my giving and allow it to speak as a testimony before You. Thank You, Lord, so much.*

RELEASING THE RIGHT TESTIMONY

Therefore if you bring your gift to the altar, and there remember that your brother has something against you, leave your gift there before the altar, and go your way. First be reconciled to your brother, and then come and offer your gift.
—Matthew 5:23–24

Jesus teaches us to bring an offering with the right testimony attached to it. We are told to not give our offering if we remember someone has something against us; this is speaking of a heart condition. If someone has something against me, then there is a strong likelihood that I also have a problem in my heart. The principle is that whatever the condition of my heart at the time I bring my offering, that is the testimony attached to it. In bringing an offering to the Lord, I must make sure my heart is free and clear of offense, anger, bitterness, or ill will toward another. If it is not, this will be the witness I am releasing through my offering into the heavenly realm. The offering will speak against me rather than for me in the Courts of Heaven. I must make sure my offering is from a pure heart of worship, adoration, and affection toward the Lord.

Lord, as I come before Your Courts, I ask that as I would honor and worship You with my offering that the right testimony would be attached to it. May my heart be free from anger, bitterness, and offense on every level. Allow my offering to speak the right things before You. I pray that You may remember me. Allow the right decisions to be rendered from Your Courts in my behalf because of what my offering is saying before You. It is my privilege to honor and worship You with the best that I have. Thank You, Lord, for my offering speaking in my behalf before You.

SILENCING THE ADVERSARY

Therefore if you bring your gift to the altar, and there remember that your brother has something against you, leave your gift there before the altar, and go your way. First be reconciled to your brother, and then come and offer your gift. Agree with your adversary quickly, while you are on the way with him, lest your adversary deliver you to the judge, the judge hand you over to the officer, and you be thrown into prison.
—Matthew 5:23–25

In these Scriptures Jesus clearly connects the condition of our heart when bringing an offering, to the adversary, our legal opponent, having a judicial case against us. When we bring an offering that is polluted because of an attitude of our heart, the adversary can grab the testimony of it in the spiritual realm and use it against us. Our money speaking the wrong things about us can be used to build legal cases to harm us. If we have ever brought an offering with a wrong testimony attached to it because of a wrong heart attitude, we should ask for that testimony to be silenced. When we do, that which the adversary could be using to speak against us is revoked and removed. We become free from his power to deliver us to the judge and seek to destroy our lives.

Lord, as I stand before Your Courts, I ask that any offering I may have ever brought with the wrong testimony attached to it would now be silenced by the blood of Jesus. Any "sound" in the spirit world that is attached to any offering I gave that the devil is using against me, would You allow Your blood to now nullify and revoke its rights to speak? I repent for bringing an offering with the wrong motive, with the wrong heart, and with the wrong speech joined to it. Thank You, Lord, that Your blood now speaks in my behalf to silence this in the spiritual realm. Let that which is from Heaven only speak in my behalf now.

FEBRUARY 16

SILENCING THE SOUND OF WRONG MOTIVES AND MONEY

So it was, when the days of feasting had run their course, that Job would send and sanctify them, and he would rise early in the morning and offer burnt offerings according to the number of them all. For Job said, "It may be that my sons have sinned and cursed God in their hearts." Thus Job did regularly. Now there was a day when the sons of God came to present themselves before the Lord, and Satan also came among them.
—Job 1:5–6

At first appearance it may seem that Job's activities in behalf of his children were godly and right. However, when the devil made his case against Job, his accusation was that he wasn't serving God from a pure heart (Job 1:9–11). Satan accused Job of only serving God because of how much He had blessed him. Where did satan get the evidence to bring such a case against Job? It came from the offerings that Job brought with a sound of fear and manipulation. It could appear that through offerings Job was seeking to manipulate God not to judge his children for their sins. This was driven by his fear and not real faith (Job 3:25). This testimony, or sound, attached to Job's offerings was grabbed by satan in the spirit world as they were presented to speak against Job rather than for him. If we have ever been party to bringing an offering to manipulate God, the testimony of this offering must be silenced so that it does not speak against us.

Lord, as I come before Your Courts, I repent of any offerings that I may have brought to manipulate rather than worship and adore You. I know Your Word declares that my offering must be from a cheerful and even hilarious heart (2 Cor. 9:7). This is what speaks before You in my behalf. May Your blood speak in my behalf before Your Courts and revoke every right of any previous offerings that had any form of manipulation and fear attached to them to speak against me. May my offerings now be from a cheerful and pure heart and speak and cause Your heart to be stirred toward me and what belongs to me.

MONEY: SPEAKING FOR
OR AGAINST US?

*Your gold and silver are corroded, and their corrosion will be
a witness against you and will eat your flesh like fire. You have
heaped up treasure in the last days. Indeed the wages of the
laborers who mowed your fields, which you kept back by fraud,
cry out; and the cries of the reapers have reached the ears of the
Lord of Sabaoth. —James 5:3–4*

In speaking concerning the rich who oppressed with their wealth rather than
blessed with it, James said what was held back would speak against them. He is
warning that if they use their riches to oppress with rather than bless, it would
"cry out" against them. The result would be judgment against them and the
oppressive economic system they controlled. Money unrighteously stewarded
to control and oppress will release a testimony against the ones who use it as
such. It will speak in the Courts of Heaven before the Judge of all the earth.
When the cries of those who have been damaged mix with the cries of the
money itself, judgments can come from the Courts of Heaven to begin to set in
order economic systems to free people from the slavery of these systems.

*Lord, as I stand in Your Courts, I repent of any agreement I have
had with oppressive economic systems. I want my money to speak
for me and not against me before Your Courts. I also, however,
add my voice to the voice of finances held back. I ask that as our
testimony comes before Your Courts, a righteous judgment will
be released against all that oppresses me and my family and even
my culture as a whole. I ask, Lord, that freedom would come, and
instead of oppression there would now be prosperity and blessings.*

OFFERINGS IN RIGHTEOUSNESS

*He will sit as a refiner and a purifier of silver; He will purify
the sons of Levi, and purge them as gold and silver, that they
may offer to the Lord an offering in righteousness. "Then the
offering of Judah and Jerusalem will be pleasant to the Lord, as
in the days of old, as in former years. And I will come near you
for judgment; I will be a swift witness against sorcerers, against
adulterers, against perjurers, against those who exploit wage
earners and widows and orphans, and against those who turn
away an alien—because they do not fear Me,"
says the Lord of hosts.* —Malachi 3:3–5*

God declares that an offering brought to Him in righteousness from a purified heart releases judgment against that which destroys lives, families, and even cultures. The testimony attached to the offerings of God's people grants the Lord the legal right He needs to render judgments that establish justice. We have a right to cry for His justice based on the offerings of righteousness we bring. When justice comes from the throne of God in Heaven, order begins to come in the earth realm. This all happens because we are bringing an offering in righteousness to the Lord. I exhort you to cry out for His justice over your life and your culture. He will hear and move based on what your offerings are speaking before Him.

*Lord, as I stand before Your Courts, I ask that I might bring
an offering in righteousness to You. May this offering speak
with a testimony that grants You as Judge the right to render
decisions that bring justice into the earth. Allow my offering to
be acceptable to You and present testimony before You that speaks
in my behalf and in behalf of the culture I represent. May Your
name be glorified among us.*

OFFERINGS PRODUCING JUSTICE IN CULTURE

"And I will come near you for judgment; I will be a swift witness against sorcerers, against adulterers, against perjurers, against those who exploit wage earners and widows and orphans, and against those who turn away an alien—because they do not fear Me," says the Lord of hosts. —Malachi 3:5

As we have seen for the last several days, our offerings and finances have a significant voice before the Lord. They do not just speak for us; they can also speak for the culture that we are a part of. When we bring an offering in righteousness as the people of God, we can be received not only as an individual but also as a representation of the culture as well. When this happens, our offerings can speak and allow God as Judge to render judgments in behalf of cultures. It can be that which allows witchcraft, adultery, perjury, oppressive economic systems, and immigration issues to have heavenly remedies. This can happen because an offering of righteousness from God's people is speaking in the Courts of Heaven. This grants God the legal right He desires to set things in order in the earth and its cultures.

> *Lord, as I come before Your Courts, I come not just as an individual but also as a representation of my culture. I ask that my offering would speak not just for me, but also for Your Kingdom passion to be done in my culture. I ask for judgments against adultery that destroys homes, witchcraft that empowers the satanic, lies and perjury and corruption, oppressive economic systems, and improper immigration policies. Lord, allow my offerings to speak and set in order Your will and purpose in the earth.*

THE HOLY MOUNTAIN OF GOD

Even them I will bring to My holy mountain, and make them joyful in My house of prayer. Their burnt offerings and their sacrifices will be accepted on My altar; for My house shall be called a house of prayer for all nations. —Isaiah 56:7

The holy mountain of God is not a geographical place; it is a governmental spiritual dimension. When we are promised being brought to the mountain, we are being granted access into a realm of the spirit where the Courts of Heaven are. Hebrews 12:22 tells us that as New Testament believers, we have *"come to Mount Zion."* This is the name of the holy mountain of God we have been allowed access to. God the Judge of all is in this realm (Heb. 12:23). This means this is where the Courts of Heaven are. As a people of prayer we are brought to this place where our function has great power, authority, and influence. Even nations can be altered and brought to divine order as we operate in these realms.

Lord, as I come to the Courts of Heaven in the holy mountain of God, I ask for grace to function here. Lord, would You allow my operation in this place to move things over my life. Lord, allow nations and cultures to be freed to come into the expression You have designed for them. Let them now become the expression of the Kingdom of God You have longed for them to be. Lord, in Your Courts I represent my nation before You. May my nation be blessed as I stand before You in Your holy mountain.

A HOUSE OF PRAYER FOR THE NATIONS

Even them I will bring to My holy mountain, and make them joyful in My house of prayer. Their burnt offerings and their sacrifices will be accepted on My altar; for My house shall be called a house of prayer for all nations. —Isaiah 56:7

That which has a right to stand in the holy mountain of God or a governmental spiritual dimension where the Courts of Heaven are is God's house of prayer. A house of prayer is a people of God who have been knit together in covenant that are now functioning as one. When these come to the holy mountain of God, their activity in this place can bring change even to nations. We must allow ourselves to be formed and fashioned into this kind of people. This is the house that Jesus is passionate about and has come to reclaim. In His earthly ministry Jesus came to the temple of God and purged it because it had lost its purity of being a house of prayer (Matt. 21:13). Will we allow the Lord on an individual level and a corporate one to cleanse us that we might be a people who from prayer can reshape nations into their God-ordained destiny? Jesus is passionately waiting for us to move into this place of authority that His will might be implemented.

Lord, as I stand before Your Courts, by faith I take a place in Your holy mountain. I move into this spiritual realm of government where not only is my life altered, but the lives of nations can change. I repent, Lord, for being any part of changing Your house to not being what You desire. You desire Your house to be a house of prayer for all nations. Allow me, Lord, to please have the right perspective and right heart as a part of Your house to see nations come into divine order. Lord, from Your Courts I ask, "Let Your will be done on earth as it in heaven."

THE HOUSE OF HIS PASSION BUILT

Do not let the son of the foreigner who has joined himself to the
Lord speak, saying, "The Lord has utterly separated me from
His people"; nor let the eunuch say, "Here I am, a dry tree."
—Isaiah 56:3

Jesus's passion is His house of prayer. In Isaiah 56 we see three groups of people mentioned that He uses to build this house or people. He uses foreigners/strangers. He uses eunuchs. He also uses the outcast (Isa. 56:8). Strangers are those who feel like they are misfits. Eunuchs are those who are frustrated that they can never reproduce or bear fruit. Outcasts are those who are rejected and made to feel useless. These are the ones God declares that will be used to build His house that shall reshape nations. They are able to stand in the holy mountain of God where the Courts of Heaven operate (Heb. 12:22–24). The Lord loves to take what others have despised and use them to do great things and accomplish His purposes. He takes the foolish and confounds the wise (1 Cor. 1:27). Today, regardless of how we see ourselves, we should be the ones that understand we are of great use to the Lord. God will fashion us into a people designed to do His will and bring about His passion in the earth.

Lord, as I stand before Your Courts in Your holy mountain, I
surrender my view of myself to You. I repent for not seeing myself
as You see me. I yield all my strengths and weaknesses to You.
Take me, Lord, and use me to be a part of Your people as a house
of prayer for the nations. I acknowledge before Your Courts that
whether I am a stranger, a eunuch, or an outcast, that it is Your
grace in me that accomplishes Your purposes. Today I give myself
to You and ask to be used by You in the holy mountain where the
Courts of Heaven are.

MISFITS FOR JESUS

Do not let the son of the foreigner who has joined himself to the
Lord speak, saying, "The Lord has utterly separated me from
His people"; nor let the eunuch say, "Here I am, a dry tree."
—Isaiah 56:3

Notice that the foreigners/strangers see themselves as separated. They consider themselves as misfits. Yet these are part of the group that God uses to build His house of prayer that can stand in the holy mountain of God, where the Courts of Heaven are. So many today in the church see themselves as misfits. Those who feel as if they are not a part. They cannot seem to find where they are joined. This may make them consider there is something wrong. It can make them think that maybe they are just rebellious. Though this may be true for some, the fact is that there is a group today that is a remnant. They cannot be happy in the traditional church setting. This is because they have a Kingdom heart and desire to see God's purposes done in the earth. They long for cultural reformation and to see the multitudes brought into salvation and functioning as Kingdom parts. These are those who desire Jesus to be glorified and His purposes to be done. This passion can make them misfits in today's church. However, they will be used of God to build a house of prayer that can stand in the holy mountain of God from where the Courts of Heaven function.

> *Lord, as I come before Your Courts in the holy mountain of*
> *God, I yield myself to You. I give You the right to search me*
> *and remove any rebellion that might be in me. Even though I*
> *might feel like a stranger/foreigner/misfit, my heart is to see Your*
> *Kingdom come and Your will done in the earth. Lord, would*
> *You use me as those that would build Your house of prayer and*

can stand in Your holy mountain and the Courts of Heaven?
Thank You, Lord, for allowing me the privilege of being a part of
Your purpose in the earth.

FRUITLESS AND FRUSTRATED

Do not let the son of the foreigner who has joined himself to the
Lord speak, saying, "The Lord has utterly separated me from
His people"; nor let the eunuch say, "Here I am, a dry tree." For
thus says the Lord: "To the eunuchs who keep My Sabbaths,
and choose what pleases Me, and hold fast My covenant, even to
them I will give in My house and within My walls a place and
a name better than that of sons and daughters; I will give them
*an everlasting name that shall not be cut off." —*Isaiah 56:3–5

The Lord encourages the eunuchs who have lost the ability to reproduce and be fruitful to not refer to themselves as a dry tree. In other words, a tree that has no juices flowing through them that would allow reproduction. God promises that as they commit to building Him a house of prayer that can stand in His holy mountain, He will give them a greater name than that of sons and daughters. He also promises to give them an everlasting name that will not be cut off. This is amazing since a eunuch's name dies with him because of lack of offspring. There would be no one to carry on the family name because of an inability to produce children. The promise God is making for those who build His house of prayer is that not only will the eunuch who would be frustrated because of fruitlessness be fruitful, but they would have generations of fruitfulness that would not be cut off. The promise is simply that when those who feel fruitless and frustrated become a part of building God a house of prayer that can stand in His holy mountain and the Courts of Heaven, God will bless them with fruitfulness now and throughout their generations. We and all that comes from us will be blessed because of our passion to build His house of prayer.

Lord, as I stand in Your Courts, in Your holy mountain, I ask that You would allow me to be a part of building Your house of prayer. I ask that even though I feel fruitless and frustrated, that because of my passion to see Your house of prayer built, that You, Lord, bless me and my generations with fruitfulness for Your Kingdom. Let every realm of barrenness be revoked and removed from me, and make me a part of Your house of prayer that can stand in Your holy mountain and the Courts of Heaven. I gladly take my place before You and in this realm of the spirit world.

REJECTED BUT NOT A REJECT

The Lord God, who gathers the outcasts of Israel, says, "Yet I will gather to him others besides those who are gathered to him."
—Isaiah 56:8

The other group God promises to use to build His house of prayer is the outcast. These are those who have been rejected. They have been made to feel unfit and not good enough. Jesus said that He Himself was the stone which the builder rejected, yet He became the chief cornerstone (Matt. 21:42). Anyone that God ever uses in a prominent way will have walked through the rejection of people. God actually fashioned Jesus through rejection to fit into the building as a chief cornerstone. If we are to fit into the building God is forming, we too will have to suffer rejection. We must allow it to fashion us into an absolute dependence upon God; the Lord must be where we gain our identity and affirmation. When this occurs, we are ready to be placed in His house of prayer as a stone of great worth and impact.

> *Lord, as I stand before Your Courts and in Your holy mountain, I thank You for the places of rejection I have walked through. I have no hurt, wound, or bitterness toward those who have rejected me. In fact, Lord, I thank You that their rejection has fashioned me to stand before You as a part of Your house in Your mountain, that can see decisions from Your Courts in behalf of nations. Thank You, Lord, that as an outcast, I have great status before You in Your heavenly Courts. Thank You so much for Your status that You set upon me.*

THE MOUNTAIN OF GOD'S HOUSE OVER NATIONS

Now it shall come to pass in the latter days that the mountain of the Lord's house shall be established on the top of the mountains, and shall be exalted above the hills; and all nations shall flow to it. —Isaiah 2:2

The Lord promises that He will have the mountain of the Lord's house established on the top of the mountains. This is the house of prayer that God promises to build, which is us. We as the house of prayer stand in *the "mountain of the Lord."* This is the governmental dimension of the spirit world. Notice that which stands in this place is a house. A house speaks of a family. God will have a family that is a government. This governmental family will be on the top or in a governmental position over all the governments of the earth. This is what the word *top* speaks of. It is the Hebrew word *rosh.* If we are to stand in the Courts of Heaven in the holy mountain of God, we must allow the Lord to fashion us into a family. Only a family will have the right to stand before the Lord in this place. A network can't; an organization can't; a ministry can't. Only a family bound and linked together by the Holy Spirit can take a place to impact the nations from these realms. We should pray for these families to come into order and that we might be a part of an expression of one of these families.

> *Lord, as I stand in Your Courts, I ask that the "mountain of the Lord's house" would be established in the top of the mountains. I ask, Lord, that You would arrange a people that is a family that You may trust with governmental authority. Lord, I ask as they stand in Your holy mountain of governmental authority*

that nations will shift into their God-ordained purpose. Lord, would You allow me to be connected, fitted, and joined in Your family/house that functions in this way? Thanks so much, Lord, for the honor.

REIGNING FROM THE TOPS OF THE MOUNTAINS

Now it shall come to pass in the latter days that the mountain of the Lord's house shall be established on the top of the mountains, and shall be exalted above the hills; and all nations shall flow to it. —Isaiah 2:2

The word *top* is the Hebrew word *rosh*. It means a *head* and "shake the head." God intends for His house of prayer to be governmental in nature. This has nothing to do with politics. This has to do with who determines what happens in the cultures of the nations. As God's house of prayer we are to be creating atmospheres that allow and promote His agenda in the earth. Instead of demonic powers creating these atmospheres, it is our job and responsibility. As we take our place as the government of God, we determine what is allowed and what is not allowed. This is what binding and loosing is all about (Matt. 18:18). In fact, our being in the "top" means that what we are in agreement with will be allowed, but what we shake our head in disagreement with will not be allowed. This is the authority and place we have been granted as the *"mountain of the Lord's house"* in the top of the mountain.

> Lord, as we stand in the Courts of Heaven in the governmental place of the Spirit called the "holy mountain of God," we ask that the culture of nations will come under Your divine rule and authority. We ask that what is not in agreement with Heaven will be denied the right to operate. We also ask that what is in agreement with Heaven will be permitted to function. Thank You for the right and privilege to stand as Your house of prayer in the top of the mountains and in the Courts of Heaven.

FAMILY BECOMING GOD'S GOVERNMENT

Now when Abram heard that his brother was taken captive,
he armed his three hundred and eighteen trained servants who
were born in his own house, and went in pursuit as far as Dan.
—Genesis 14:14

Abraham's house became an army, which is an expression of government. They were able to bring down several kings and their armies. This was because a "house" began to function as a "government" in the spirit realm. The principle is before we can be a governmental people, we must first be a house. In other words, there must be covenant and knitting that allows a house to begin to function as a governmental people and shift culture into its divine order. It is the responsibility of each part of the Body of Christ to be a part of the expression of family. We are to be joined and connected. As we do this, we are allowing the Lord the right to bring us into a governmental place of the spirit as the church Jesus died to birth. We are no longer strangers and foreigners but now members of the household of faith (Eph. 2:19).

> *Lord, as I come before Your Court, I ask that You turn the family*
> *of God into a governmental expression that can affect the culture*
> *of nations. Thank You that You allow me to be rightly connected*
> *into Your house that is a family. As I do this, allow us, Lord, to*
> *express Your government and authority in the earth. Would You*
> *allow our cultures to become a demonstration of Your Kingdom?*
> *Thank You so much, Lord, for this honor.*

BORN IN THE HOUSE

Now when Abram heard that his brother was taken captive,
he armed his three hundred and eighteen trained servants who
were born in his own house, and went in pursuit as far as Dan.
—Genesis 14:14

Abraham's house became an expression of government that had the power to destroy kings, powers of darkness, that were tormenting and warping culture. This house is a picture of what the church is to be. We are to be a house that is a government. We are to be God's governing family. The first thing that allowed this house to be an expression of government in the spirit was those "born" in the house. In other words, they had the DNA of the house. There is a certain DNA that comes from being born in a house. We also could say you are "born for" a house. In other words, one of the main reasons you exist is to be a part of a specific house. In that house you will find destiny, purpose, and empowerment. When you are born for a house, you take on the very spirit and life of that house. You think the way that house thinks. You have the same goals and vision that the house has. Your passion comes from the passion of the house. The thing that allowed Abraham's house to be a government was because they *all* walked in the same spirit, unity and like-mindedness because they were born for this house. There is a house for everyone, even those who feel like they do not fit. God will fit you in the Body as it pleases Him (1 Cor. 12:18). You will find the place you were born for. This allows a house to become His expression of government.

> *Lord, as I stand before Your Courts, I ask that You fit me in the*
> *Body as it pleases You. I ask that the place I have been born for*
> *would be revealed to me. I ask that I might be joined in Your*
> *house as a living stone made and prepared by You. Lord, as I*

do this would You let this house I am born to be a part of now, become an expression of Your government. Lord, allow life to change in the world because Your house, the church, is expressing Your life, power, and authority.

TRAINED FOR PURPOSE

Now when Abram heard that his brother was taken captive,
he armed his three hundred and eighteen trained servants who
were born in his own house, and went in pursuit as far as Dan.
—Genesis 14:14

Part of being in a house is being trained. Not only were there those who had been born in and for Abraham's house, they also were trained. The word *train* comes from a Hebrew word that means "to narrow." This implies that God takes our wild, unrestrained nature and begins to modify it. He works discipline into our lives. Even the gifts that we have must come under submission, so they are honed to bring forth the maximum results. Jesus even spoke of the blessing of being meek (Matt. 5:5). To be meek means "to be bridlewise." In other words, the strength and power of a gallant horse has to be harnessed for it to be the most useful. The horse has to go through a process of coming under submission so that its power might be the most effective. So it is with us in a house; we must submit ourselves to discipline, training, and being "narrowed." As we do, the house becomes filled with the unified power of all those born in it and begins to express government in the earth.

> *Lord, as I stand in Your Courts, I come to submit myself to the training of Your house. I ask that I would be brought into surrender and submission to Your Lordship, even through those within Your House. Lord, I desire to be a part of a house that begins to express government and glory. Thank You, Lord, for working deeply in me that I might be useful to You and Your purposes.*

ARMED AND DANGEROUS

Now when Abram heard that his brother was taken captive,
he armed his three hundred and eighteen trained servants who
were born in his own house, and went in pursuit as far as Dan.
—Genesis 14:14

The third dimension that was necessary for Abraham's house to become an expression of government was being armed. In the house we are to be armed with gifting, ability, authority, and power. This is required for us to be an expression of government as His house. *Armed* in Hebrew means "to pour forth." We are to be equipped in such a way that who we are can now be poured out and sacrificed for the purposes of God to be done. Being armed isn't about us getting to practice our gifting and receive applause for it. Being armed is about taking the gifting we have been granted and graced with and being poured out in sacrifice for God and for others. Being armed isn't about manifesting a gift. Being armed is about sacrificially giving ourselves away to see God's delight fulfilled. This means we don't get to function in our gift only when we want to. Our gift will bring responsibility with it. I must steward and use the gift I have primarily to advance God's desire. As we all do this as a house, government is expressed and the Kingdom of God in culture is advanced.

> *Lord, as I stand before Your Court, I repent for any and every place that I have thought my gift was for me. I now see it is for You. I gladly yield my life and allow You to pour me out for Your delight to be done. Forgive me for every place I have walked in vainglory and pride. I repent. I ask that I might steward correctly the gift You have given me for Your passion to be seen.*

NATIONS FLOWING TO THE HOUSE

*Now it shall come to pass in the latter days that the mountain
of the Lord's house shall be established on the top of the
mountains, and shall be exalted above the hills; and all nations
shall flow to it.* —Isaiah 2:2

Nations are to be affected through God's house of prayer established in the top of the mountains. They will be drawn and caused to come to this expression of God's government. There is something about the governmental authority of God being manifested in His people that will cause nations to come and bring glory to the Lord. The earth is yearning for a demonstration of God's presence and power. As the mountain of the Lord's house is set in place and cultures began to be affected, people from all realms will be drawn to it. They will come to partake of the breakthrough that they can gain from being a part of such a people. This is the key to nations being touched. A people where God dwells in the midst of them, and from them great power and authority issue forth. The nations will not be forbidden. Out of great hunger and desire they will come to the glory and government of God in and through His people.

Lord, as I stand in Your Courts, You are causing the mountain of the Lord's house to be established on the top of all other mountains and what they represent. I thank You that You will have a people of great government and glory that will allow Your name to be known even in the nations of the earth. Thank You that all nations together will flow to this expression of who You are. Thank You for allowing me to be a part of such a people.

TAUGHT AND EMPOWERED TO WALK

*Many people shall come and say, "Come, and let us go up to the
mountain of the Lord, to the house of the God of Jacob;
He will teach us His ways, and we shall walk in His paths."
For out of Zion shall go forth the law, and the word
of the Lord from Jerusalem. —Isaiah 2:3*

As the house of prayer that has the right to stand in the holy mountain of God where the Courts of Heaven function, people will be taught and empowered. Not only will people be taught His ways and Kingdom concepts, they will also be empowered to walk in them because of their connection to mountain of the Lord's house. How we are joined and connected is very important to the power to walk out the ways of God. We are told here that we will have not only the right information but also the right impartation. Being taught is great; walking, however, determines the authority we are able to function in. As we come and are attached in the spirit word to the mountain of the Lord's house, we will discover the new realms of authority we can function in because of the alignment we have gained with God's house of prayer and governmental people.

> *Lord, as I come to stand in Your Courts of Heaven as a part of
> the mountain of the Lord's house on the top of the mountains, I
> thank You that new revelation impacts my heart. I also thank You
> that I begin to walk in new places of authority and breakthrough
> because of the people I by faith am now a part of. Thank You for
> the right and privilege to stand in these places of the spirit realm
> and function here. I thank You that I have new dimensions of
> victory because of my placement before You.*

THE LAW AND THE WORD SHAPING CULTURES

Many people shall come and say, "Come, and let us go up to the mountain of the Lord, to the house of the God of Jacob; He will teach us His ways, and we shall walk in His paths." For out of Zion shall go forth the law, and the word of the Lord from Jerusalem. —Isaiah 2:3

We are told that the law will go forth from Zion and the word of the Lord from Jerusalem. Zion and Jerusalem are expressions of this mountain of the Lord's house ruling over nations and cultures in the spirit world. They are actually the title of this house and mountain. Zion is the mountain (Heb. 12:22). Jerusalem is representative of the house (Ps. 116:19). As God's governing family, there is to be the law of God and the Word of the Lord going forth that shape the cultures of the earth. We see this happening in Ephesus in the New Testament as the *"word of the Lord...prevailed"* and ordered the function of culture (Acts 19:20). As we function as a house of prayer in the Courts of Heaven, the cultures of the earth can begin to be shaped by the Word and law of God. Who we are before the Lord will allow all resistance to the law and Word of God to be removed. The result will not be just individuals being saved but also cultures of nations being transformed by the Word and law of God.

Lord, as we stand before You in Your Courts, we thank You that Your law goes forth from Zion, the mountain of the Lord, and from Jerusalem, the house of the God of Jacob. I thank You that the impact upon the cultures of the nations is glorious. Thank You, Lord, that You have granted us the right as Your people to stand in this holy place to see this done and Your glory revealed for all flesh together to see it (Isa. 40:5). Lord Jesus, we thank You that You will be revered, honored, and worshipped in the nations. Your name, Lord, shall bring salvation to all people.

LEARNING WAR NO MORE

He shall judge between the nations, and rebuke many people;
they shall beat their swords into plowshares, and their spears
into pruning hooks; nation shall not lift up sword against
nation, neither shall they learn war anymore. —Isaiah 2:4

As we walk as the house of prayer in the holy mountain of God, where the Courts of Heaven are, we can see nations brought to peace and tranquility. It might seem unimaginable, yet God grants us the right as His house of prayer in the holy mountain of God to bring conflict to an end on the earth. We are told as we take our place as the mountain and house of the Lord that nations' conflicts that produce war will end. Instead of war there will be production and prosperity. This is because we as the people of God are able to stand in the Courts of Heaven and undo all the things causing conflict from the realm of the spirit. The first step toward this is to believe the Word of God. We must believe that the place God has given us is real. We can actually stand as the Lord's house of prayer and deal with spiritual realities in the unseen realm. When we do this, that which is stirring up war is neutralized, and peace and tranquility can come to the nations. The Lord has given us a great place of authority as His people. May we take that place and see the nations brought to peace and prosperity.

> *Lord, as I stand before Your Courts, I repent for not seeing myself and the Body of Christ the way You see us. I ask for revelation of who we are in You. I also ask that we might stand before You in the holy mountain of God in Your Courts and see all that would stir up strife and conflict be neutralized and subdued. May the nations come to peace as we as Your people position ourselves in agreement with You and Your heart.*

THE HOUSE OF GLORY AND PEACE

"The glory of this latter temple shall be greater than the former,"
says the Lord of hosts. "And in this place I will give peace," says
the Lord of hosts. —Haggai 2:9

The Lord promises that the glory and peace of the latter house will be greater than the former. This is the house of prayer that God would build that stands in the Courts of Heaven for nations. When we are a part of this latter house, we will walk in new levels of glory and the peace of God. This house will manifest and reveal the glory of God into nations. We are told that in the early church people would come into the church and fall on their face and confess that God was truly among them (1 Cor. 14:25). The glory of God would so manifest His presence and power that hearts would be convicted, changed, and empowered for righteousness and purpose. As we walk in connection to God's house of prayer, the same glory can touch in us and through us. We can not only manifest the glory of God but also God's peace and presence. My cry and longing is to be a part of this kind of people. A people who are joined and connected as a house of prayer where nations are changed through the glory of God and peace abounds in them.

Lord, as we stand in Your Courts as a part of Your house of prayer, we thank You that glory and peace are our portion. We thank You that the glory of this latter house of prayer will supersede the glory of that which has been before. We humbly position ourselves and join in the spirit those called to be this kind of house. May others so sense Your presence that they fall before You in reverence and honor Your Holy name.

THE PLACE OF HIS FEET

The glory of Lebanon shall come to you, the cypress, the pine,
and the box tree together, to beautify the place of My sanctuary;
and I will make the place of My feet glorious. —Isaiah 60:13

The Lord calls the house of prayer He would build the place of His feet. This speaks of this house not only being His dwelling place, but also the place of His dominion. Feet in Scripture almost always speak of dominion. God told Joshua that every place his feet touched had been given to him as a possession (Josh. 1:3). The house of prayer that God is building to stand in His Courts is to possess for the Lord new territory and places. It is our job to claim the realms of the earth for the purposes and passion of the Lord. As we stand before the Lord in the Courts of Heaven, our main purpose is to remove every illegal claim being asserted by the devil to rule nations and cultures. We are to set in place the claims of the Lord Jesus from His cross and resurrection. Through His grace the Lord grants us the rights and privileges to stand before Him for the purpose of seeing His government and peace increased (Isa. 9:7). This is the honor the Lord extends to us. We as His house of prayer become the place of His feet that possesses all Jesus died to reclaim.

> *Lord, as we stand in Your Courts from the holy mountain of God, we thank You that we are the place of Your feet. Lord, use us to extend the increase of Your government and peace in the spirit realm. We want to see even the nations reflect the glory and power of who You are. We desire to see all demonic claims over nations and cultures revoked and Your claims established. Lord Jesus, would You allow us to stand in this holy place with You and see this done? Thank You for the privilege of this. Do in us what is necessary for this to happen.*

THE PLACE OF HIS PLEASURE

*Thus says the Lord of hosts: "Consider your ways! Go up to the
mountains and bring wood and build the temple, that I may
take pleasure in it and be glorified," says the Lord.*
—Haggai 1:7–8

As a house of prayer for the nations, God would take pleasure in us as His people. The Lord is exhorting His people through Haggai the prophet to build that which He could take pleasure in. Notice that God's pleasure in something brings His glory to it. The sign that God takes pleasure is the glory of God's presence on it. When something has been built according to the pattern of God, God is pleased. When Moses built the original tabernacle according to what was shown him, the glory of God filled it with such power that no one could even enter or stand in it (Exod. 40:33–35). As we allow ourselves to be "built" into an expression of God's heart and passion, His glory will fill us. We will be allowed to be a living depiction of the majesty and power of the Lord. As a house of prayer for the nations, we will function in and from the glory of God because God delights in us. May we be built according to the pattern of His heart and manifest His ways in the earth.

> *Lord, as we stand in Your Courts as Your house of prayer, may
> we be built according to Your pattern. May we not substitute our
> own ideas and concepts for what You desire. Our passion is to
> please You and be a house of Your pleasure. Lord, would You
> honor this desire You have created in us and fill us with the glory
> of God. Then and only then will we be able to reflect to the earth
> the nature and goodness of who You are.*

CLOTHED TO STAND IN HIS COURTS

Now take Aaron your brother, and his sons with him, from among the children of Israel, that he may minister to Me as priest, Aaron and Aaron's sons: Nadab, Abihu, Eleazar, and Ithamar. And you shall make holy garments for Aaron your brother, for glory and for beauty. —Exodus 28:1–2

Aaron's and his sons' right to operate as priest before the Lord required them to wear the right clothes. Clothing is important in the spirit world. We all are "wearing" something in the spirit realm. What we have on determines the function we are allowed. To function in the Courts of Heaven requires the right attire. We can see this with Joshua the high priest. His unclean garments were being used to forbid him the right of function in his office as priest (Zech. 3:1–3). We must endeavor to be clothed with the "right garments" so we can be recognized in the spirit world as those who may function there. We as the kings and priests of our God are to have on the right clothing for this function (Rev. 1:6). As we repent and stand before the Lord, His blood will cause us to have on the right garments that we may stand in His presence without fear and operate as His priest in His Courts.

> *Lord, as we stand in Your Courts, we ask that we might be clothed with the right garments. We ask that we would have on garments for glory and beauty that would allow us to function as kings and priests before You in the spirit realm. Lord, take away any and all shame associated with us, and allow us to stand before You completely confirmed and welcomed. Let us be clothed with the right garments provided for us through Your atoning blood.*

OVERCOMERS' CLOTHING

You have a few names even in Sardis who have not defiled their
garments; and they shall walk with Me in white, for they are
worthy. He who overcomes shall be clothed in white garments,
and I will not blot out his name from the Book of Life; but I
will confess his name before My Father and before His angels.
—Revelation 3:4–5

The Lord causes white garments to be placed on those who are worthy and have overcome. As a result of the white garments we wear in the spirit realm, we are recognized there. We again see this in Joshua the high priest (Zech. 3:7). Joshua is told that he will be granted to walk among these who stand there. In other words, he will be allowed to function in the unseen realm of the Courts of Heaven because he now has on clean and undefiled garments. The garments they are wearing both in Joshua's day and here in Sardis were the result of overcoming. As we walk an overcomer's life, we are allowed to wear clothing in the spirit realm that lets us be recognized. When Jesus says He will *confess* our name before the Father and the angels, He is declaring we will be recognized in the spiritual realms. This grants us a place of influence, impact, and authority in these dimensions. May we walk as overcomers and be dressed in garments of white before Him.

> *Lord, as I come before Your Courts, I thank You that Your grace*
> *empowers me to live an overcomer's life. Lord, I desire to "have a*
> *walk worthy of the calling" (Eph. 4:1). Help me, Lord, to stand*
> *before You as an overcomer who has on white garments in the*
> *spirit world that are not defiled. Let me be dressed in this attire*
> *that allows me to be proclaimed as worthy before You. Lord Jesus,*
> *thank You for confessing my name before the Father and the angels*
> *that I might be recognized and walk among these who are here.*

GARMENTS CAUSING RECOGNITION

But when the king came in to see the guests, he saw a man there who did not have on a wedding garment. So he said to him, "Friend, how did you come in here without a wedding garment?" And he was speechless. —Matthew 22:11–12

Again today we see the importance of what we wear in the realm of the spirit. Jesus speaks of a man who came into a wedding feast but did not have on a wedding garment. In Jewish custom, the bridegroom would provide all invited guests with garments. These garments caused it to be known they were a part of the wedding. The garment speaks of the *nature* of the one who gave it. We are told that when we are born again we receive His divine nature (2 Pet. 1:3–4). We are provided a garment that reflects Him. The result of this man not having on the proper wedding garment was him being kicked out and removed. It was the absence of the garment that caused him to not be recognized. One of the principles is that if we try to operate in a place of the spirit where we are not "clothed" to function, the penalty can be severe. We must make sure we are allowing the nature and life of who our Bridegroom is to be formed in us that we might wear the right clothing. This will allow us the place to function in the realms of the spirit, including the Courts of Heaven.

Lord, as I come standing in Your Courts, I thank You that I have received Your divine nature. Lord, thank You that as a result I have on the right clothing that allows me to be recognized in the spirit world as Your son/daughter. From this place, Lord, allow the continuing forming of Your nature to be in me. May I reflect the glory and majesty of who You are in all I do. Lord, allow me, I pray, to stand with the right clothing on that I might be welcomed into these places before You.

PUTTING OFF THE OLD MAN

Do not lie to one another, since you have put off the old man
with his deeds, and have put on the new man who is renewed
in knowledge according to the image of Him who created him.
—Colossians 3:9–10

Paul uses verbiage of putting off and putting on. It is the picture of *changing clothes*. As believers and followers of Jesus, we are to make sure we have the right clothing on before Him. Just like in the natural, we do not put on one set of clothes over another, so we don't do this in the spirit as well. We must *undress to redress*. In other words, we must *put off* the old man and his deeds. The *old man* is the old nature whose desires are against God and His ways. According to the Word of God, when we were saved, this *old man* died. Even though *he* is now dead, we have to put him off like changing a set of clothes. Changing clothes is not a hard process, but it does involve *change*. However, because of the power of who Jesus is in us, we now can make the *changes* that are necessary. As a result of the *old man* dying, we simply discard his ways through repentance. It is not a difficult issue. The Holy Spirit in us has regenerated us to love what God loves and to hate what God hates (Titus 3:5). We are now free to see our behavior come into agreement with God's nature and passion.

> *Lord, as I stand before Your Courts, I thank You that the old man has died with You at the cross. When You died on the cross, this old man/old nature in me died with You. I now by faith discard this old man like a set of unwanted clothes. The passions and desires associated with this old man no longer have control over me. Thank You, Lord, that You now empower me to be clothed with the newness of Your nature and life.*

PUTTING ON THE NEW MAN

...put on the new man which was created according to God, in
true righteousness and holiness. —Ephesians 4:24

As we have put off the old man like an old set of clothes, we now should put on the new man that reflects the nature of the Lord Jesus Himself. As we endeavor to wear the right clothes in the spirit world, this is essential. We do not simply stop doing what is displeasing to the Lord. We also must be proactive and function in true righteousness and holiness. In other words, we live a life of sanctification by giving ourselves to that which pleases the Lord. We allow our thoughts, mind, conduct, and activities to be in agreement with the new nature that we have received. Having received the very nature of the Lord Himself, whose seed is in us, we now love what He loves and hate what He hates (1 John 3:9). As a result of this new nature, we now put on the new man like a set of new clothes. The very spirit we live life from has now changed. The desires we have are now for holiness and true righteousness. We are free to live and demonstrate who God is to the world because His nature is in us, and we are putting on through holy conduct the new man like a set of fresh, clean clothes.

> *Lord, as I stand in Your Courts, I thank You that I am clothed*
> *in true righteousness. Thank You that I have the nature of who*
> *You are in me. Lord, I declare that I love what You love and hate*
> *what you hate. Lord, as I stand before You, I put on the new man*
> *like a set of fresh clean clothes. I thank You that I stand before You*
> *accepted and pleasing to You. Thank You that I manifest the very*
> *nature of You as my Lord and Savior.*

ROBES OF RIGHTEOUSNESS

I will greatly rejoice in the Lord, my soul shall be joyful in my God; for He has clothed me with the garments of salvation, He has covered me with the robe of righteousness, as a bridegroom decks himself with ornaments, and as a bride adorns herself with her jewels. —Isaiah 61:10

As we receive the new clothing of garments of salvation and robes of righteousness, we walk in great joy and rejoicing. The old has passed away, and everything is now new (2 Cor. 5:17). As we now stand in the spirit realm freshly clothed with the nature of the Lord Himself, we have great joy and life. We are also granted a new realm of authority to function in by virtue of the clothing we now are wearing. Our clothing in the spirit realm determines the dimension of authority we carry and function in. This clothing is what testifies that we are righteous and therefore have the right to stand in this holy place called the Courts of Heaven. Righteousness is necessary for the *right* to stand and function before the Lord in His Courts. We are righteous by faith in who Jesus is and what He has done (Rom. 4:3). Our faith in Jesus and His atoning work in our behalf on the cross is what deems us righteous. However, from the new birth that this produces, we now stand clothed as a new man manifesting His righteousness from His nature that is in us. This righteousness grants us realms of authority to function in from the Courts of Heaven.

Lord, as I stand in Your Courts, I receive from You the garments of salvation and the robe of righteousness. Thank You for all that Your body and blood has provided for me. Thank You, Lord, that I am righteous before You not because of my performance but my faith in who You are and what You have done. Thank You,

Lord, that my nature has now changed. From this new nature I express the righteousness of who You are into the earth. This, Lord, grants me authority to stand before You in Your Courts. Thank You so much, Lord Jesus.

THE RIGHTEOUSNESS THAT DELIVERS

"Even if these three men, Noah, Daniel, and Job, were in it,
they would deliver only themselves by their righteousness," says
the Lord God...."Even though these three men were in it, as I
live," says the Lord God, "they would deliver neither sons nor
daughters; only they would be delivered, and the land
*would be desolate." —*Ezekiel 14:14, 16

It is righteousness that grants us the authority to present cases in the Courts of Heaven that allows deliverance and mercy to be shown. We see this as a result of Noah, Daniel, and Job only having *enough* righteousness to deliver themselves. They did not have *enough* effect in the heavenly realm to secure mercy for the wickedness of Israel. Their righteousness was insufficient for this. The level of righteousness we possess is what gives us a place of influence before the Courts of Heaven. We know however that our righteousness is a gift as a result of Jesus's activity in our behalf (Rom. 5:17). This gift empowers us to reign in life through Jesus Christ. We are responsible to walk in obedience to the Lord, but our righteousness is from Him. This means that apart from works we are righteous because of Jesus working in our behalf. It also declares that because of this transaction I now have a new nature that is established in righteousness and true holiness (Eph. 4:24). I now have a desire and longing to live out this righteousness in the earth. The more I function in this, the more authority I can carry before His Courts.

Lord, as I stand before Your Courts, I thank You that I am
righteous because of what Jesus has done for me. My righteousness
is separate from the works of the law. My righteousness is a result
of faith in Jesus and His works for me. I also thank You that this

produces in me a desire and cry to be holy and righteous as You are. Lord, allow me to stand in true righteousness before You that I might appeal and petition Your Courts from a place of authority and influence.

THE PRAYER OF THE RIGHTEOUS

Confess your trespasses to one another, and pray for one another,
that you may be healed. The effective, fervent prayer of a
righteous man avails much. —James 5:16

The authority of the righteous to pray brings great results. The Greek word for *fervent* is *energeō*. It means "to be active and effectual." It is the word we get our word *energy* from. So, effective praying flows out of a righteous life that has energy in the prayer. I have often said, "If you don't feel your prayers, then it is doubtful God does." Praying is an activity that should be full of passion. Praying is an unclothing of the soul where the deepest recesses of our hearts are manifest to Him. When this cry comes from a righteous heart that has purposed to not defile itself with unclean things, there is great power. This was the case of Daniel and the three Hebrew children. They purposed in their hearts to stay clean and free from the defilements of the *"king's delicacies"* (Dan. 1:8). This simply speaks of partaking of anything that brings a defiling effect into our hearts and lives. We must walk with all integrity and innocence before Him with the power of the Holy Spirit. When we do, there is an empowering of our prayers that gains the attention of Heaven.

> *Lord, as I stand before You in Your Courts, I ask that I might walk in a way that does not bring a sense of defilement into my life. May the words of my mouth and the meditations of my heart be acceptable to You (Ps.19:14). As I stand before You in true righteousness, may I be granted great power and authority to make my request. I ask, Lord, that I may be esteemed in Your Courts as one who has the right to stand here. Lord, I ask that my prayers may be used by You to accomplish Your will in the earth and answer the deepest cries of my heart.*

PRIESTLY GARMENTS

*So you shall speak to all who are gifted artisans, whom I have
filled with the spirit of wisdom, that they may make Aaron's
garments, to consecrate him, that he may minister
to Me as priest. —Exodus 28:3*

There were certain garments that Aaron had to wear to stand before the Lord.
As we have read in earlier days, we all are *wearing* something in the spirit world.
What we have on determines our realm of authority, function, and operation.
The Lord's instruction was for certain articles of clothing to be made that would
allow Aaron to minister to the Lord as priest. The Bible clearly declares that we
are *"kings and priest to our God"* (Rev. 5:10). Just like Aaron's ministry as high
priest required a certain attire, so does ours. Notice that what is worn *consecrates*
us to function in these realms. This is the Hebrew word *qadash,* and it means
"to observe or pronounce as clean." The clothing of the priest allowed them
to be proclaimed to be clean, and therefore worthy to stand in the holy place
and minister to the Lord. Notice also that our primary purpose is to *minister
to the Lord* as priest. This is what the prophets and teachers were doing as God
spoke to them in the early church (Acts 13:1–2). Out of the place our attire has
granted us, we must always begin in ministering to the Lord. It is our highest
calling. As we minister before Him and to Him, He will draw near and speak.

> *Lord, as we stand before Your Court attired in the garments You
> provided for us, we come to minster to You. We do not come to
> just ask and request. We come to seek to bless Your heart and
> love You from the deepest places of our life. May our words and
> thoughts be pleasing before You. We desire to stand before You in
> our role as priest, rightly clothed and consecrated. Thank You,
> Lord, for granting us this place.*

HOLY GARMENTS

And these are the garments which they shall make: a
breastplate, an ephod, a robe, a skillfully woven tunic, a turban,
and a sash. So they shall make holy garments for Aaron your
brother and his sons, that he may minister to Me as priest.
—Exodus 28:4

The breastplate, ephod, robe, tunic, turban, and sash were all articles of clothing the priest were required to wear to stand before the Lord and minister to Him. Each item speaks of a certain necessity to stand in the holy place of the spirit realm and function in the Courts of Heaven. The priest's job was to legally secure from Heaven the blessing of the Lord over His people. This is still our job as priests today. Through the clothing we have on in the spirit world, we are to stand before the Lord and legally secure blessings for ourselves and others God has given us responsibility for. Through our ministry as priests, we cause the rulership of God to come into the earth (Rev. 5:10). We *"reign in life through the One, Jesus Christ"* (Rom. 5:17). We can stand with confidence, rightly attired, and present our case and petitions before Him and His Court. This will allow the mercy of God to be secured and blessings to come on us and people assigned to us. God grants us the privilege to be His priest rightly clothed and allowed the rights of presenting cases in the holy place called the Courts of Heaven.

> *Lord, as we stand before Your Courts, we take the clothing You*
> *have provided for us in the realms of the spirit. We thank You that*
> *we may stand as the priest of old and secure from Your Courts*
> *the mercy of Your heart toward us. Thank You for the sacrifice of*
> *Jesus that we now take and use to see Your loving passion toward*
> *us fulfilled. May I and all assigned to me walk fully under Your*
> *mercy and kindness. Thank You so much, my God.*

THE EPHOD CALLING GOD TO REMEMBER

With the work of an engraver in stone, like the engravings of a signet, you shall engrave the two stones with the names of the sons of Israel. You shall set them in settings of gold. And you shall put the two stones on the shoulders of the ephod as memorial stones for the sons of Israel. So Aaron shall bear their names before the Lord on his two shoulders as a memorial.
—Exodus 28:11–12

One of the items of clothing the priest wore was the ephod. This was an apron-like piece that was attached as an outside part of his clothing. On this ephod were two stones with the twelve names of the sons/tribes of Israel inscribed. The priest was to wear this to cause God to remember His covenant with His people. As the priest would go before the Lord to do his priestly duty, these names being upon his shoulders would be a memorial speaking to the Lord. This speaks to us of one of the things we are to do as priests before our God in the Courts of Heaven. We are to call God to remembrance those we are assigned to represent before Him. Paul spoke of *making mention* in his prayers (Rom. 1:9). This was Paul functioning as a priest before the Lord. It was as if he was carrying these upon his shoulders and feeling the weight of responsibility for them. This is a part of our role as priest unto our God. We carry in intercession those God has appointed us to carry before His Courts and in His presence. They are inscribed upon us, and we bear them before the Lord to secure His blessing and mercy over them.

Lord, as we come to stand in Your Courts, I thank You that I am called by You to be Your priest (Rev. 5:10). As I stand in this function, thank You that You have clothed me in the spirit world with garments for this function. Lord, I know on these garments are the names of those You have assigned me to carry before You. I ask that You remember them as I stand before Your Courts. Allow, Lord, Your blessing and life to flow over them and be so very close to them. I thank You for this before Your Courts.

THE BREASTPLATE OF JUDGMENT

So Aaron shall bear the names of the sons of Israel on the breastplate of judgment over his heart, when he goes into the holy place, as a memorial before the Lord continually.
—Exodus 28:29

The breastplate of judgment that the priest wore had on it the twelve names of the tribes of Israel over his heart. The ephod had a representation of them on the shoulders that speaks of carrying something in responsibility. These names, however, were over the priest's heart in that it spoke of his love, care, and desire for their well-being. This would also cause God to remember them as the priest stood in the holy place and the Courts of Heaven and ministered in their behalf. The Lord doesn't desire our ministry as priest in behalf of others to be only from a sense of responsibility and duty. He wants it to also be out of a deep heart of care and love for them. Paul spoke of people being in his heart to live and die with (2 Cor. 7:3). He didn't see his function as a job; he saw it as a holy assignment to manifest the heart and love of Jesus in behalf of others before the Lord. There is no higher call than this. We, as His priests, are to carry in our hearts a deep care and concern for those God would have us represent before Him. This comes from the power and influence of the Holy Spirit as we stand in the Courts of Heaven as the priest of the Most High God. We can't manufacture this, but the Holy Spirit can and does fashion it in our hearts.

> *Lord, as I stand before Your Courts as Your priest, thank You for the honor of bringing to Your remembrance those assigned to me. Thank You that You have placed them in my heart to carry before You out of Your love through me. May Your Holy Spirit please fashion in me deep concern and love that would allow me*

to carry them that You may be brought into remembrance of them. Thank You, Lord, for this awesome honor and privilege to be Your priest and stand in Your Courts.

THE BREASTPLATE
AND URIM AND THUMMIM

And you shall put in the breastplate of judgment the Urim and
the Thummim, and they shall be over Aaron's heart when he
goes in before the Lord. So Aaron shall bear the judgment of the
children of Israel over his heart before the Lord continually.
—Exodus 28:30

Also within the breastplate of the priest's attire was something called the Urim and Thummim. It is unclear what these actually were, but we know that through *consulting* them, God's direction could be affirmed for a given situation (1 Sam. 28:6). They would place their hands into a pouch, and by *feel* they could know the will of God. As priests before our God we are to be outfitted with the ability to discern His direction and voice. Through a sensitive spirit we are to be able to *feel* what God is saying and doing. This is essential to standing before the Lord in His Courts as priest. As we perceive His direction and desire, we can then begin to agree with it and pray in unison with Him. This is so often the key to answered prayer. When Elijah prayed for it to rain, he was successful because he first heard the sound of an abundance *of rain* (1 Kings 18:41). He simply prayed in agreement with what he was *hearing*. Having the ability to discern the heart of God in a matter sets us on the course to our petitions being answered before Him. The Lord would desire to outfit us in our spiritual clothing with a gifting to hear Him. This is not so much so we can prophesy something as it is to stand before Him and pray something into being. This is to be a very necessary part of the clothing we wear in the spirit world as priest standing in His Courts.

Lord, as I stand in Your Courts, I thank You that I am outfitted with a heart that can feel and hear from You. Thank You that You make me sensitive and able to discern Your impressions and Your touch. Lord, I ask that You might empower me with an ability to recognize the gentle whisper of Your voice and even Your breath upon me. As I walk in this part of my attire, I thank You that I can more adequately present my cases before Your Courts as Your priest.

MARCH 24

THE PRIESTLY ROBE

You shall make the robe of the ephod all of blue. There shall be an opening for his head in the middle of it; it shall have a woven binding all around its opening, like the opening in a coat of mail, so that it does not tear. —Exodus 28:31–32

The priest wore a robe made of all blue and constructed so that it wouldn't tear. The color blue speaks of that which is heavenly and spiritual, while the inability to tear speaks of no division and separation. The blue means that we as priests have a right to stand in and operate from the heavenly realm. We are to be a part of this activity. This is why we are told we *have come* to heavenly functions (Heb. 12:22–24). My participations are absolutely essential to God's desires being done. God *needs* us for His passions to be fulfilled. We also are to labor to *"keep the unity of the Spirit"* (Eph. 4:3). Unity is necessary to our function as priests before our God. Even husbands and wives are admonished to live together in unity so their prayers are not hindered (1 Pet. 3:7). Unity and like-mindedness help produce the clothing we are wearing in the spirit world that allows us to exercise authority there. From this heavenly dimension and place of unity we can see awesome breakthroughs come. We can stand as priests of the Most High God in His Courts and heavenly realms.

> *Lord, as I stand in Your Courts as a priest, I ask that I might be clothed with what allows me to function in these dimensions. I thank You that I can stand being clothed in blue, which speaks of my right to be here. Thank You also that I am walking in unity in my most intimate relationships. Let there be no division or separation that would allow my prayers to be hindered. Thank You, Lord, that I am clothed and in right standing before Your Courts.*

CLOTHED WITH GIFTS AND FRUIT

*And upon its hem you shall make pomegranates of blue, purple,
and scarlet, all around its hem, and bells of gold between them
all around: a golden bell and a pomegranate, a golden bell
and a pomegranate, upon the hem of the robe all around. And
it shall be upon Aaron when he ministers, and its sound will
be heard when he goes into the holy place before the Lord and
when he comes out, that he may not die. —Exodus 28:33–35*

Gold bells and pomegranates were on the hem of the garments the priest was required to wear in the holy place. The bells that made a sound speak of the gifts of the Holy Spirit (1 Cor. 12: 4–7). The pomegranates speak of the fruit of the Holy Spirit in our lives (Gal. 5: 22–23). This is to be a part of the clothing we are wearing as we stand in the Courts of Heaven. Through the gifts of the Holy Spirit we know how to maneuver, speak, and pray as we stand before the Courts. The Holy Spirit helps our weakness in these moments (Rom. 8:26). We are empowered from revelation to function in His Courts. This is the ringing of the bells on the hem of the garments. It would be intercession that would cause the priest not to die in this holy place. The Holy Spirit Himself would be making intercession in his behalf (Rom. 8:26–27). Through us, as we stand in this place, the Holy Spirit is releasing intercession. The gifts of the Spirit are used to empower us in our intercession. These are the bells ringing. We also have the fruit of the Spirit, which speaks of the character of the Lord in us. The very nature of the Lord in us allows us to stand in this place and beseech Him for His mercies, judgments, and breakthroughs. We become the very reflection of who He is through these character qualities and traits. We are then received before His Courts as priests.

Lord, as I stand in Your Courts, I thank you that I operate in the gifts of the Holy Spirit. Thank You that my life of prayer is empowered by the Holy Spirit and His abilities. Through these abilities I am effective in prayer from revelation. Thank You also that Your nature and character are in me through the fruit of the Spirit. May I be a reflection of You as I stand in this holy place of power and authority. Thank You, Lord, for allowing me to be clothed and equipped with these heavenly garments.

OPERATING IN THE MIND OF CHRIST

You shall also make a plate of pure gold and engrave on it, like the engraving of a signet: HOLINESS TO THE LORD. And you shall put it on a blue cord, that it may be on the turban; it shall be on the front of the turban. So it shall be on Aaron's forehead, that Aaron may bear the iniquity of the holy things which the children of Israel hallow in all their holy gifts; and it shall always be on his forehead, that they may be accepted before the Lord. —Exodus 28:36–38

The priests were to wear a turban on their heads. It had on it a plate with the inscription *"Holiness to the Lord."* As we seek to stand in the Courts of Heaven and function there as priests, we must have a pure, clean mind. For Aaron to function as priest in behalf of the nation and be accepted, this had to be on his forehead. If we are to stand before the Lord, we must allow the mind of Christ to be in us (1 Cor. 2:16). We must allow every thought to be taken captive and brought under His authority (2 Cor. 10: 5). As we do, we are wearing the clothing of one who can stand as a priest before our God. Our minds are now *Holiness to the Lord.* We are allowing the governing power of the Holy Spirit to remove every unclean and unrighteous thought and replace it with that which is holy and pure. We are walking in the disciplines of *thinking* as God would *think.* We are thinking with the mind of Christ on things true, honest, just, pure, lovely, of good report, that which is virtuous, and those things that are praiseworthy (Phil.4:8). We are wearing a turban in the spirit world that allows our mind to be *Holiness to the Lord.*

Lord, as I stand in Your Courts, I ask that I might operate in the mind of Christ. Lord, remove every unclean and unrighteous thought in me and place in me thoughts that please You. I want to stand before You in true holiness and righteousness with my mind being "Holiness to the Lord." Let there be a consecration of my mind to You that allows me to stand here for myself and in behalf of others. Thank You, Lord, that my mind belongs to You and Your desires in the earth.

ALIGNED AND EQUIPPED

For Aaron's sons you shall make tunics, and you shall make
sashes for them. And you shall make hats for them, for glory
and beauty. So you shall put them on Aaron your brother and
on his sons with him. You shall anoint them, consecrate them,
and sanctify them, that they may minister to Me as priests.
—Exodus 28:40–41

Not only was Aaron outfitted with proper attire to function as priest, but his sons were also. Sons in the spirit realm speaks of alignment. Not everyone is a natural-born son. There are those who have joined and connected to another through the principle of alignment (Eph. 4:11–12). Through this principle they become sons/daughters in the spirit realm. This gives them the right to function in a dimension that otherwise they would be forbidden from. As a result of being Aaron's sons, they were allowed the privilege of being priest. We are priests because we are the heavenly Father's sons and daughters. However, we also must be rightly joined in the Body of Christ. This alignment will allow us privileges that we otherwise would not have. Proper alignment under the leading of the Holy Spirit will grant us authority to stand in the Courts of Heaven. Alignment is that which is legal in nature. The spirit world must adhere to it and recognize it. The Lord is setting in place proper spiritual alignments that is granting new places of authority before His Courts. From these places of authority decisions are being obtained from the Courts, and new places of victories are being won!

Lord, as I stand before Your Courts, thank You that You help me
discern my proper alignment. Allow me, Lord, to be recognized
in the spirit world because of whose son/daughter I am. Thank
You that first I am Your son/daughter. Thank You for this

wonderful privilege. However, Lord, thank You that I am rightly joined, connected, and aligned in Your church. Lord, allow this alignment to grant me new places of power and influence before You. Thank You so much for this, Lord Jesus.

NAKEDNESS COVERED

And you shall make for them linen trousers to cover their nakedness; they shall reach from the waist to the thighs. They shall be on Aaron and on his sons when they come into the tabernacle of meeting, or when they come near the altar to minister in the holy place, that they do not incur iniquity and die. It shall be a statute forever to him and his descendants after him. —Exodus 28:42–43

Nakedness in the Scripture speaks of something being uncovered and of shame. The Lord provided for Aaron and his sons a covering for their nakedness. After Adam's and Eve's sin in the Garden, God covered their nakedness (Gen. 3:21). After Adam sinned and saw his nakedness, he was ashamed. God in His mercy provided clothing for Adam and Eve. The nakedness of the priests had to be covered before they could stand in the holy place in behalf of themselves and a nation. Otherwise their iniquity would speak against them and they would die. The trousers were so their nakedness would not appear. We must cover those things that would be exposed. Through our repentance and humility we ask for the blood of Jesus to cover our nakedness. We ask that His love would cover a multitude of sins (1 Pet. 4:8). We ask that there would be no exposure of our shame and disgrace. This is what we are to be clothed with as the priest of the Most High God. That we might stand before Him without shame having our sins washed, cleansed, and covered. That there would be no place where exposure would be seen. God in His mercy provides covering and atonement for us through the blood of Jesus that we might stand before Him without fear as His priests in His Courts.

Lord, as we stand in Your Courts, I ask that our nakedness would not be exposed. Lord, would You allow every disgraceful and shameful place in us and our history to be washed, cleansed, and covered. Lord, I am sorry for any and all places of nakedness and shamefulness. Please, Lord, I ask that these places now be covered and that I might stand before You without fear and guilt. Thank You so much for Your blood that is now speaking in my behalf and providing this covering.

THE LEGAL RIGHT OF CURSES

Like a flitting sparrow, like a flying swallow, so a curse without cause shall not alight. —Proverbs 26:2

Curses are unseen spiritual forces that sabotage the future you are appointed to. We are told that a curse cannot land on us or our family without a *cause*. The *cause* of a curse means its right to operate is legal in nature. Curses are like birds looking for a place to put their feet down and land. In the spirit world they have to find a legal right to do this. This legal right is *usually* one of three things. Sin, transgression, and iniquity are the most prevalent legal rights of a curse to operate (Ps. 32:1–2). *Sin* means to fall short of God's glory; *transgression* means to *step across a boundary*; *iniquity* is the sin connected to our ancestry. To effectively deal with a curse seeking to deny our and/or our family's destiny from being fulfilled, we must deal with any legal right. We must repent for our own sin and transgression but also for that which is in our bloodline. This will give God the legal right to revoke every voice demanding a right to afflict you and your family and allow what is written in the books of Heaven about you to be your future and nothing less.

> *Lord, as I stand in Your Courts, I thank You that Your blood does speak for me and my family. I thank You that any voice demanding a right to curse me is silenced and revoked. I repent for any and all sin of falling short of Your glory. I repent for any and all places I have stepped across boundaries set by You. I also repent for any and all rebellion against You in my bloodline. Thank You, Lord, that Your blood is now speaking for me and silencing every voice that could allow a curse to operate, in Jesus's name!*

THE FULL REMOVAL OF CURSES

And there shall be no more curse, but the throne of God and of the Lamb shall be in it, and His servants shall serve Him.
—Revelation 22:3

We know that when Jesus died on the cross, He became a curse for us and delivered us from the curse of the law (Gal. 3:13). Many would say that because of this, curses no longer affect us. However, the Bible clearly declares in this verse that only in the millennial reign of Christ will there be *"no more curse."* In other words, until this time, to be free from curses we must aggressively take what Jesus did for us on the cross, His body and blood, and use it in the Courts of Heaven to silence all voices demanding the right to land curses against us. We then get the benefits of Jesus's work and sacrifice for us. If we do not take the voice of the blood that is speaking for us and stand in the Courts of Heaven with it to silence curses and the voices in the spirit world that drive them, curses will continue to operate. They will seek to deny us the future that God has for us and what we love. We have everything we need to stand before the Lord and silence curses and the voices driving them. Jesus's sacrifice has provided everything necessary for life and godliness (2 Pet. 1:3). With aggressive faith we must take all that belongs to us and use it before His Courts to silence any and all voices demanding the right of cursing.

> *Lord, as we stand before Your Courts, we thank You that You have already provided everything that pertains to life and godliness. We thank You that the sacrifice of Your body and blood is even now speaking in my behalf. As a result of this, I ask that all curses lose their right to hurt, harm, and afflict me. I thank You that in Your millennial reign all curses will be fully removed. However,*

as I stand before You in behalf of me and my family, I ask that I might see the full manifestation of what You have done for me even now. Allow me, Lord, before Your Courts, to see every curse against me personally revoked and removed. I thank You, Lord, that I receive a full manifestation of my salvation presently and in the times to come.

REACHING INTO THAT WHICH IS TO COME

...whom having not seen you love. Though now you do not see Him, yet believing, you rejoice with joy inexpressible and full of glory, receiving the end of your faith—the salvation of your souls. —1 Peter 1:8–9

The Apostle Peter is telling us here that we can *receive the end of our faith, the salvation of our souls.* In other words, there is an *end* or something that is to come. A full salvation that will manifest will be ours in the fullness of time. Peter, however, tells us that we can reach into what is yet to come and by faith pull it into the now. We can see every curse that would try to claim us now removed. Even though in the millennial reign there will be no more curse (Rev. 22:3), we can get that benefit now and have a full salvation. We do this through believing and operating in faith. This means we exercise confidence in all that Jesus has done for us on the cross and through His burial and resurrection. As we place our faith in this and stand in the Courts of Heaven, all things against us are forced to line up with is ultimate truth. Curses and limitations against us must bow, as from the Courts of Heaven decisions are rendered in consistence with the cross and its legal transactions. The Lordship of Jesus is seen in and through our lives as curses' rights are revoked and removed.

> *Lord, as I stand before Your Courts, I thank You that I can gain and have now the end of my faith. I thank You that as I stand before Your Courts that I receive the fullness of my salvation and its operation in my life. Every curse's power must be broken and removed. It no longer will hold me or control me. A decision against it is released from Your Courts, and I am free to fulfill my destiny and purpose.*

REMOVING THE PURPOSE OF A CURSE

Therefore please come at once, curse this people for me, for they are too mighty for me. Perhaps I shall be able to defeat them and drive them out of the land, for I know that he whom you bless is blessed, and he whom you curse is cursed. —Numbers 22:6

Balak the king of Moab calls for Balaam to come and curse the people of God. His reasoning and desire for them to be cursed is so they can be *weakened*, and he can defeat them. He understands that they are too strong for him to destroy. He therefore needs a curse working against them to weaken them so they can be routed. This is one of the main purposes of curses. The devil uses them to weaken us, so he is able to defeat us. When a curse is working against us, it brings us to a place of weakness that makes us vulnerable, whereas otherwise we are strong and can overcome. The devil knows this. Therefore, he looks for the legal right in us and our bloodline to land a curse against us. When there is a curse against us, our health may be weakened, our finances could be diminished, our relationships might be strained, our mental faculties may be under attack, and other infirmities might be seen. This can be because a curse has landed and is methodically eroding strength and creating weakness so that we might be defeated. As we stand in the Courts of Heaven however, we can see these curses' rights revoked, and our strength will return and be replenished!

> *Lord, as I stand before Your Courts, I thank You that any voices "hired" to speak against me and bring a curse is silenced. I thank You that the devil's desire to weaken me through an operating curse is revoked and destroyed. Let there be a decision rendered in my behalf based on what the blood of Jesus is speaking for me right now. Let every curses' claim be removed and all limits come off my life.*

REVOKING THE AGGRESSIVE CURSE

Moreover all these curses shall come upon you and pursue and overtake you, until you are destroyed, because you did not obey the voice of the Lord your God, to keep His commandments and His statutes which He commanded you.
—Deuteronomy 28:45

In this Scripture we are shown that a curse is not something that is neutral or inactive. It is not passive. A curse by nature will come upon you, pursue you, and overtake you until you are destroyed. This means curses are aggressive. We cannot be passive or neutral in dealing with them. If we take a less than aggressive posture in dealing with curses, they will be allowed to work against us effectively. We must with great zeal attack any and all curses that would seek to fashion our future. Curses that are not dealt with will form our experiences in life rather than the passion and desire of the Lord toward us. We are to take that which is speaking in our behalf before the Lord and revoke the aggressive curse and deny it its right to function. That which is speaking for us is the body and blood of the Lamb of God. It is standing for us and legally removing any curses' rights to determine our future and purpose!

> *Lord, as I stand before Your Courts, I thank You that the aggressive curse that desires to destroy me is undone. I thank You that because of the sacrifice of Your body and blood for me any and all curses have lost their power to function against me and my family. Lord, from Your Courts allow a decision to be rendered to undo all curses speaking and claiming a right to operate.*

CURSES AND INIQUITY

*"Therefore I will judge you, O house of Israel, every one
according to his ways," says the Lord God. "Repent, and turn
from all your transgressions, so that iniquity will not
be your ruin." —Ezekiel 18:30*

Iniquity that has not been dealt with will be our ruin. Iniquity is the sin associated with our ancestors. The devil will seek to use the transgressions, covenants with demons, sin, and other rebellious activities in our family heritage against us. He will claim the legal right to thwart the destiny and future God has prepared for us. We are told that we must repent and turn away from any transgression and iniquitous pattern of sin in our family lineage. Otherwise this can cause ruin to come to our lives and future. Notice that God says He will judge us according to our ways. This is legal activity. God as Judge can only render decisions based on evidence presented Him in His Courts. As You stand before the Lord as Judge, repent of any agreement with the sins of your family's history. Repent of your sins and your ancestor's activities. Then ask for all that Jesus has done for you to speak now in your behalf. God as Judge will have the legal right He needs to free us from every curse and the ruin the devil would intend to bring against us.

*Lord, as I stand before Your Courts, I repent for any and all my
sins, transgressions, and the iniquity connected to my bloodline.
I ask for Your forgiveness and cleansing. I ask that Your sacrifice
would now speak in my behalf and give testimony before You
as Judge. Thank You that all You need to deliver me from every
curse that would seek to ruin my life is now in place. Let what
You say about me determine my destiny and future!*

REVOKING CURSES THAT DELAY AND DENY DESTINY

Put Me in remembrance; let us contend together; state your case, that you may be acquitted. Your first father sinned, and your mediators have transgressed against Me. Therefore I will profane the princes of the sanctuary; I will give Jacob to the curse, and Israel to reproaches. —Isaiah 43:26–28

As a result of improper courtroom activity Jacob was given over to a curse and Israel to reproaches. When curses are operating, they seek to form the destiny of a person, family, or even a nation. Reproaches are that which is being spoken against someone in the Courts of Heaven. These reproaches are used to determine the future of someone or something. Through repentance and the blood of Jesus we can silence the voices against us that is allowing curses to operate. So many people's lives and experience are being determined by the voices against them in the spirit realm. As we repent and present our case to the Lord, these voices are silenced. No longer will these voices of reproach that are allowing curses to operate produce our future. Instead, what God has said and is saying over us will determine the future we have. The right of curses and the reproaches driving them will be silenced!

Lord, as I stand before Your Courts, I thank You that any and all reproaches producing curses against me are silenced. I repent for any and all sins that would be allowing these voices to speak. I ask that Your blood would now speak and silence these things seeking to shape my destiny and future. Instead, Lord, let Your voice and the voices of Heaven speak for me now.

SILENCING INNOCENT BLOODSHED

Surely for your lifeblood I will demand a reckoning; from the
hand of every beast I will require it, and from the hand of man.
From the hand of every man's brother I will require the life of
man. "Whoever sheds man's blood, by man his blood shall be
shed; for in the image of God He made man." —Genesis 9:5–6

The standard of God's Word was that if one was guilty of shedding blood, then his blood must be shed. This would mean that there would be premature death. Many families find that premature death is in their bloodline. This causes fear and dread to be in people's lives. They are afraid and are even convinced that they will die young prematurely. This can be a result of the shedding of innocent blood in the history or ancestry of their family. The devil will claim a legal right to bring this against them. Through repentance and the work of Jesus, however, in our behalf, we can see this claim of the devil annulled and long, satisfying life be our portion. This is the promise of God's Word (Ps. 91:16). We must come into agreement with what Heaven is speaking for us. Every voice clamoring in the spirit world for our demise will be silenced. Instead, there will be the promises of God's Word speaking for us as we live long, productive, fruitful, and satisfying lives filled with the goodness of God.

Lord, as I stand before Your Courts, I thank You that every voice
speaking against me and claiming the right to cause premature
death in me or my family is now silenced. Any place we have
been guilty of shedding innocent blood and causing premature
death, we ask for You to forgive. Lord, I ask that any right the
devil is claiming as a result of this in my bloodline would now
be silenced. I thank You, Lord, that my reward is long, satisfying
life for generations to come. I am filled with the goodness of God.

REMOVING THE RIGHTS OF DISOBEDIENCE TO GOD'S VOICE

Then to Adam He said, "Because you have heeded the voice of your wife, and have eaten from the tree of which I commanded you, saying, 'You shall not eat of it': Cursed is the ground for your sake; in toil you shall eat of it all the days of your life."
—Genesis 3:17

Adam listened to Eve's voice rather than the voice of God. This produced a disobedience that caused a curse. Anytime we allow another voice to outrank the voice of God in our life, we grant a legal right for a curse to land or alight (Prov. 26:2). The intimidation of someone else's voice can produce disobedience in us. Whether it is because we fear that person, believe that person more than God's voice, or simply desire to please that person, our willingness to disobey the voice of God can open the door to a curse. Notice that the curse that came on Adam was a diminished return for his labors. Many are laboring it would seem under this curse. They work diligently but never seem to receive a full return for their labors. They live in a perpetual place of need, lack, insufficiency, and a sense of never being able to come into the abundance promised in the Word of God. It could be because the devil is claiming a legal right based on our disobedience to God's voice in preference for obeying someone else's voice. We must repent for any place someone in our bloodline or we have done this. When we do, we grant God the legal right to revoke and silence the devil and his accusations against us. We are freed to see a full return from our labors and efforts.

Lord, as I come to stand before Your Courts, I repent for any and every place I or those in my bloodline have transgressed against Your voice and not obeyed You. I ask that any place I have chosen to obey another's voice in the place of Yours, that I would be forgiven. I repent for this rebellion and sin. Lord, allow Your blood to speak for me, forgive me, and justify me before Your Courts. Let the curse of diminished returns be lifted off me, and let me prosper and succeed as You have purposed and promised.

REVOKING THE CURSE ASSOCIATED WITH COVENANT BREAKING

Now there was a famine in the days of David for three years, year after year; and David inquired of the Lord. And the Lord answered, "It is because of Saul and his bloodthirsty house, because he killed the Gibeonites." —2 Samuel 21:1

David was perplexed as to why there was a famine in the land that had lasted for three long years. After it was clear it wasn't just a natural occurrence, David asked God why this was happening. The principle here is anytime we see a reoccurring pattern it can be a sign of a curse. The Lord told David it was because Saul, his predecessor, had broken the covenant Joshua made with the Gibeonites. The result was famine. Broken covenants can allow the devil the legal right to bring famine and need into our lives. It can be divorce, an agreement in a business deal that was not honored, or as simple as breaking a promise we made to someone. The devil can grab this as a legal right and use it against us to rain down a curse on us and our family. We must repent for any place we have not honored a covenant or our word. As we do, the blood of Jesus will speak for us and cause the legal right of the devil to be removed.

> *Lord, as I stand before You and Your Courts, I repent for any place I have not honored covenants and words I have spoken. I ask for Your blood to speak for me as I repent. I ask that I would be forgiven and any place in my bloodline where covenants have been dishonored. Lord, I'm asking for a decision to be rendered from Your Courts to deny the devil the right to use this against me and land a curse of famine in my life. Thank You so much for this.*

THE CURSE OF SEXUAL SIN

Thus says the Lord: "Behold, I will raise up adversity against you from your own house; and I will take your wives before your eyes and give them to your neighbor, and he shall lie with your wives in the sight of this sun. For you did it secretly, but I will do this thing before all Israel, before the sun."
—2 Samuel 12:11–12

As a result of David's sin with Bathsheba (2 Sam. 11:2–5), a curse came on David and his house. It was a curse that propagated illicit sexual sin in the lineage of David. Because of this sin with Bathsheba, other events also took place in David's family. One of David's sons committed incest and fornication with his sister (2 Sam. 13:1–19). The result of this was not only the defilement of David's daughter, but later murder and revenge. The result of this sin that David entered into with Bathsheba had effects in the family for generations to come. We must repent of the places where there has been sexual sin and immorality. The devil can use it as a legal right to bring about destruction in a family line and heritage. Through our repentance and the blood of Jesus speaking for us, this right is revoked.

> *Lord, as I come before Your throne and Court, I repent for any and all places in my bloodline and in me where sexual sin has been allowed. I ask that Your blood would speak for me and my family based on my repentance and faith in who You are and what You have done. Lord, please allow every voice of the accuser that would be driving any curse against us to be silenced and dismissed before Your Courts. Let the curses working against me and my family allowed through sexual misconduct be removed from me and my lineage!*

REVOKING A CURSE CAUSED BY DOING EVIL AGAINST THOSE WHO HAVE BLESSED US

Whoever rewards evil for good, evil will not depart from his house. —Proverbs 17:13

Perhaps we or somewhere in our bloodline there has been those who hurt and harmed ones who had previously blessed them. If this is the case, the Scripture declares that evil will come upon that family and it will not be lifted. If the devil in searching the bloodline finds a place where this kind of activity has occurred, he can claim the legal right to visit harm and bring destruction against that family and its members. It is a wise thing to repent of any known place where such a thing might have been done. It is also good to take inventory of our own lives and see if we have been guilty of such things. If we have, harm and hurt can come to us and our heritage. We must not justify ourselves and say we were in the right to damage those who had done us good or to use them for our own selfish purposes to their hurt. This self-justification can produce a legal right for the devil to visit and devour our families. The safe thing is to repent and ask forgiveness for any and all activity that would fall in this category. With all seriousness we should ask the Lord to forgive us for activities that damaged those who previously had blessed us and were our friends. May the Lord grant grace to accept any place of responsibility and repent so that the devil's rights to destroy our family and lineage is removed.

> *Lord, I ask that You would forgive me for every place I might have wounded, injured, or hurt those who have done me good. Forgive me for this and any place in my bloodline where this*

would have occurred. I stand and repent before You and Your Courts and ask that the curse seeking to destroy me and my family would be lifted. Allow its claim to work against me to now be annulled and removed. Forgive me, Lord, for any wound I have inflicted upon another through selfish ambition. Lord, I repent before You.

ABUSING AUTHORITY AND THE RESULTING CURSE

Woe to those who devise iniquity, and work out evil on their beds! At morning light they practice it, because it is in the power of their hand. They covet fields and take them by violence, also houses, and seize them. So they oppress a man and his house, a man and his inheritance. Therefore thus says the Lord: "Behold, against this family I am devising disaster, from which you cannot remove your necks; nor shall you walk haughtily, for this is an evil time." —Micah 2:1–3

Notice in this Scripture that people are afflicting, stealing, and through violence taking away someone else's inheritance. They are doing this because it is *in the power of their hand.* In other words, they have been granted a place of authority they are misusing. Instead of using the position of authority to bless and serve, they are using it to afflict, persecute, and oppress. God declares that whoever does this will not be able to remove themselves from a disaster. If any in our history or ancestry operated in this manner, we should repent in their behalf and ask for any right the devil is claiming to destroy us to be revoked. We should also search our own heart and repent for any place we might be guilty of using our placement in authority to steal from others and their family. This must seriously be dealt with or the devil will claim a legal right to bring disaster on us and our family. Places of authority trusted to us must be walked in carefully and in the fear of the Lord. As we do, we will bring blessings on ourselves and our family and not curses.

Lord, as I stand before Your Courts I repent for any place where I or my ancestry have used a position of authority to afflict. Any place we have stolen, deceived, or taken away inheritance, we repent and ask for forgiveness through what the blood of Jesus would be saying about us. Lord, please allow restoration to come to any we have damaged. We are so sorry for this activity. Please, Lord, let Your blood speak and remove the vengeful right of the devil to destroy us. We would further say that any place we can bring restitution of what was stolen, we would do. Help us, Lord, and forgive us for these activities.

REVOKING THE CURSE OF REBELLION AGAINST AUTHORITY

Therefore whoever resists the authority resists the ordinance of
God, and those who resist will bring judgment on themselves.
—Romans 13:2

Walking under proper family, civil, and spiritual authority is absolutely essential to life, success, and protection. Authority is not our enemy. I would acknowledge that there are those who abuse their place of authority and even wound and destroy with it. This, however, is no reason to rebel against it. David always honored the authority and position of King Saul even though he was in rebellion to and rejected by the Lord. David's refusal to strike or seek to hurt Saul caused the favor of the Lord to be upon him (1 Sam. 26:8–9). We are told that if we resist authority, it can bring judgments on us. If there is rebellion in us coming even from the wounds of authority, this can grant the devil legal right to land curses. We must repent for any wrong attitude and/or action against authority and ask for the blood of Jesus to speak for us. Even when authority cannot be obeyed because it would violate our conscience before the Lord, it is to be honored. This is what Paul did before the high priest. When Paul was unaware that he was speaking to the high priest, he spoke with accusation and disdain when he was struck at the command of the high priest. However, when he became aware to whom he was speaking, he softened and repented (Acts 23:2–5). Paul did not want to be in rebellion to the high priest and give any legal right for judgment to come on him even though the high priest himself was in disobedience to the ways of God. We too must walk in humility before any and all that function in places of authority. It will produce the favor of God.

Lord, as I stand before Your Courts, I repent for every place I have rebelled against Your legitimate authority. Lord, forgive me for the rebellion that would be in me and would seek to defend myself. I submit myself before You and seek to honor authority. Even when I might not obey because of conscience's sake, I choose to honor those who are in these places of authority and power. In doing so, I am honoring You (Rom. 13:1). Cleanse me from every place of insubordination, and produce in me a spirit of humility that You may bless from Your Courts.

RESTRAINTS AGAINST THE DEVIL
FROM THE COURTS OF HEAVEN

So Satan answered the Lord and said, "Does Job fear God for nothing? Have You not made a hedge around him, around his household, and around all that he has on every side? You have blessed the work of his hands, and his possessions have increased in the land." —Job 1:9–10

The word *hedge* is the Hebrew word *suwk*. It means *restraint* or *protection*. The devil is complaining that he has no access to Job because God has a restraining order in the spirit world in place. This legal document in the spiritual realm prohibited the devil from being able to touch Job. In fact, from the power of this restraining order his family lived in divine strength, health, and prosperity. He was blessed and kept on *every side!* There was an increase of possessions and tranquility that was enjoyed. We too can live under a divine restraining order. Jesus even said we would walk on serpents and scorpions and no power of the devil could touch us (Luke 10:19). There can be a decision rendered from the Courts of Heaven that produces these restraining orders. The result will be an environment and atmosphere surrounding us that no demon can penetrate. We can literally be inaccessible and untouchable to the devil (Prov. 18:10). From this place our families are immune to the powers of darkness, and health and prosperity and blessings are our portion and lot. Let us beseech the Lord as Judge of all to render a decision that allows this hedge of a restraining order to be set in our life and denies the devil any access or entrance.

Lord, as I approach Your Courts, I ask for a divine restraining order to be set into place. Lord, set a hedge about me and all that

I love so we are inaccessible to the devil and his forces. I submit myself to You, Lord, and from this place I resist the devil (James 4:7). I say, as I stand in this place, let the devil flee and have no right to touch, harm, or afflict in any way. Let me and all that belongs to me be off-limits to him and his works. Thank You, Lord, for the restraining order of Heaven working in my behalf.

SETTING RESTRAINING ORDERS IN PLACE

Then the Lord said to Satan, "Have you considered My servant Job, that there is none like him on the earth, a blameless and upright man, one who fears God and shuns evil?" —Job 1:8

The restraining order of the Lord against the devil in our behalf is no accident. Just as in the days of Job, his life and choices allowed God to place a restraining order in place. The Lord actually told satan why there was a restraint against him that prohibited him from touching Job. There is always a lifestyle associated with those who live life under the restraining hand of God. They live under the divine protection and order of God. In Job's case there were six distinct things that caused God's restraining order to be set. Job was the servant of the Lord. There was none like him in the earth. In other words, he did what others didn't and wouldn't do. He was blameless. He was upright. He was one who feared God. He also shunned and ran from evil. As a result of these six things speaking in his behalf before the Lord, God as Judge set a restraining order that forbid the powers of darkness from touching him. As we too operate in these six things we can petition the Courts of Heaven to set a restraining order in place for us and our families. Thank You, Lord, so much for loving us and setting this in order.

Lord, as I stand before Your Courts, I thank You for Your love and care for me and my family. I ask that You would help these six things operate in my life so that Your divine restraining and protective order can be in place in my life. Thank You, Lord, that You revoke the rights of the devil to touch me and my family in any way. Lord, we declare that You are our protection, care, life, and strength. Nothing can touch us because of who You are and Your rendering from Your Court in our behalf. We live under the divine canopy of God.

THE SERVANT OF THE LORD— PROTECTED BY GOD

Then the Lord said to Satan, "Have you considered My servant Job, that there is none like him on the earth, a blameless and upright man, one who fears God and shuns evil?" —Job 1:8

God referred to Job as His servant. This word in the Hebrew is *ebed*. It means *a bondman or bondage.* Being the bondservant of the Lord is what grants God the right to put a restraining/protective order in place against the devil in our behalf. Paul spoke of himself as the prisoner of the Lord (Eph. 3:1). Being a servant of the Lord isn't just about serving; it's about ownership. In other words, just serving will not necessarily give God the right to set a restraining order in place. However, serving from a place of being owned by Him will. Our hearts and lives surrendered and yielded to Him as our Master and Lord allow God to restrain the devil against us. This is why we must not be our own but rather owned by the Lord (1 Cor. 6:19–20). We are bought with a price, even the blood of the Lamb. When we understand this, the gratefulness of our hearts cries to be His. The expensive price that was paid to redeem us and purchase us demands we give our lives to Him as His servants. As a result of this choice and transaction, God as Judge can set restraining and protective orders in place that stops satan from bringing harassment and destruction into our lives. He cannot touch us because we are His bondservants.

> *Lord, as the servant and bondslave of the Lord I come and ask that Your restraining order against the devil be set in place in my life and family. Lord, I ask that every right the devil would claim be revoked because of Your hedge and restraint against the devil and his forces. I decree that I am kept and preserved by You from Your Courts. We are safe and protected.*

DOING WHAT OTHERS WON'T

Then the Lord said to Satan, "Have you considered My servant Job, that there is none like him on the earth, a blameless and upright man, one who fears God and shuns evil?" —Job 1:8

One of the most significant things that allowed God's restraining order over Job was there was none like him on the earth. When we walk the way others don't walk or won't walk, we get what they don't and won't get. If we want what is uncommon, we must live uncommon lives. This is not from our own efforts, but from responding to the grace of God in our lives. The Apostle Paul said he labored more abundantly than others because of the grace of God in his life (1 Cor. 15:10). If *living like none others on the earth* was a result of our own effort, then it wouldn't be fair. If, however, it is a result to choose to embrace God's grace and empowerment, it is available to all. When we by grace *live like none others on the earth,* we get restraining orders in place that forbid the devils activities against us. The widow of Zarephath got what others didn't because she by faith did what others wouldn't and gave the prophet her last; Namaan was healed when others died of leprosy because he by faith obeyed the prophet's word (Luke 4:25–27). There was *none like them on the earth.* May we embrace the grace of God to live uncommon lives of faith so that God can set restraining orders in place over our lives and families. The result will be favor, blessing, protection, and prosperity. Thank You, Lord, for the rendering of decisions from Your Courts in our behalf.

Lord, as I stand before You, I repent for every place I have made excuses for not living an uncommon life. Today I embrace Your grace and choose to obey on another level. Lord, as I do, would You empower me and help my weakness. Let a decision be set in place from Your Courts that allows the restraining of God against every work of the devil. Thanks so much for this.

BLAMELESS LIVING

Then the Lord said to Satan, "Have you considered My servant Job, that there is none like him on the earth, a blameless and upright man, one who fears God and shuns evil?" —Job 1:8

God's testimony concerning Job was that he was blameless. This allowed the Lord the right to set a hedge/restraining order in place against the devil concerning Job and his house. The word *blameless* in Hebrew is *tam*, from the root word meaning "gentle, dear, coupled together." So to be *blameless* is to walk in *union* with the Lord in intimacy. Everything we get from the Lord flows from intimacy with Him. Jesus walked in such union with God that He could declare *"he who has seen Me has seen the Father"* (John 14:9). We are to seek such union, and *coupling together* with Him, we manifest the Lord as well. This is a result of deep intimacy with Him. The power to live blameless and undefiled lives before Him isn't from willpower. It is a result of deep connections in the spirit as a result of a coupling together through intense times of devotion with Him. As we set our heart and face toward Him, the Holy Spirit will reveal the beauty of Him to us. We will have no choice but to fall desperately in love with who He is. Our hearts will be joined with Him in union. This will empower our walk of purity before Him. The result will be a rendering from the Courts to set a restraint against all the powers of the devil. He will by no means hurt us or be able to do damage to us. We are the protected of the Lord.

Lord, as I approach Your Courts, I ask for deep places of union and coupling with You that will result in new realms of purity and blamelessness. I cannot produce this in my own strength. However, Lord, from a joining with You the strength and power to live holy is set in my life. Lord, let my life be a demonstration of who You are. Lord, let Your restraining order be established over me and my family.

STRAIGHT AND TRUE

Then the Lord said to Satan, "Have you considered My servant Job, that there is none like him on the earth, a blameless and upright man, one who fears God and shuns evil?" —Job 1:8

The Lord testified of Job that he was upright. This was an additional thing that allowed God to set a restraining order against the powers of darkness. In the Hebrew the word for *upright* is *yashar*. It means *to be straight*. It is not crooked, twisted, or perverse. In other words, Job's thinking, activities, and life were straight before the Lord. There was no compromise little or small in his life. He lived his life from the standard of God and His word. The word *iniquity* in the Hebrew comes from the root *avah*, which means "to make crooked." Job being straight meant that he was not allowing the iniquity in his bloodline to twist him. When iniquity is not dealt with, it will produce a twisting and crookedness in us morally, ethically, and spiritually. Job did not allow this. He was straight through the word of the Lord in his life. His thinking was in line with the word of God. As we repent and ask for the blood of Jesus to cleanse us, every crooked thing will be taken out of us. The nature of God we received at salvation will work in us cutting off any and all effects of iniquity to shape us and fashion us (see 2 Pet. 1:4). We will be made straight and upright. The result will be that God can render a decision to set a restraining order in place for us. The power of iniquity is broken, and we become demonstrations of God and His life.

> Lord, as I stand before You and Your Courts, I ask that any crooked place in me would be made straight. I repent for any iniquity in my bloodline seeking to fashion me and twist me. I ask for Your blood to speak for me and for the Holy Spirit to

cleanse any and all perverse places in me. Lord, make me upright and straight before You that You might testify in my behalf. Let Your Courts set in place a restraining order against every power of darkness.

FEARING GOD

Then the Lord said to Satan, "Have you considered My servant Job, that there is none like him on the earth, a blameless and upright man, one who fears God and shuns evil?" —Job 1:8

Job's fear of God caused a restraining order from the Courts of Heaven to be set in place. Fearing God is when we have an awareness of the spirit realm. We understand that if we obey God, He is free to bless and empower us. However, if we disobey, we grant the devil the legal right to devour and destroy. This should cause a sobriety to be in us that causes us in fear and trembling to seek to always obey the Word of the Lord and His precepts. This cuts off the devil's rights against us and establishes God's passion to bless us. Our awareness of the weakness of our humanity also plays into this. The result of this weakness causes us to push into the Lord to gain His strength from His grace and Spirit. Only through this empowerment can we obey and find the blessing of God. The early church walked in this fear. It was not a tormenting fear but one that births a holy reverence for God and His ways. The result was great demonstration of power and miracles (Acts 2:43). The fear of the Lord creates an atmosphere that allows the majesty of God to be displayed. May we walk more and more in the fear of God. As we do, He will set restraining orders in place over those who fear Him and obey His ways.

> *Lord, as we stand before You in Your Courts, we ask that the fear of who You are would be established in our hearts. We thank You that as we fear You and obey Your Word, the rights of the devil are revoked from us. I thank You that through the revelation of You, I walk in a right perspective and honor You. Lord, because of this set Your restraints against the enemy in my life.*

SHUNNING EVIL

Then the Lord said to Satan, "Have you considered My servant Job, that there is none like him on the earth, a blameless and upright man, one who fears God and shuns evil?" —Job 1:8

Job shunned evil. The word *shun* in the Hebrew means "to turn off." Job knew how to *turn off temptation*. Everyone gets tempted. The Scripture says even Jesus was tempted, yet He did not sin (Heb. 4:15). As born-again believers with the nature of God now inside us, we have power over sin. The Scripture actually says we don't have to sin (1 John 3:9). As a result of His seed or nature in us we now have the power of choice. We can choose to *turn off* temptation and not allow it to seduce us. This is the discipline that Job walked in. This caused God to issue a restraining order in behalf of him and his house. Job's resistance to temptation and saying no to all that would lead him astray spoke before the Lord. Based on this testimony, God set this restraining/protective order in place. When we are tempted, we must know how to *turn off* the desire of the flesh to go that way. When we make that choice, it has great power before the Lord. The Lord actually said to me years ago, "Every time you say no to sin, you are saying, 'I love You more.'" In other words, because of a passion to please Him out of a love for Him there is the power to resist temptation. When this is done, we are *shunning evil* and obtaining a restraint from Heaven against the desire of the devil toward us.

> *Lord, as I stand before Your Courts, I ask for a restraining order against the powers of darkness. I repent for all the places I have not shunned evil. I repent for the times I haven't turned off "the lust of the flesh, the lust of the eyes, and the pride of life" (1 John 2:16). I ask for Your blood to speak for me. I ask that any rights*

the devil would be claiming to devour or destroy me would now be revoked. Lord, please allow a restraint from Your Courts to be set in place. Empower me, O God, by Your Spirit to turn off temptation and serve only You.

A PURE HEART

So Satan answered the Lord and said, "Does Job fear God for nothing? Have You not made a hedge around him, around his household, and around all that he has on every side? You have blessed the work of his hands, and his possessions have increased in the land. But now, stretch out Your hand and touch all that he has, and he will surely curse You to Your face!" —Job 1:9–11

Satan's accusation against Job, which caused his troubles, was that Job wasn't serving God with a pure heart. Satan contended before the Lord as Judge that Job's supposed loyalty to Him was simply because of how much God had blessed him. This tells us that our motives and heart attitude is important. Not only are we to serve God with right actions but also with a right heart. Everything in the spirit realm is open and manifest. We are told that all things are naked and open before Him (Heb. 4:13). Not only are our actions on display, but apparently the motives that drive them are as well. As a result of this accusation against Job, the Lord as Judge allowed satan to bring destruction into Job's life. This accusation allowed the restraining order Job and his family had been functioning under to be lifted. The tranquility of their life was disrupted and destroyed. We too must make sure that our hearts are pure before the Lord. We must allow the evaluation of the Holy Spirit to search us to make sure what we are doing is from a right motive and heart (Ps. 139:23–24). We grant the Lord the right to examine us and make sure that a pure clean heart is operating in us. This will remove any right the devil might be trying to claim to have a restraining order lifted off our life. We can get in place and maintain the restraining order of God in our behalf.

Lord, as I approach Your Courts I give You the right to search me and examine my actions and motives. May any place the devil would claim a right based on unrighteous motives, be silenced. I'm asking that the purity of who You are would be in my life. Let there not be a reason found in me for the devil to request a lifting of the restraints of Heaven against him. Thank You, Lord, for Your restraining order being in place and being unmovable.

REMOVING EVIDENCE THAT LIFTS RESTRAINING ORDERS

And his sons would go and feast in their houses, each on his appointed day, and would send and invite their three sisters to eat and drink with them. So it was, when the days of feasting had run their course, that Job would send and sanctify them, and he would rise early in the morning and offer burnt offerings according to the number of them all. For Job said, "It may be that my sons have sinned and cursed God in their hearts." Thus Job did regularly. —Job 1:4–5

This verse sounds as if Job was doing something right, yet upon closer examination we can see that the motive of his heart at least was a mixture. Out of fear of his children being judged, he brought an offering to try and *appease* God, not *please* God. This offering had a testimony attached to it that satan used to question Job's motives and sincerity before God. Our money does speak in the Courts of Heaven (Heb. 7:8). The sound of this offering was manipulated by satan to question Job's motives and heart before the Lord. We even know that later Job declared, *"The thing I greatly feared has come upon me"* (Job 3:25). This offering was out of fear not faith toward the Lord. This was enough for satan to have evidence to back up his accusation of impure motives against Job. We must make sure that the offerings we bring are from a pure, unadulterated heart. When we do, our offerings are acceptable and speak right things before the Lord. If our hearts are not pure, then the offering carries that sound. It can actually speak against us rather than for us. Sometimes we need to silence the sound of an improper offering in our history, so satan doesn't use it as a legal right to question us before the Lord and His Courts.

Lord, as I stand before You, I ask that any offering I have brought that wasn't from a heart of faith and purity would not be allowed to speak before You. Lord, would You let this sound of any offering speaking now be silenced, so satan cannot use it to question me and my motives. Lord, help me to bring only offerings attached to a right heart of faith that they may speak before You. Lord, allow every restraining order to be in place before You concerning me and my family. Forbid the devil from using any offering to question my heart.

THE SEVEN SPIRITS OF GOD
BEFORE HIS COURTS

*John, to the seven churches which are in Asia: Grace to you and
peace from Him who is and who was and who is to come, and
from the seven Spirits who are before His throne, and from Jesus
Christ, the faithful witness, the firstborn from the dead, and
the ruler over the kings of the earth. To Him who loved us and
washed us from our sins in His own blood.*
—Revelation 1:4–5

Scripture says that the seven Spirits are before the throne of God. The throne is the judicial center of Heaven (Ps. 97:2). So these Spirits being before His throne means they operate in and from the Courts of Heaven. In fact, it could be that to gain the advantage these Spirits bring, we must function in and from the Courts of Heaven to receive the anointing they carry. When we speak of the seven Spirits, we are speaking of the Person of the Holy Spirit and His major characteristics. Paul was clear that there is *one* Spirit (1 Cor. 12:8). The same Spirit ministered all nine of the spiritual manifestations mentioned in First Corinthians 12. Even though there are nine different expressions mentioned, they are from the *same* Spirit. So we cannot think of there being seven Holy Spirits. There is one Holy Spirit with seven characteristics, personalities traits, or expressions. These are before the throne of God from where the Courts of Heaven operates. They are called lamps (Rev. 4:5) and eyes (Zech. 4:10). These seven bring illuminations and are the eyes of the Lord scanning the whole earth, looking for those with perfect hearts before Him (2 Chron. 16:9). As we stand before the throne of God and His Courts, we should agree with and ask for the empowerment of these seven Spirits to come upon our lives. From the Courts of Heaven the anointing of who they are can come upon our lives.

> *Lord, as I stand before Your throne in the midst of the Courts of Heaven, I request the empowerment and anointing of the seven aspects of the Spirit of God. I yield and humble my heart before You and ask that the strength of these seven would come upon my life. I acknowledge my need for the empowerment of these seven. Lord, allow them to impact me from Your Courts and throne.*

SEVEN SPIRITS OF GOD REVEALED

There shall come forth a Rod from the stem of Jesse, and a Branch shall grow out of his roots. The Spirit of the Lord shall rest upon Him, the Spirit of wisdom and understanding, the Spirit of counsel and might, the Spirit of knowledge and of the fear of the Lord. —Isaiah 11:1–2

We are told that these seven Spirits will rest upon the Rod from the stem of Jesse and the Branch growing from its roots. This prophetically is speaking of Jesus, who was of that lineage. So we know that Jesus functioned in His earthly ministry under the influence of these seven. When the Holy Spirit came on Him in the Jordan River, these seven aspects and characteristics of the Holy Spirit anointed Jesus's life (Luke 3:21–22): 1) the Spirit of the Lord, 2) the Spirit of wisdom, 3) the Spirit of understanding, 4) the Spirit of counsel, 5) the Spirit of might, 6) the Spirit of knowledge, and 7) the Spirit of the fear of the Lord. From the anointing of these seven, Jesus impacted the earth and its people. We should petition the Courts of Heaven about the throne where these seven are in operation. We should ask for these seven aspects of the Person of the Holy Spirit to come into our life even as they did Jesus at the Jordan River. Among other things, these seven will grant us the power to function before the Courts of Heaven. The Holy Spirit is called the *Comforter* (John 14:16). This is the Greek word *parakletos*, which means an *advocate, intercessor,* or *one who stands in behalf of another.* It can also imply a legal aid. The Holy Spirit and His seven characteristics empower us to function in the Courts of Heaven as our legal aid. He instructs us and directs our movements before the Court as we listen and are sensitive to His direction.

Lord, I come to stand before Your Courts. I thank You that the Holy Spirit is my advocate and legal aid. He helps me in my weakness to know how to maneuver the realms of the Courts (Rom. 8:26). I ask that the seven aspects of the Spirit of God would now help me function effectively before You. Lord, help me listen to, pay attention to, and be directed by Your precious Spirit and the anointing of these seven.

THESE SEVEN AND THEIR ANOINTING

The Spirit of the Lord is upon Me, because He has anointed Me to preach the gospel to the poor; He has sent Me to heal the brokenhearted, to proclaim liberty to the captives and recovery of sight to the blind, to set at liberty those who are oppressed; to proclaim the acceptable year of the Lord. —Luke 4:18–19

In these verses Jesus famously declares what He is anointed to do. We have seen that the prophet Isaiah spoke of the sevenfold Spirit of God that was upon Jesus (Isa. 11:1–2). Here in Luke we see that Jesus declares He is also anointed to do seven things. It would seem that the order of these seven correspond to the order given in Isaiah 11. In other words, here the *Spirit of the Lord is upon Him to anoint.* Isaiah 11:2 declares that *"the Spirit of the Lord shall rest upon Him."* These are connected. This would mean that the Spirit of wisdom is what produces the gospel being preached to the poor. Following this train of thought, the Spirit of understanding anoints to heal the brokenhearted. The Spirit of counsel sets the captives free. The Spirit of might causes recovery of sight of the blind. The Spirit of knowledge causes liberty to come to the oppressed, and the Spirit of the fear of the Lord brings about the acceptable year of our God or the time of Jubilee. Isaiah 11:1–2 is connected to Luke 4:18–19, which is a quote from Isaiah 61:1–2. As we petition the Courts for the anointing of these seven, we should be aware of that which they do. They are here to empower us to minister life to others in need. The power of the Holy Spirit released through these seven aspects allows God to set people free and restore destiny and future.

Lord, as I come before Your throne and Your Courts, I thank You for the anointing of these seven aspects of the Spirit. I ask that the sevenfold anointing of the Spirit of God would come on me. I ask that the poor would be freed from poverty, the brokenhearted be healed, the captives freed, the blind made to see, the bruised liberated, and the restoration of Jubilee would come. Thank You, Lord, for allowing the power of the Holy Spirit work this in me and through me.

THE RESTING SPIRIT OF GOD

*The Spirit of the Lord shall rest upon Him, the Spirit of wisdom
and understanding, the Spirit of counsel and might, the Spirit
of knowledge and of the fear of the Lord.* —Isaiah 11:2

In both Luke 4:18 and here we are told that the Spirit of the Lord comes to rest and anoint. The word *rest* in the Hebrew word is *nuwach*. It means "to settle down." The Holy Spirit comes to rest and settle down upon us as He anoints us for His service. This implies that the Spirit comes to stay on our lives. Jesus said that when the Holy Spirit came, He would be with us forever (John 14:16). The Holy Spirit by His nature looks for a dwelling place. We become the dwelling place of God by His Spirit (Eph. 2:22). In that the Holy Spirit is looking to dwell upon us and in us, we should be careful not to *grieve* Him. We are cautioned that the Spirit can be grieved through unholy living (Eph. 4:30). The word *grieve* in the Greek is the word *lupeo*, and it means "to distress, cause grief, and sadness." When the Spirit of God comes to rest and settle down on us and in us, we must learn to accommodate Him. Our efforts should be to make Him feel welcome and comfortable with us. The more we receive the Spirit of God and His *resting* upon us, the more He will commune with us and we will be His dwelling place. We must welcome Him and always endeavor to make Him feel warmed and at home with us.

> Lord, as Your Spirit comes to rest upon and settle down in us and
> on us from Your throne and Courts, help me to live in a way that
> He is welcomed and comfortable. I repent for any place I have
> grieved the Holy Spirit in any way. Lord, help me to always be
> aware of my attitudes and conduct that the Spirit of God within
> me will feel warmed and welcomed.

WISDOM THAT DESTROYS POVERTY

The Spirit of the Lord is upon Me, because He has anointed Me to preach the gospel to the poor; He has sent Me to heal the brokenhearted, to proclaim liberty to the captives and recovery of sight to the blind, to set at liberty those who are oppressed.
—Luke 4:18

The Spirit of wisdom is that which anointed Jesus and us to deliver a word that destroys poverty. Many people think that lack, need, and poverty are solved by money. Money gained outside of wisdom, however, will usually result in sorrow and loss of that which was gained. Wisdom is always righteously connected to the obtaining of wealth and prosperity. We are told that Solomon *"surpassed all the kings of the earth in riches and wisdom"* (2 Chron. 9:22). Riches and wisdom are connected. If we are to break out of poverty, it is not money we need; it is wisdom. This is why God could promise Solomon wisdom and also riches and wealth (1 Kings 3:11–13). The wisdom that Solomon carried would allow him to become wealthy and prosper in an unprecedented way. As we receive the Spirit of wisdom as one of the sevenfold spirits of God, it will produce in us the strategies, favor, and empowerment to gain wealth. I believe it could be said that *power to get wealth* spoken of in Deuteronomy 8:18 is this anointing of wisdom. Let's ask for this anointing from the Courts of Heaven and allow it to saturate our lives.

> *Lord, as I stand before Your Courts, I thank You for the sevenfold Spirit of God. I ask You from this place in the spirit realm that You would anoint me with this Spirit of wisdom. Lord, would You allow this wisdom to empower me with principles, strategies, and insight that allow the good news of the gospel to free us from debt, poverty, lack, and need. Thank You, Lord, for this anointing.*

THE PROFITS OF WISDOM

Happy is the man who finds wisdom, and the man who gains understanding; for her proceeds are better than the profits of silver, and her gain than fine gold. —Proverbs 3:13–14

We are told that happiness is found in finding wisdom and gaining understanding. This Scripture can mean that wisdom will purchase for us what gold, silver, and finances never could. This is true. However, wisdom also causes us to gain the profits of silver and gold. Through wisdom we will not miss the opportunities presented to us. Through wisdom we will see what others miss. Through wisdom we will have perceptions that others never realize. The result of this will be an ability to prosper and increase. The ability to see increase of wealth is not necessarily about working harder than another. The prosperity of the Lord can be a result of us seeing what others are missing. When we can recognize these opportunities and not let them pass us by, we can prosper. This is a result of wisdom. We must ask the Lord to make us sensitive to His voice in the midst of opportunities. From the voice of the Lord there is wisdom (Prov. 2:6). The mouth of the Lord speaks wisdom that the wise in their own understanding miss. Those who have an ear to hear will obtain wisdom that brings the proceeds of wealth and prosperity.

> *Lord, as I stand before Your Courts, I ask that You would make me sensitive to Your voice from Your mouth that brings wisdom. Allow Lord the Spirit of wisdom to rest upon me that would produce wealth, prosperity, and riches. Thank You, Lord, that this anointing comes from the Courts upon my life and purpose.*

THE DELIGHT OF PROSPERITY

Let them shout for joy and be glad, who favor my righteous
cause; and let them say continually, "Let the Lord be
magnified, who has pleasure in the prosperity of His servant."
—Psalm 35:27

As we believe God for the Spirit of wisdom that brings the prosperity of the Lord, we must know that God delights and has pleasure in His servants' prosperity. It brings joy to God's heart when we prosper. It is not the desire of the Lord for His people to wane in lack and need. He desires to prosper those who belong to Him and have set their hearts toward Him. Prosperity is simply an extension of a soul who has come to a realm of wholeness through their relationship with the Lord. Third John 2 tells us that we should prosper and be in health as our soul prospers. So prosperity is something that occurs from the inside out. As we come to wholeness on the inside, we are able to walk in the wisdom of the Lord. The result will be prosperity inside and out. The more we surrender and yield our lives to the ways of God and order our *inner world,* the more we can be trusted with prosperity. The wisdom of the Lord will not be missed but recognized as it comes to us. The result will be a prosperity that delights the heart of God and brings pleasure to His soul.

> *Lord, as I stand before Your Courts, I ask that any adjustment*
> *in my perception of who You are would come. Any place where I*
> *might think that You delight in my lack and need I repent of. I*
> *thank You that You take delight and pleasure in my prosperity.*
> *Lord, allow my soul to prosper on the inside that I might also*
> *prosper from Your wisdom on the outside.*

APRIL 29

WISDOM TO TILL

He who tills his land will have plenty of bread, but he who follows frivolity will have poverty enough! —Proverbs 28:19

We are instructed that those who work their land will prosper. This is a piece of wisdom from the Spirit of wisdom that breaks poverty. If we work our land, it will bring forth a harvest. However, whoever is frivolous and unstable will have poverty to contend with. Working and tilling our land speaks of investing ourselves, energies, talents, and plans in the enterprise under our hand. In other words, we must prepare the soil, plant the seed, watch over the growth, and give ourselves diligently to the process. The result will be a harvest that brings plenty. So many do not till their land. They are lazy, lack oversight, and expect something to magically happen. This will not occur. The wealthy can always point to diligence and investing of themselves in the process that produced the harvest they enjoy. They know how to work the process until harvest has come. This will result in prosperity and enrichment that allows blessing and increase.

> *Lord, as I stand in Your Courts, I repent for any place where I have not followed the Spirit of wisdom. Every place where I haven't tilled my land, I repent of this. Any place I have waited magically for something to happen, I repent of this. I yield myself to You and choose to walk in the Spirit of wisdom that brings prosperity.*

THE WISDOM TO STAY AWAY FROM DISHONESTY

Wealth gained by dishonesty will be diminished, but he who gathers by labor will increase. —Proverbs 13:11

There are no shortcuts to wealth and prosperity. The consistent application of principles of wisdom from the Spirit of wisdom will produce lasting increase. If we seek to shorten the process and involve ourselves in questionable and even dishonest activity, we will see diminishment. The Bible warns us of get-rich-quick schemes. Proverbs 21:5 tells us the plans of the diligent bring plenty. In other words, their business plans work. However, those who are in a hurry come to want and need. We must never substitute a get-rich-quick mindset for consistent labor of gathering methodically our wealth and blessing. We desire lasting results that bring blessing to us and even our coming generations. The more we guard ourselves from dishonesty and unscrupulous practices, the more we will increase by labors that produce lasting results.

> *Lord, as I stand in Your Courts, I repent for any place of misguided focus. Every place where I have sought a get-rich-quick rather than practical, methodical labor of gathering, I repent. I ask, Lord, that any tendency toward dishonesty and a violation of ethical standards, I repent of. Lord, I purpose to apply the wisdom of God from the Spirit of wisdom and see blessing, increase, and prosperity come.*

THE WISDOM OF MORAL LIVING

*Remove your way far from her, and do not go near the door of
her house, lest you give your honor to others, and your years to
the cruel one; lest aliens be filled with your wealth, and your
labors go to the house of a foreigner.* —Proverbs 5:8–10

We are warned from the Spirit of wisdom that immoral living and sexual sin can result in the wealth appointed to us going to others. When we yield to sexual temptation, we open the door to the powers of darkness devouring what is supposed to be ours. The wealth meant for our family and us can be taken away because of a legal right granted to these spirits. We must repent for any and every place where we have been ruled by the lust of the eyes and the lust of the flesh. We must ask for the blood of Jesus to speak in our behalf at our sincere repentance and revoke the right of aliens and foreigners from taking away what is meant for us from the Lord. When we live moral and ethical lives filled with a commitment to the Lord and His ways, the rights of the devil and his forces to steal away our wealth is removed. We will be able to enjoy the goodness of the Lord in the land of the living and flourish before Him in all things. The wealth apportioned to us will be for us and our descendants to enjoy.

> *Lord, as I approach Your Courts, I repent for any and all places
> of immoral thoughts, actions and living. I ask that Your blood
> speak for me. I want to be a good steward of all that You have
> trusted me with. I yield my heart to You and allow You to cleanse
> and wash me of any and all defilements. Thank You, Lord, for
> speaking in my behalf and removing any claim of the devil to
> take away the wealth You appointed me to steward.*

THE WISDOM OF RIGHT PRIORITIES

Prepare your outside work, make it fit for yourself in the field;
and afterward build your house. —Proverbs 24:27

The Spirit of wisdom that produces wealth and prosperity will cause us to operate in proper order. We are told that before we build our house, we should get into place that which will bring consistent income into our lives. The field is where our money is made. If we try to live in a realm of prosperity that we do not have an ongoing income stream to sustain, we will come to trouble. The wisdom of the Lord is to get the income in place first then build the house you are able to sustain. One of the biggest problems we have is people living beyond their means. This is because they don't pay attention to this principle of wisdom. We try to live a life of comfort we don't have resources for from our field. Prepare the outside work first, and then live the life you can maintain from that income produced. The bigger the income stream, the bigger the life that can be lived. We must operate in the wisdom of the Lord and set the right priorities that allow sustained lifestyles and blessings.

> *As I stand in Your Courts, I receive from the Spirit of wisdom*
> *for wealth and prosperity. Lord, I repent for any places I have*
> *tried to live a life I don't have an income stream to sustain. Lord,*
> *I purpose to make things right in my field, and then build my*
> *house. I follow the priorities set forth in Your Word, and I prosper*
> *according to Your passion over me.*

WISDOM THAT PRODUCES THE RIGHT PERSPECTIVE OF MONEY

Do not overwork to be rich; because of your own understanding, cease! Will you set your eyes on that which is not? For riches certainly make themselves wings; they fly away like an eagle toward heaven. —Proverbs 23:4–5

In the midst of obtaining wealth and prosperity from the wisdom of the Lord, we must not allow money to be our god or idol. If we allow money to rule us through greed and covetousness, we will not be able to enjoy the wealth God blesses us with. We are told that what we set our heart on could make wings and fly away. Then what we have given our life to is all in vain and for nothing. We must have the right perspective about money for the Lord to trust us with it. We are not to overwork and give all our time to obtaining it, sacrificing more important things such as family, relationships, and purpose in life. If we do, we will awaken one day and realize we have sold ourselves for something that didn't live up to what it promised. We will be pierced through with much sorrow all because what we sought to gain we found to be a cruel taskmaster. This was because it was never supposed to rule us but rather to be our servant. May the Lord grant us the wisdom to walk with a right perspective of finances and wealth.

> *Lord, as I stand in Your Courts, I repent for every wrong perspective of money I have walked in. Help me, Lord, not to give my life for that which can suddenly make wings and vanish. Help me invest in the true treasures of life and receive the right reward for that investment. May my ways please You as I seek to walk in the Spirit of wisdom that brings prosperity and wealth.*

UNDERSTANDING THAT HEALS THE BROKENHEARTED

The Spirit of the Lord is upon Me, because He has anointed
Me to preach the gospel to the poor; He has sent Me to heal the
brokenhearted, to proclaim liberty to the captives and recovery
of sight to the blind, to set at liberty those who are oppressed.
—Luke 4:18

Jesus declared that the anointing He received enabled Him to heal the broken-hearted. This was the third anointing Jesus spoke of. The third aspect of the Spirit of God spoke of in Isaiah 11:2 is the Spirit of understanding. Through the Spirit of understanding the brokenhearted are healed. The word *brokenhearted* means "to crush completely," while the word *understanding* means "the ability to put things back together." Through the Spirit of understanding the broken-hearted are mended and healed. So often we are broken in our hearts and spir-its. As human beings we are *"fearfully and wonderfully made"* (Ps. 139:13–14). This means we can be complicated, and without revelation of the anointing of understanding we may not realize where our real struggles emotionally, men-tally, spiritually, and even physically are rooted. As God through understanding unveils this, we are able to allow healing to come to our broken places. When the anointing of understanding is unlocked from the Courts of Heaven, we can clearly see the deepest places of our hearts that have been crushed and see them put back together again. For instance, perhaps someone struggles with depres-sion but cannot understand why. When through the Spirit of understanding a trauma is remembered or a hurt is uncovered, the root of the depression can be found. It is now ready to be healed because now that person can see where the empowerment of this thing working against them is coming from. Through the Spirit of understanding broken and crushed hearts can be mended!

> *Lord, as I approach Your Courts, I ask that the Spirit of understanding would be unlocked and manifest. I need to clearly see the pieces of my life that have been broken, crushed, and perhaps even scattered. Lord, please allow the Holy Spirit to bring understanding to put these pieces back together again. Thank You so much as the Spirit of understanding is unlocked from the Courts of Heaven.*

DISCERNING HOW WE ARE MADE

*For You formed my inward parts; You covered me in my
mother's womb. I will praise You, for I am fearfully and
wonderfully made; marvelous are Your works, and that my soul
knows very well.* —Psalm 139:13–14

David declared that he was fearfully and wonderfully made. We are a triune made in the image and likeness of God. We are spirit, soul, and body (1 Thess. 5:23). Even though we are made in three separate dimensions, they overlap and are connected. If there is trouble in one dimension of our being, it can manifest in another. For instance, a wounded and bitter soul can cause problems physically. Proverbs 14:30 declares that envy can decay the bones. This is a prime example of how the spiritual, soulish, and emotional makeup of our beings can have effects in the physical realm. Therefore, many times the problems of sickness, depression, mental illness, and other maladies can be traced to a trauma or other emotional consequences. This is because we are fearful and wonderfully made. We can be a complicated entity that takes the revelation of the Holy Spirit to reach into the innermost places of our heart and bring healing. This is where the Spirit of understanding is able to piece together the fractured places of our hearts, emotions, and feelings. The Holy Spirit is the One who reaches the deepest places of our being and heals the wounded places.

*Lord, as I stand before Your Courts, I surrender my being
before You. I thank You that I am fearfully and wonderfully
made. Through the Spirit of understanding unveil any place of
brokenness in me and make me whole in this place. Let every
affected place now be made well through the power of Your Spirit.*

COUNSEL TO SET THE CAPTIVES AT LIBERTY

The Spirit of the Lord is upon Me, because He has anointed
Me to preach the gospel to the poor; He has sent Me to heal the
brokenhearted, to proclaim liberty to the captives and recovery
of sight to the blind, to set at liberty those who are oppressed.
—Luke 4:18

The fourth thing Jesus declared He was anointed to do was to declare liberty to the captives. This corresponds to liberty coming to the captives through the Spirit of counsel (Isa. 11:2). *Captives* is a reference to prisoners of war. Many times in the course of life and events people are taken captive in wounds, hurts, and bondages. This is because we are in a spiritual conflict whether we want to be or not. As with any war that has ever been fought, there are prisoners of war. There are those who in the course of conflict are taken captive. So it is in the spiritual realm. Through the Spirit of counsel, however, they can be freed. Paul speaking to his spiritual son Timothy in Second Timothy 2:26, speaks of those who have been taken captive of the devil to do his will. Through the Spirit of counsel they can be freed from this bondage. The Spirit of counsel that sets prisoners free can come through different venues. It can come through preaching (Luke 4:18). It can come through the prophetic as it did through Jesus when He answered the accusers of the woman caught in adultery (John 8:5–11). It can come through dreams as in the days of Daniel and Nebuchadnezzar (Dan. 4:19–27). If we are sensitive, the Lord will bring His Spirit of counsel to liberate those in bondage from their captivity. The Lord turns the captivity of Zion and sets people free (Ps. 126:1).

Lord, as I stand before Your Courts, I thank You for the Spirit of counsel that liberates me from every captivity. Any place the devil has taken me prisoner I ask, Lord, for Your counsel to come to me to set me free. Thank You, Lord, that through Your counsel I am freed from the bondages of the powers of darkness as Your Holy Spirit brings me counsel from Your Courts.

COUNSEL THROUGH PREACHING AND PROCLAMATION

The Spirit of the Lord is upon Me, because He has anointed
Me to preach the gospel to the poor; He has sent Me to heal the
brokenhearted, to proclaim liberty to the captives and recovery
of sight to the blind, to set at liberty those who are oppressed.
—Luke 4:18

Notice that Jesus was anointed with the sevenfold Spirit of God to *proclaim liberty* to the captives. One of the ways the Spirit of counsel manifest is through the power of preaching. Paul spoke of God using the foolishness of preaching (1 Cor. 1:18). He said the preaching of the cross released the power of God. There can be power revealed through anointed preaching. A Spirit of counsel can be loosed upon people who are sitting under the anointed declaration of the Word of God. We should never underestimate the power of proclamation. Preaching is not just the impartation of information. Preaching should bring an encounter with the Holy Spirit Himself that brings counsel that sets the captives free. The prisoners of war are loosed from the bonds as the Word of God impacts their lives. This is foolishness to those who are perishing but the power of God to those who are being saved (1 Cor. 1:18).

> *Lord, thank You that as I stand before Your Courts, through the*
> *preaching of Your Word, the Spirit of counsel comes to set me free.*
> *I am loosed from my bonds as this anointing comes upon me. I*
> *receive from this wonderful expression of who You are from the*
> *sevenfold Spirit of God.*

THE SPIRIT OF COUNSEL
THROUGH THE PROPHETIC

So when they continued asking Him, He raised Himself up and said to them, "He who is without sin among you, let him throw a stone at her first." And again He stooped down and wrote on the ground. Then those who heard it, being convicted by their conscience, went out one by one. —John 8:7–9

Jesus waited on the Holy Spirit to give Him the prophetic answer in this intense situation where a woman's life hung in the balance. As Jesus lingered before the Lord, the Holy Spirit whispered the answer. As Jesus spoke it, the entire situation was defused and solved. This was because the Spirit of counsel came upon Jesus to give an answer in an unanswerable situation. As He heard the prophetic voice of the Father, He spoke, and the circumstance was remedied. We too must listen for the voice of the Father through the Holy Spirit. He will bring us counsel that will solve what would seem to be unsolvable problems. This woman was liberated from a sentence of death for her sin. All because Jesus could operate under the Spirit of counsel. May we also receive this Spirit of counsel to see ourselves and others freed.

> *Lord, as we stand before Your Courts, we thank You that the Spirit of counsel rests upon us. We thank You that through the prophetic voice of the Father through the Holy Spirit we are able to declare counsel that brings life in what would seem to be certain death. Thank You, Lord, that You are the Prince of Life. We receive Your counsel and walk in it.*

COUNSEL TO STAY FREE

*When Jesus had raised Himself up and saw no one but the
woman, He said to her, "Woman, where are those accusers of
yours? Has no one condemned you?" She said, "No one, Lord."
And Jesus said to her, "Neither do I condemn you;
go and sin no more." —John 8:10–11*

Not only did Jesus give a word of counsel from the prophetic that delivered the
woman from death, He also spoke a word to keep her free and liberated. He
lifted all condemnation off her and empowered her to *"go and sin no more."* This
was His counsel to her to stay free. Jesus did the same thing to the man healed
at the pool of Bethesda in John 5:14. After this man was healed, Jesus found
him, and through the Spirit of counsel told him to *"sin no more lest a worse thing
come"* on him. Jesus was not just content to set people free. Through the Spirit
of counsel He showed them how to stay free. If we are to walk in liberty and
the freedom of the Lord, we must pay attention to the Spirit of counsel. This
anointing will cause us to walk in the freedom and liberty of the Lord appointed
to us. We will not just be delivered; we will be sustained in the liberty and freedom of our God.

> *Lord, as I stand in Your Courts and receive from the Spirit of
> counsel, I thank You for the insight on not just getting free but
> staying free. I receive from You and the rendering of Your Courts
> the Spirit of counsel that empowers me to walk in liberty and
> freedom from every bondage and hold of the devil. I am free in
> Jesus's name.*

THE COUNSEL OF DREAMS

Therefore, O king, let my advice be acceptable to you; break off your sins by being righteous, and your iniquities by showing mercy to the poor. Perhaps there may be a lengthening of your prosperity. —Daniel 4:27

Nebuchadnezzar had a dream where he saw a tree that was cut down. Daniel interpreted the dream for him, then from the dream gave him counsel. Many times the Lord will bring counsel to us from dreams. This happened to Joseph when God directed him to take Jesus and Mary to Egypt to escape the wrath of Herod (Matt. 2:13). As a result of this dream God preserved the life of Jesus when He was young and vulnerable. This was because Joseph received counsel through the dream. We should pay attention to our dreams. They can be the counsel of the Lord coming to us and delivering us from the intents of the devil. They can keep us from his traps and move us into the future God has for us. We can be preserved and kept through the Spirit of counsel setting us free from any and every form of captivity.

Lord, as I approach Your Courts, I thank You that the Spirit of counsel comes to me in my dreams. I ask, Lord, that I might be sensitive to these manifestations and learn to receive that which this anointing would bring to me. I repent for any time I have missed Your communications to me. Lord, help me to receive fully Your Spirit of counsel to give direction to my family and life.

RESTORING VISION THROUGH THE SPIRIT OF MIGHT

The Spirit of the Lord is upon Me, because He has anointed
Me to preach the gospel to the poor; He has sent Me to heal the
brokenhearted, to proclaim liberty to the captives and recovery
of sight to the blind, to set at liberty those who are oppressed.
—Luke 4:18

Jesus declared that He was anointed to recover sight to the blind. The corresponding anointing in Isaiah 11:2 is the Spirit of might. Through the Spirit of might, vision is restored to the visionless and hopeless. We are told that without a vision, people cast off restraints (Prov. 29:18). Vision or the ability to see the destiny and future God has for you is critical to living life with passion and success. God told Abraham to lift up his eyes. He was told that as far as he could see God had given him the land (Gen. 13:14–15). Seeing is imperative to getting what God has ordained us to have. Only when we see can we then receive. The problem is many have lost the ability to see. It takes the Spirit of might to restore this. The word *might* in Isaiah 11:2 means *force*, *valor*, or *victory*. The reason people lose the ability to see so often is because they don't think there is enough *power* to accomplish the impossible. Only when we have an encounter with the Spirit of might are we empowered to look again and see. Our hopes are not foolish wishes or desires. They are very real potentials because of the anointing of might that can actually produce them! As the Spirit of might comes on us, we will be able to look and see once again with expectation and real faith.

Lord, as we stand in Your Courts, we ask that the Spirit of might
would come upon us and restore our ability to see again. Lord,

we ask for true vision from Your heart to come again into our lives. Let the Spirit of might empower us to see and believe to the point of laying our lives down for Your will to be done through us. We receive again the power to see!

LOOK AGAIN

So Ahab went up to eat and drink. And Elijah went up to the top of Carmel; then he bowed down on the ground, and put his face between his knees, and said to his servant, "Go up now, look toward the sea." So he went up and looked, and said, "There is nothing." And seven times he said, "Go again." Then it came to pass the seventh time, that he said, "There is a cloud, as small as a man's hand, rising out of the sea!" So he said, "Go up, say to Ahab, 'Prepare your chariot, and go down before the rain stops you.'" —1 Kings 18:42–44

While Elijah prayed for rain, he commanded his servant to go and look seven times before the servant finally saw a cloud the size of a man's hand on the horizon. Six times he came back with the report of *"there is nothing."* There was a need for the servant to go and *look again*. In the midst of our praying we must always also be *looking* for the answer to appear. This may require us to *look* and see nothing six times. Yet if we will continue to pray and *look*, we will see the cloud the size of a man's hand forming. Elijah's prayer caused this cloud to form, and it became a torrential downpour and broke the drought and famine off Israel. There was a need, however, in the process *to keep looking*. They could not be detoured by the six times they saw nothing. There had to be a faith that propelled them forward even when nothing seemed to be happening. This faith allowed them to *see* the big thing in the little thing. The cloud the size of a man's hand wasn't a drought-breaking rain, but it became one. We must be able to see the big in the little as we look. Otherwise we will miss what God is doing many times. We must not despise the day of small beginnings (Zech. 4:10). We must have eyes to see as the Spirit of might restores sight to the blind.

Lord, as I stand before Your Courts, I repent for the places of discouragement that I have allowed when I have seen nothing. I repent for my faithlessness. May I humble my heart before You and receive through Your Spirit of might the power to see again. I will arise, Lord, and look again for Your answer and demonstration of power.

IF YOU SEE YOU WILL HAVE

So he said, "You have asked a hard thing. Nevertheless, if you see me when I am taken from you, it shall be so for you; but if not, it shall not be so." —2 Kings 2:10

Elisha had asked for a double portion of the spirit of Elijah. Elijah's answer was that if Elisha saw him when he was taken away, it would be his. Elisha's ability to receive the double portion was connected to his *seeing*. We can only receive what we first are able to *see*. In other words, if we can *perceive* it, we can *receive* it. Everything we get must first be conceived through revelation. As we walk in intimacy and relationship with the Father, we will begin to *see* or *conceive* dreams from His heart for us. This is when we begin to attach to that which we are seeing through faith. We use our faith to pull into place what is meant to be ours. What we are seeing in the unseen world, we are able to see manifest in the seen realm. As we *see* something, it can then be ours. Jesus said that the ability to see and perceive was critical to possessing. This is why having eyes to see, ears to hear, and hearts to perceive is essential. Without them, what could be ours will never occur (Matt. 13:14–15). The Lord restores sight to the blind (Ps. 146:8). Because of this, we will see and receive.

Lord, as I come before Your Courts, I thank You that You restore my ability to see. By faith I look and see that I might receive all that You have for me. I even receive by faith a double portion of Your kindness, goodness, and life for me. Thank You that I have eyes to see, ears to hear, and a heart to perceive all that is available to me.

THE POWER TO SEE

But He answered and said, "It is not good to take the children's bread and throw it to the little dogs." And she said, "Yes, Lord, yet even the little dogs eat the crumbs which fall from their masters' table." —Matthew 15:26–27

A Canaanite woman came to Jesus for the healing of her daughter. As a result of Jesus's mandate to go to the Jews first, He refused to heal her daughter. Yet this woman continued to press and push the Master to release the word of healing. Jesus then tells her it isn't right or time for the children's bread/healing to be given to her, a Gentile. The woman then makes an incredible statement. She asked for only the *crumbs*. She was literally asking for the *crumbs of His power*. She had such a revelation of how powerful God was that she said she needed only the *crumbs* of it to heal her daughter. As a result of her awareness of His power, she could *see* her daughter being healed, if only Jesus would release the word. When we know the power of God, it will birth faith in us to see again. It will cause us to reach out and grab hold of the power of God that is available to bring our breakthrough. A revelation of the awesome power of God and the Spirit of might will cause our vision to be recovered and our faith to rise again. May this revelation and awareness come to us through the ministry of the Holy Spirit.

> *Lord, as I stand before Your Courts, I thank You for Your awesome power. It is Your power revealed in the resurrection of Jesus that we believe in and hold to. I repent for every place I have doubted You or Your power. I ask that I might have my sight recovered to see again even as this woman asked for only the crumbs of Your power. Thank You for birthing a believing and faith-filled heart in me as I believe in the power of God toward me.*

LIBERTY FOR THE OPPRESSED THROUGH KNOWLEDGE

The Spirit of the Lord is upon Me, because He has anointed
Me to preach the gospel to the poor; He has sent Me to heal the
brokenhearted, to proclaim liberty to the captives and recovery
of sight to the blind, to set at liberty those who are oppressed.
—Luke 4:18

Jesus claimed He was anointed to bring liberty to the oppressed. Isaiah 11 corresponds the Spirit of knowledge to this anointing. In other words, it is the Spirit of knowledge that sets at liberty those who are oppressed. The oppressed were those who were under the bondage of legalism. They were living under the dictates and mandates of a religious structure designed to control them through fear. This is why the Apostle Paul declared that as New Testament believers we had not received the spirit of bondage again to fear (Rom. 8:15). This was a reference to always feeling condemned because of an inability to keep the law. It is the Spirit of knowledge that sets us free and at liberty. This is not knowledge gained through natural means, but knowledge garnered through the revelation of the Holy Spirit. We come to a knowledge that sets us free from the mandate of religion. We understand through this Spirit of knowledge that it is not the keeping of the law but the communion of the Holy Spirit that sets us free. We have not received the spirit of bondage again to fear but the spirit of adoption that cries out, "Abba Father."

> *Lord, as I come before Your throne and the Courts of Heaven, we*
> *thank you that the seven Spirits of God are released to minister*
> *Your life to me. I thank You that the Spirit of knowledge is*

breaking every false concept and idea I have of You and Your ways. I thank You that because of this I am being freed from the oppression of religion, legalism, and fear. I receive this from Your Courts in Jesus's name.

KNOWLEDGE THROUGH REVELATION

*What shall we say then? Shall we continue in sin that grace
may abound? Certainly not! How shall we who died to sin live
any longer in it? Or do you not know that as many of us as were
baptized into Christ Jesus were baptized into His death?*
—Romans 6:1–3

Paul makes a statement. As he is seeking to challenge believers to live above sin
and a life of holiness, he declares *"Or do you not know."* In other words, he is
asking, "Don't you know by revelation that we died to sin when Jesus died for
us and that baptism is an agreeing and reckoning of this reality?" This knowledge through the revelation of the Holy Spirit breaks the power of oppression
over our lives and frees us to live a righteous life. Revelation is the most powerful thing there is. More powerful than miracles, signs, and wonders, revelation
changes our minds and the way we think about ourselves. Through the Spirit
of knowledge we are empowered to *know* things that set us free. Knowledge
born of revelation alters our thinking process to agree with God's thoughts concerning us. Through this power we can begin to function in the mind of Christ
concerning us and not our own degenerate thought process (1 Cor. 2:16).

*Lord, as we come before Your Courts where the Spirit of knowledge
as one of the seven Spirits of God is, we ask that this anointing
would bring revelation of my true status in the spirit world. We
ask, Lord, that this anointing would flow from Your throne and
empower us to know the right things about You, what You have
done, and what we have already received. Thank You so much for
this impartation in my life from the Courts of Heaven.*

REVELATION KNOWLEDGE FREES US FROM SIN

For if we have been united together in the likeness of His death, certainly we also shall be in the likeness of His resurrection, knowing this, that our old man was crucified with Him, that the body of sin might be done away with, that we should no longer be slaves of sin. For he who has died has been freed from sin. —Romans 6:5–7

When Jesus died on the cross, He didn't just die for us. He also died *as us*. Because of this we died with Him. Paul is asking if this piece of powerful revelation has penetrated our hearts and minds. He is making the point that if through the Spirit of knowledge we are aware of this, sin would no longer have a power over us. He reasons that if we truly died at the cross with Jesus, then the one who has died can no longer sin. Death is the end of the struggle against sin. When we die and transition into the heavenly realm, there will be no more desire for sin. Therefore, if we by faith in who Jesus is and what He has done, know we have *died now*, sin and its power is presently broken over us. Our desires change, and we have the ability to say no to sin and its pull. This is a *knowledge* we have through the Spirit of knowledge that has come to free us from the oppression of sin.

> *Lord, as I stand in Your Courts, I thank You for the empowerment of the Spirit of knowledge that brings me these key revelations for my life. I thank You that as a new creation in Christ Jesus the sin nature I had died with Jesus at the cross. Therefore, through the anointing, I now live a life above sin and its grasp. Its powers against me are now destroyed, in Jesus's name, amen.*

LIVING IN NEWNESS OF HIS LIFE

*Now if we died with Christ, we believe that we shall also live
with Him, knowing that Christ, having been raised from the
dead, dies no more. Death no longer has dominion over Him.*
—Romans 6:8–9

As the Spirit of knowledge brings revelation, we will have a *knowing*. We are
progressively *knowing* that Christ has been raised from the dead and dies no
more. We don't just *know that which has happened; we know new things every
day of our life with Jesus.* We are *knowing* the power of the resurrected life we
are now living. It is bringing us into places in the Lord because death has been
destroyed against us. Death no longer having any dominion or power over Him,
and it is the same for us in Him. Through this *knowing* we come to newer and
newer understanding of the life we are now living in Christ Jesus. This revelation allows old things to progressively pass away and all things to become new
(2 Cor. 5:17). Everything that is associated with death, poverty, sickness, disease, troubles, and all other negative issues have been broken against us. We are
living a life of resurrection where these things have no authority to subdue us.

> *Lord, as we stand before Your Courts, we thank You that the
> Spirit of knowledge brings a "knowing" of that which is ours
> through the resurrected life of Jesus Christ. Thank You so much,
> Lord Jesus, for all You have done for us. May I see these realities
> come into my life. I receive abundantly from all that You have
> legally done for me, in Jesus's name, amen.*

KNOWING THE TRUTH AND BEING LIBERATED

Then Jesus said to those Jews who believed Him, "If you abide in My word, you are My disciples indeed. And you shall know the truth, and the truth shall make you free." —John 8:31–32

This Scripture gives us great insight into *knowing the truth. Knowing the truth* is another means of saying *"revelation has come."* This Scripture is quite often quoted as *the truth shall set you free.* This is not what it says. It declares, *"You shall know the truth, and the truth shall make you free."* There is a vast difference. The revelation by the Spirit of knowledge has the power to liberate from oppression and make us free. Notice that Jesus speaks of abiding in His word. This makes us His disciples, which in turn unlocks the Word and causes revelation to come. This revelation is the *truth* Jesus is speaking of. In other words, Jesus gives the secrets of *truth* to His disciples that are continuing and abiding in His Word. This brings us out of every false idea and concept that has put us in prisons. These can be prisons of sin, religion, legalism, or other forms of oppression. When the truth of God penetrates our spirits, we then *know* that which changes everything and sets us free.

> *Lord, as we approach Your throne and Courts, we ask that we might truly be Your disciples that abide in Your Word. As we faithfully apply Your Word, Lord, we ask that through revelation of the Spirit of knowledge we might know the truth that sets us free from every bondage. Lord, whether it is demonic bondages, religious bondages, or even self-made prisons, please set us free. In Jesus's name, amen.*

KNOWING THE FATHER AND THE SON

All things have been delivered to Me by My Father, and no one knows the Son except the Father. Nor does anyone know the Father except the Son, and the one to whom the Son wills to reveal Him. —Matthew 11:27

Knowing the Father requires that Jesus the Son has to reveal Him. Knowing who God is as our Father is crucial to a life of peace and blessings. Jesus is explicit here that only He as the Son *knows* the Father. Only those who Jesus decides to share this intimate awareness with can *know* the Father as well. Jesus does this through adoption (Rom. 8:15). As the Holy Spirit, who was given by Jesus, comes into our lives, He unveils the ways of the Father and the Father's heart for us. Also, *knowing* the Father is a result of the Spirit of knowledge revealing Him and His ways to us. The secrets and mysteries hidden for ages become our possession. Through these secrets we are able to step into a brand-new life and experience as the sons and daughters of God. The deeper our awareness of God as Father, the more we are liberated from old ways of thinking and function.

Lord, as we stand in Your Courts, thank You for the Spirit of knowledge that unlocks the revelation of who Jesus as the Son is. Jesus, we thank You for then revealing to us the Father and His ways. We ask that every false idea and concept we have of God would be removed and destroyed. We ask that we might function in fresh revelation of who You are and who the Father is. In Jesus's name, amen.

REST FROM OUR LABORS
THROUGH "KNOWING"

Come to Me, all you who labor and are heavy laden, and I will
give you rest. Take My yoke upon you and learn from Me, for
I am gentle and lowly in heart, and you will find rest for your
souls. For My yoke is easy and My burden is light.
—Matthew 11:28–30

In yesterday's devotional we saw that knowing the Son and the Father are the result of revelation. This revelation produces in us a rest from all our religious labors and efforts. Jesus declares that as this *knowledge* comes through the Spirit of knowledge, we discover His true posture toward us. He is gentle and lowly in heart. Out of who Jesus the Son is and who the Father is we find rest to our weary souls. His yoke is easy, and His burden is light! There are many sincere believers who are consistently under a heavy load trying to be righteous and holy. Trying to earn acceptance from the Lord. Jesus comes through the revelation of the Spirit of knowledge to lift this from us. As this is taken from us, our torment is removed. This in turn frees our hearts to serve God from a true love relationship. Instead of working to be righteous, we accept by faith who Jesus is and what He has done. As this burden is lifted and the yoke is destroyed, we take His yoke and His true burden upon us. It becomes a joy again to serve the Lord.

> *Lord, as we approach Your Courts, we ask that the true Spirit of*
> *knowledge would free us from our own self-efforts to be righteous.*
> *Lord, for those of us who have become weary from this effort,*
> *would You by revelation show us what we should know about*
> *You as the Father. Bring us into the place of Your burden being*
> *light and Your yoke being easy. In Jesus's name, amen.*

KNOWN BY GOD

Now concerning things offered to idols: We know that we all
have knowledge. Knowledge puffs up, but love edifies. And if
anyone thinks that he knows anything, he knows nothing yet as
he ought to know. But if anyone loves God, this one
is known by Him. —1 Corinthians 8:1–3

The real revelatory knowledge of God never puffs up. When we have gained understanding from the Spirit of knowledge, we will not be arrogant; we will have a love for God. If the knowledge we have makes us proud against people, this knowledge hasn't been derived from the Spirit of knowledge. It can be from the tree of the knowledge of good and evil that we are not to eat from (Gen. 2:17). We are told that if we eat from this, we will surely die. Knowledge that puffs up will lead to spiritual death because of the arrogance it creates. The knowledge, comes from the Spirit of God that brings intimacy with the Father brings life. We are told that if we are proud in our knowledge that we know nothing yet that we ought to know. We are still ignorant in our pride and false self-esteem. We must repent and ask for the true knowledge of the Spirit of knowledge to birth in us an awareness of who Jesus is and His ways.

Lord, as we stand before Your Courts, we ask that any and all
pride derived from eating from the tree of the knowledge of good
and evil be revoked. Lord, we only want the knowledge that
births a love for You, not an arrogance against people. I confess,
God, that I am no better than anyone. In fact, I ask that I might
become the servant of all men (1 Cor. 9:19). In Jesus's name,
amen.

NO OTHER GOD BUT ONE!

Therefore concerning the eating of things offered to idols, we know that an idol is nothing in the world, and that there is no other God but one. For even if there are so-called gods, whether in heaven or on earth (as there are many gods and many lords), yet for us there is one God, the Father, of whom are all things, and we for Him; and one Lord Jesus Christ, through whom are all things, and through whom we live. —1 Corinthians 8:4–6

Paul is making a revolutionary statement here. He is declaring that the only true God is the One we serve. This revelation is about to bring the people of God into a new realm of liberty. Paul is about to free people to function in real life without the religious restrictions that have been on them. This will be the result of the *knowledge* we have from the Spirit of knowledge. Paul declares that from this understanding an idol is nothing in the world, neither is that which is offered to idols. Because of this, God's people will be liberated from legalistic forms that have bound them. As this revelation begins to penetrate the heart of the believer, that which has made life less enjoyable will be removed. We will be able to enjoy things that have been forbidden all the while giving glory to God.

Lord, as we stand in Your Courts, I ask for the true Spirit of knowledge to bring Your real revelation. Lord, allow me to never grant my flesh the right to sin. Deliver me from self-deceit. However, through Your revelation knowledge allow me to function as a free person in this life. I honor You, Lord, and give glory to You, the One true God. In Jesus's name, amen.

TO EAT OR NOT TO EAT?

*However, there is not in everyone that knowledge; for some,
with consciousness of the idol, until now eat it as a thing offered
to an idol; and their conscience, being weak, is defiled. But food
does not commend us to God; for neither if we eat are we the
better, nor if we do not eat are we the worse.*
—1 Corinthians 8:7–8

Eating means "to participate and engage in an activity." This is not about just the eating of that which has been offered and dedicated to idols. Remember that Paul said that as far as he was concerned there was only one true God. When this verse speaks of the weak, it is speaking of those inferior in *knowledge*. In other words, they were still living under religious restrictions because of their view of what was right and wrong. Paul said, however, that if they *ate or engaged* in activities with the idea that it was sinful, then it was to them, even if God was OK with it. We all are to live with the convictions we have from the knowledge we are carrying. Our knowledge or understanding of what God requires of us forms our convictions. We must live in these convictions to be right and acceptable before the Lord. As we grow in the Lord, however, we can come to new revelations of what is allowed and what is not allowed. We must live according to the knowledge we have as we progress in our adventure and journey with the Lord.

> *Lord, we ask that from Your Courts You would cause a Spirit of knowledge to enlighten us concerning that which pleases You and that which doesn't. May You bring revelation to us that would free us from religious restrictions not of You. However, bring awareness of that which we are to walk in regarding the holiness of God. In Jesus's name, amen.*

STANDING OR FALLING

Receive one who is weak in the faith, but not to disputes over doubtful things. For one believes he may eat all things, but he who is weak eats only vegetables. Let not him who eats despise him who does not eat, and let not him who does not eat judge him who eats; for God has received him. Who are you to judge another's servant? To his own master he stands or falls. Indeed, he will be made to stand, for God is able to make him stand.
—Romans 14:1–4

Remember that the weak here are those who have not come to knowledge of what God does or does not permit. Again Paul is speaking of eating or engaging in activities that some religious people said were forbidden. We are being told to allow each person the liberty to live by their own conscience. Each person must let God be their Judge and determine what is permissible and what is not permissible for them. We are not to allow this to cause quarrels or inner fightings among the people of God. We are to have maturity that lets each person follow the Lord out of his or her own personal convictions and the dictates of his or her own heart. The Holy Spirit is the One who helps the sincere come to awareness of what the Lord is asking of them. It can be different from person to person. We must allow this liberty for all. *"To his own master, he stands or falls."*

Lord, as we stand before Your Courts as the Judge, we thank You that we are not the judge of others. You determine whether someone is living by the standards You have set for them. I ask, Lord, that there would be a Spirit of knowledge that would progressively bring us into new liberties all the while moving us to new levels of holiness in You. In Jesus's name, amen.

THE LIFTING OF THE VEIL

But their minds were blinded. For until this day the same veil remains unlifted in the reading of the Old Testament, because the veil is taken away in Christ. But even to this day, when Moses is read, a veil lies on their heart. Nevertheless when one turns to the Lord, the veil is taken away.
—2 Corinthians 3:14–16

Paul is teaching the Corinthians that the Jews could not really see what God was communicating through the Old Testament and the law. They could not see that it was a shadow of the good things to come. However, when we see who Jesus is as the Christ, the Old Testament makes sense and becomes relative to our day. As David declares in Psalm 119:18: *"Open my eyes, that I may see wondrous things from Your law."* David was aware that there were secrets, truths, and ideas concealed in the law of God. It wasn't just a lot of dos and don'ts. It was filled with a revelation of His heart, passion, and desire for us. His cry was for the veil to be taken away that we might see past what was legalistic and into the life of God contained in His commandments. There are still things to be revealed to us so that we might come into the Spirit of knowledge that frees us from the oppression and control of the devil and his religious order. Jesus's heart is that we be free.

> *Lord, as I stand before Your Courts, I ask that You would open my eyes to behold the wondrous things from Your law. May I gain knowledge through Your Spirit of knowledge that I might walk in the revelation of who You are and Your ways. Thank You, Lord, for unlocking these realms in Jesus's name, amen.*

WHAT IS LIBERTY?

Now the Lord is the Spirit; and where the Spirit of the Lord is,
there is liberty. But we all, with unveiled face, beholding as in
a mirror the glory of the Lord, are being transformed into the
same image from glory to glory, just as by the Spirit of the Lord.
—2 Corinthians 3:17–18

Many times when the word *liberty* is used, we think of freedom in worship to dance, shout, or act out in some other exuberant way. I have countless times heard this Scripture used to encourage others to let loose and be free in these moments of praise. Although this might be good and fine, this is not what Paul was referring to. He was speaking of a revelation of Jesus as the Christ that sets people free from the bondages of legalism and religious oppression. He was communicating that through the Spirit of knowledge we can come into a new liberty and be transformed into a true expression of the Lord Himself. What the law could never produce in us, the Spirit of the Lord was now accomplishing. We can be freed from the bondage, fear, and shame of the law and turned loose into the glory of the Lord while being transformed into His image. We are free to take the veil from our face without fear of rejection and look into the perfect law of liberty that sets us free (James 1:25). Out of a relationship with the Holy Spirit we are being ushered into a place of acceptance, love, and forgiveness. In this place we are free.

Lord, as I stand before Your Courts, I thank You that You as
my Lord have brought me to liberty. I thank You that who the
Son sets free is free indeed. I am no longer hinged to the law that
produced condemnation. I am now joined to the Spirit of God
and have come to liberty and into Your glory. Thank You that
this glory changes me into Your image from glory to glory, even
as by the Spirit of the Lord. In Jesus's name, I receive this. Amen.

LED BY THE SPIRIT

For if you live according to the flesh you will die; but if by the Spirit you put to death the deeds of the body, you will live. For as many as are led by the Spirit of God, these are sons of God.
—Romans 8:13–14

As we come into the knowledge of who Jesus is, what He has done, and where we are now positioned and placed by Him, we are empowered. We no longer are to be bound by the flesh or the lust of it. We now have the authority to win over its desires, appetites, and intents. We are told even as believers that if we give into the flesh, we will die. This means we will forfeit the good thing God has for us. However, through the power of the Holy Spirit that now lives in us and transforms us, if we put these things to death, we will live out the fullness of what God's passion is for us. This is what it means to be *led by the Spirit*. It is not so much about direction for life as it is the pressing of us to a place of freedom and holiness. The word *led* in the Greek is *agō*. It means "to lead, bring forth, go." This is not a passive act. It is something that is pushing us in the right direction. When we are *led* by the Spirit, there is an impulse to go into that which God desires and approves. It will take us away from the flesh and into the things that are holy and pure. This is because the holy nature of God is now in us. The Spirit of God that lives in us is causing us to live as the sons of God manifesting the nature of our Father.

> *Lord, as I stand in Your Courts, I thank You that I am empowered to live by the Holy Spirit and not according to the flesh. I repent for every place I have surrendered to the flesh and not the impulse of Your Spirit. I now yield to You and ask that I might be led by Your Spirit into the holiness and desire of My Father. Thank You, Lord, that I am Your son/daughter manifesting Your nature, in Jesus's name, amen.*

SEEING AND KNOWING

A little while longer and the world will see Me no more, but you will see Me. Because I live, you will live also. At that day you will know that I am in My Father, and you in Me, and I in you. —John 14:19–20

Jesus was not speaking of His second coming in these verses. He was actually speaking of the Day of Pentecost when the Holy Spirit came into the upper room (Acts 2:1–4). When the Holy Spirit entered the earth at that moment, it was Jesus coming again to His disciples in this form. It is clear in Scripture that the Godhead is revealed in three persons: the Father, the Son, and the Holy Spirit. Yet the Holy Spirit is here to reveal and glorify Jesus (John 16:13–14). So when Jesus said in just a little while the world wouldn't *see* Him but His disciples would, He meant that He would come into their hearts through the person of the Holy Spirit. In that day there would be revelation that would permeate and penetrate them. They would *know* that Jesus was in the Father, that we are in Him, and He is in us. In other words, we would have a deep revelation of who He is, who the Father is, and who we are in them and them in us. We would be greatly secured and empowered from this revelation. We would *know* this in an unshakable way that secured us now and forever.

> *Lord, as I stand before Your Courts, I thank You that the Holy Spirit has come to let me see You. Through His ministry I am aware and established in who the Father is toward me, who You are, and who I am in you. Thank You for this revelation and knowledge that I now have, in Jesus's name, amen.*

TAUGHT BY THE HOLY SPIRIT

But the Helper, the Holy Spirit, whom the Father will send in My name, He will teach you all things, and bring to your remembrance all things that I said to you. —John 14:26

As we receive the Spirit of knowledge, the Holy Spirit teaches us all things. Being taught of the Spirit means a progressive understanding of God and His ways. The Holy Spirit takes that which Jesus has said and brings them to our remembrance. He causes us to be stirred and quickened with understanding. This happened when Jesus purged the temple and His disciples *remembered* it was written of Him that God's zeal would eat Him up (John 2:16–17). Through the quickening of the Scripture the disciples could see who Jesus was and what He was doing. It brought confirmation and assurance that Jesus was who He said He was, the Son of God, the Messiah. One of the best ways to hear from the Lord is through the Holy Spirit bringing to our remembrance what Jesus said. This can only occur if we have put the Word of God, the Bible, into our spirits. When we read the Bible, we are preparing ourselves to be taught by the Holy Spirit, our Helper. He will quicken us with the Word of God that is in our spirit the moment we need to know Him and what He would say to us.

> *Lord, as I come before Your throne, the Courts of Heaven, I thank You that You are progressively teaching me. I thank You that You, Holy Spirit, are bringing to my remembrance all things that Jesus has spoken. Your Word is a light to my path and lamp unto my feet (Ps. 119:105). Lord, direct me and speak to me as I stand before Your Courts and speak to You as the Judge. Thank You so much for hearing my cry and answering my plea. In Jesus's name, amen.*

CHOOSING THROUGH
THE SPIRIT'S POWER

For if you live according to the flesh you will die; but if by the
Spirit you put to death the deeds of the body, you will live.
—Romans 8:13

Most if not all of us know the struggle of dealing with fleshly desires and temptations. We understand the pull of sin that operates in our lives and fights against what the desires of the Lord would be for us. We are told however that the Holy Spirit empowers us to put to death these activities and deeds. In other words through the Holy Spirit we find the strength and ability to say "No" to our flesh! As we walk in this power, we live or experience the life of who Jesus is flowing through us. The new nature we received from the Holy Spirit's regeneration of us, grants us the privilege of choice. Before our redemption we were held in sin with no way out. When we are saved however, we are given the right to choose. I must determine from this choice whether I pick the flesh and death, or the Spirit and life. The devil would want to make us believe that we are powerless against sin. We have been given, however, the power, strength and ability to choose the ways of the Lord for our life. When we believe this, to our astonishment we find it to be so.

> *As I stand before Your Courts Lord, I repent for believing the lie*
> *that I am powerless. You have empowered me by the Holy Spirit*
> *and granted me the right to choose Your ways. I therefore choose*
> *to walk in the new creation that I am today. I would ask that*
> *it would be recorded in Your Courts of this choice that it might*
> *speak in my behalf before You. In Jesus's name, Amen.*

THE CONVINCING OF THE HOLY SPIRIT

And when He has come, He will convict the world of sin, and of righteousness, and of judgment. —John 16:8

One of the main functions of the Holy Spirit is to *convince* us of sin, righteousness, and judgment. When we read the word *convict*, we might think conviction is to make us to feel ashamed. However, this is the Greek word *elegchō*, and it can mean to admonish and convince. If we are convinced of something, it is because we have become persuaded beyond doubt. The Holy Spirit brings us to an awareness of the things we must know and be convinced of. He actually brings us to conclusions about things. This is absolutely necessary for us to be willing to lay our lives down and give ourselves to the pursuit of His will in our lives. The Holy Spirit brings us to this place in our convictions. In other words, we are not just brought under conviction, but convictions are formed in us that propel us to the right decisions necessary for God's will to be done. Hebrews 11:13 tells us of the people of faith who died in faith waiting on the fulfillment of the promises, because they were assured that He who promised could not and would not fail. May this kind of faith be formed in us as well through the convincing of the Spirit of God.

> *Lord, as I come before Your Courts, I lay aside all doubt, fear, and confusion. I allow the convincing of the Holy Spirit to work in me. I ask that my faith, formed by the Spirit of God, would speak before Your Courts and give testimony of my hope and confidence in You. May it be recorded before You that I believe and agree with who You are and what You have done and do. In Jesus's name, amen.*

CONVINCED OF THE SIN OF UNBELIEF

And when He has come, He will convict the world of sin, and
of righteousness, and of judgment: of sin, because they do not
believe in Me. —John 16:8–9

As the Holy Spirit functions in the world and our lives, He convinces us of the sin of not believing in Jesus. When we do not believe in the Lord and who He is, it produces sin. The unbelief of the children of Israel in the wilderness caused them to progressively rebel. Their slave mentality, which was absent of faith, would not allow them to believe the Lord and move into the promises God had made for them. Therefore, they wandered in the wilderness unnecessarily for forty years. Hebrews 3:12 calls unbelief an evil heart. We are to seek to protect ourselves from this evil thing before the Lord. Unbelief is not just a part of our humanity and something we are to excuse. Unbelief is an evil thing that the Holy Spirit proclaims war against to eradicate from our lives. Through the convincing of the Holy Spirit we become aware of this in our lives and allow it to be removed from us. The Holy Spirit's function in us exposes this and helps us to move from fear and rebellion to faith and obedience born of the Spirit of God.

> *Lord, as I stand before Your Courts, I ask that any and all*
> *unbelief in me would be exposed by the Holy Spirit. That which I*
> *am excusing as a part of my humanity, let it become exceedingly*
> *sinful in my sight (Rom. 7:13). Thank You, Lord, that You*
> *convince me of this and bring me into new realms of faith. I*
> *declare before Your Courts that You, Lord, are the author and*
> *finisher of my faith (Heb. 12:2). In Jesus's name, amen.*

RIGHTEOUSNESS BEFORE HIM

...of righteousness, because I go to My Father and you
see Me no more. —John 16:10

The Holy Spirit convinces us of righteousness. In other words, He teaches us what real righteousness is. Righteousness is not from the keeping of the law (Gal. 2:21). Righteousness comes from obedience to the Holy Spirit and His leading. This is why we are told that whoever is led by the Spirit is no longer under the dictate of the law (Gal. 5:18). When Jesus said that the Holy Spirit would help us determine the righteous standard of God, He was saying that through His empowerment we would be propelled into real, true righteousness. This would not be the result of keeping rules and regulations and walking legalistically. This righteousness would come from a relationship with Jesus through the Holy Spirit. This intimate life with Him would birth in us the true righteousness that God is after in us. It would unveil for us what pleases God from a deep place of intimacy with Him.

> *Lord, as I come before Your Courts, I thank You that I stand righteously before You. My righteousness is not because I am keeping rules or even laws. My righteousness is a result of a living faith in You born from the Holy Spirit. Even as Abraham believed God and it was accounted as righteousness before You, so let it be for me (Gal. 3:6). Allow me, my God, to stand before You in the righteousness of who Jesus is by faith and out of my relationship with You through the Holy Spirit. I declare I am righteous because of who You are, Lord, and what You have done for me, in Jesus's, name, amen.*

EXECUTING THE VERDICT OF THE CROSS INTO PLACE

...of judgment, because the ruler of this world is judged.
—John 16:11

The Holy Spirit convinces us of the verdict of the cross speaking in our behalf. When Jesus died on the cross, the Lord rendered a judgment and verdict against the devil and the powers of darkness. Every legal right the enemy was claiming against us was abolished because of what Jesus did. However, a verdict not executed into place has no power. As we stand in the Courts of Heaven, we are executing what Jesus did for us into place. This causes the full effect of Jesus's judgment against the devil to be forcibly set in place. This is what it means to overcome the accuser with the blood of the Lamb (Rev. 12:10–11). The Holy Spirit, as the One who helps, strengthens, and convinces us through the revelation of these truths, empowers us to see this reality. The result is the breakthrough and full manifestation of all Jesus died for becoming ours.

> *Lord, as I come before Your Courts, I thank You that the Holy Spirit is convincing me of all that Your cross did for me. The devil's legal claims have been revoked. Lord, I agree with Your blood and all it is speaking for me. I thank You that satan's rights to harass, hinder, and hurt me are revoked and removed. I receive the fullness of what You have provided for me as I stand in repentance and agreement with You and Your work for me. In Jesus's name, amen.*

THE SPIRIT OF THE FEAR OF THE LORD

The Spirit of the Lord shall rest upon Him, the Spirit of wisdom and understanding, the Spirit of counsel and might, the Spirit of knowledge and of the fear of the Lord. —Isaiah 11:2

The last of the seven Spirits of God is the Spirit of the fear of the Lord. Remember that these seven are before the throne of God as lamps giving witness in the Courts of Heaven (Rev. 4:5). This anointing correlates with the last thing Jesus said He was anointed for in Luke 4:19, which was to preach and proclaim the *"acceptable year of the Lord."* This is a reference to the year of Jubilee that occurred every fifty years in Israel. In this year, at the sounding of the trumpet, everything went free and was returned to its original owners (Lev. 25:9–10). Jesus was declaring that He was that trumpet that had come to restore all things. There was no longer a need to wait for a fifty-year period to pass. Jesus was here to bring restoration to all who would believe in Him. Through the Spirit of the fear of the Lord this restoration would be secured and maintained. The anointing of the fear of the Lord brought by the Spirit of the fear of the Lord would bring us into and maintain us in our Jubilee. Jesus is our Jubilee. We secure this through what this spirit is witnessing before His Courts.

> *Lord, as I stand before the Courts of Heaven, I agree with the witness of the Spirit of the fear of the Lord. I thank You that this brings me into the acceptable year of the Lord. I thank You that You, Jesus, are my Jubilee. I come into full restoration of all that belongs to me in and by You. I receive the return of all that has*

been lost. I thank You that from Your Courts things are in place for the fullness of all Your benefits in my life. Thank You, Lord, that I am restored and receive fully of Your kindness, goodness, and acceptance, in Jesus's name, amen.

THE FEAR OF THE LORD AND JUBILEE

Therefore you shall not oppress one another, but you shall fear your God; for I am the Lord your God. "So you shall observe My statutes and keep My judgments, and perform them; and you will dwell in the land in safety." —Leviticus 25:17–18

This Scripture is spoken in connection with Jubilee. Every fifty years things were returned to the original owners; if property was sold to someone, the price was determined based on how many years of use there was before it was returned to the original owner. The Lord is declaring that out of the fear of the Lord, people were to be dealt with fairly and justly. They were not to be taken advantage of and oppressed. If these things were abided by, God promised them safety in their land. Operating in the fear of the Lord brings us into a safe place and security. The fear of the Lord produces in us a right attitude and behavior toward others. We realize that God is watching, and how we behave toward others can determine the benefits we get from the Lord. If we treat others well, the devil's rights to hurt us are revoked by the Lord. Our fear of the Lord is that which causes us to believe and obey Him in every area of life.

Lord, as I come before Your Courts, I thank You for the Spirit of the fear of the Lord resting upon me. From this anointing, I experience Jubilee, the times of Your restoration in my life. I thank You that in this place I dwell in safety before You. No intent or purpose of the devil may prosper against me. I am delivered from any and all of his schemes. Thank You, Lord, for any rights he would claim to devour me, being revoked as I walk before You in the fear of God. In Jesus's name, amen.

RETURNING TO
FORTUNES AND FAMILY

And you shall consecrate the fiftieth year, and proclaim liberty throughout all the land to all its inhabitants. It shall be a Jubilee for you; and each of you shall return to his possession, and each of you shall return to his family. —Leviticus 25:10

In the year of Jubilee, when the trumpet sounded, everyone returned to his possession and everyone returned to his family. Jubilee was a time of restoration of fortunes and family. As we stand before the Courts of Heaven, we can ask for the Spirit of the fear of the Lord to bring us into our Jubilee. We can ask that what has been lost, all fortunes and family, be returned to us. Whatever it would seem that is ours, that has been granted by the Lord, that the devil has stolen, would now be returned to us in abundance. In the process of life, as time progresses, it can seem like great loss occurs. Life can take its toll. Perhaps you look back to happier times when everything was good. However, great losses have occurred, and you are now filled with grief over those lost things and people. Perhaps you have lost financially. God will return your wealth to you. Perhaps relationships have been strained or even destroyed. God will heal these places. As we stand in the Courts of the Lord, we can ask the Lord to bring us into the fear of the Lord in a new way and that Jesus would manifest as our Jubilee. This would allow us to return to that which God originally planned for us.

> *Lord, as I come before Your Courts, I step into the Spirit of the fear of the Lord. As I do, I ask for You to be my Jubilee. I asked that decisions would be rendered from Your Court that would return me to my fortunes and my family. Lord, allow all things to be restored and all relationships to be healed. I thank You for this, in Jesus's name, amen.*

LETTING THE FIELD REST

That fiftieth year shall be a Jubilee to you; in it you shall neither
sow nor reap what grows of its own accord, nor gather the grapes
of your untended vine. —Leviticus 25:11

Every fifty years at Jubilee the Israelites were required to let the land rest. This also was required every seven years (Lev. 25:3–4). The Lord ordained a rest period for the land as an act of obedience to the Lord, but also so the land could replenish itself and bear much fruit. This was also the reasoning behind the weekly Sabbath's rest. Every seven days there is to be a rest period to honor the Lord and replenish ourselves. Without this exhaustion will creep in and creativity will be diminished. We will experience diminished returns from our labors because we have skipped the necessary rest period out of our own wisdom and even greed. This is what began to happen after Nehemiah brought restoration to Jerusalem. The people began to do business and commerce on the Sabbath against the law of God. Nehemiah dealt quickly and rigorously with this. He told them this was one of the reasons God judged Israel and allowed them to go into captivity. He required repentance and adherence to the law of the Sabbath (Neh. 13:16–21). Even though we are no longer under the law and required to keep the Sabbath, the principle is still the same. God created man to need rest to replenish. As we rest our mind, soul, emotions, body, and spirit, we are replenished in His presence. The result will be a greater effectiveness and fruitfulness from our labors.

> *As I come before Your Courts, I repent for any place I have broken*
> *Your principles. Where I have worked and not adhered to the idea*
> *of rest for replenishment, I repent. I ask that You would forgive*
> *and strengthen me to obey in this area that I might be more*
> *effective in my labors for You and in life. In Jesus's name, amen.*

CHOOSING THE FEAR OF THE LORD

Do not be deceived, God is not mocked; for whatever a man sows, that he will also reap. For he who sows to his flesh will of the flesh reap corruption, but he who sows to the Spirit will of the Spirit reap everlasting life. —Galatians 6:7–8

When we talk about walking in the fear of the Lord connected to Jubilee, we should define what that is. The fear of the Lord is not a tormenting fear. It is the awareness that God's Word is true and is applied without respecter of persons. In other words, whoever obeys God's Word is blessed, and whoever doesn't, will reap undesired consequences. We are told that we shouldn't allow ourselves to be deceived. This principle applies to everyone. If we *sow* good things according to God's Word, we will *reap* good things. If, however, we consistently *sow* from a fleshly or ungodly place, we will *reap* things we do not want. This idea should produce in us a fear of the Lord that would drive us to obey Him and walk in agreement with His Word. This is of great value before the Lord and has great reward associated with it. It causes us to walk in holiness in the areas of our life that people see, but also in the secret places as well.

Lord, I thank You as I come before Your Courts that I walk in the fear of the Lord before You. I ask that You empower me to obey you and sow good things in obedience to You and Your ways. Forgive me, Lord, for all the places where I have disregarded You and Your ways. Cleanse me from these places, that I may walk righteously before You. Thank You that as I walk in the Spirit of the fear of the Lord, that I experience You as my Jubilee. In Jesus's name, amen.

THE PONDERING EYE OF GOD

*For the ways of man are before the eyes of the Lord, and He
ponders all his paths.* —Proverbs 5:21

When we speak of the fear of the Lord as one of the seven Spirits of God, we speak of living under the scrutiny of God's watchful eye. To *ponder* means "to weigh." In other words, it means to consider and to evaluate our actions. It is not just a glancing at something, but rather a true investigation of the intent, motives, and desires that are producing certain actions. There is nothing hidden before the Lord. Everything is naked and opened before Him (Heb. 4:13). God sees all things and is aware of all things. Even though we may have secrets from people, there are no secrets before God. This should birth in us a fear of the Lord that impacts the decisions we make in every place of our life. Not only does this effect this life, but it also has ramifications in the life that is to come. We will all stand before the judgment seat of Christ and give an account for what we have done (2 Cor. 5:10). There is nothing hidden from the Lord. Whoever will order their life in reference to this according to the fear of the Lord will have a good report of Him in this life and the life to come.

> *Lord, as I stand before Your Courts, I thank You that all things
> are open and manifest before You. I repent for every place I have
> walked in an ungodly and unrighteous way before You. I ask that
> Your blood, Lord Jesus, would speak for me and cleanse me from
> every accusation against me. Let me be acceptable before You in
> all my ways, as I live under Your pondering eye and watchful
> gaze. In Jesus's name, amen.*

NO SECRETS BEFORE THE LORD

*Let us hear the conclusion of the whole matter: Fear God and
keep His commandments, for this is man's all. For God will
bring every work into judgment, including every secret thing,
whether good or evil. —Ecclesiastes 12:13–14*

The conclusion of the whole matter, or the point of it all, is we are to fear God
and keep His commands. When it is all said and done, God will bring every
work into judgment. All the secrets of our life will be seen and known. The
places where we have repented and asked for the blood of Jesus to speak for us,
are forgiven and cleansed (Heb. 12:24). If, however, we are living in outright,
known rebellion, these things will be judged. This should produce in us a desire
to live holy and purely before the Lord. The fear of the Lord should progressively
press us forward to a life that is pleasing and acceptable before Him. Walking
in the fear of the Lord has great promises for us in this life and the one that is
to come. Whoever will receive the Spirit of the fear of the Lord, will experience
the power of Jubilee. We will live a life of progressive restoration. We will come
into the fullness of what Jesus died for us to have as we walk tenderly and softly
before the Lord in obedience to His Word and cause.

> *Lord, as I come to stand before Your Courts, I make myself
> manifest before You. I ask that You purge and cleanse any
> place in me that is not pleasing to You. I thank You that Your
> blood through the power of the Spirit cleanses me from every
> unrighteousness. Thank You that as I walk before You in the
> Spirit of the fear of the Lord, I come into a full expression of
> Jubilee and receive a complete restoration of all things. In Jesus's
> name, amen.*

THE ATMOSPHERE OF THE FEAR OF THE LORD

And they continued steadfastly in the apostles' doctrine and fellowship, in the breaking of bread, and in prayers. Then fear came upon every soul, and many wonders and signs were done through the apostles. —Acts 2:42–43

In the New Testament church a deep sense of the fear of the Lord was present. This created an atmosphere for the miraculous to occur. When God is reverenced, honored, and obeyed, the atmosphere that allows signs and wonders to happen is unlocked. In this atmosphere there is a love for God, a soft heart toward Him, and a faith that believes Him without question. This allows supernatural things to manifest among the people of God. So often in today's church we do not see this environment. It would seem to be much more flippant and casual. However, in the early church because the Word of God was being taught, the disciples were walking in fellowship, they were partaking of communion and praying together, the Spirit of the fear of the Lord came. The result was a Jubilee occurring with signs and wonders bringing restoration and life among God's people. May we step into this place as well today.

> *Lord, as we come before Your Courts, we ask for the Spirit of the fear of the Lord to come upon us corporately. May the fear of the Lord be on every soul. May it unlock a true manifestation of Jubilee among us as the people of God. Let signs and wonders invade us, where the fear of the Lord is now present. In Jesus's name, amen.*

THE PROPHETIC ANNOUNCEMENT OF JUBILEE

Then you shall cause the trumpet of the Jubilee to sound on the
tenth day of the seventh month; on the Day of Atonement you
shall make the trumpet to sound throughout all your land.
—Leviticus 25:9

Any time we read of a trumpet in the Scripture, it is speaking of that which is prophetic (1 Cor. 14:8–9). It was a trumpet blast/prophetic sound that signaled Jubilee had come. The blast of the trumpet announced that Jubilee had arrived. This meant that everything that had been lost was now restored. What was captive could now go free. There was a resetting of things back to their original place and position. This all took place at the sound of the trumpet. The trumpet sound/prophetic set in motion that which would reorder the society of Israel and personal lives. The trumpet sound/prophetic voice demanded that restraints now be released. It demanded that what was lost was to now be restored. Each of us should *prophesy* our Jubilee. As a result of who Jesus is and what He has done, we can now be liberated into the goodness of the Lord. Anything that has been lost we should prophesy its restoration. This is our privilege in light of who Jesus is and what He has done. As we walk in the Spirit of the fear of the Lord, our prophetic declarations set our Jubilee into motion.

Lord, as I stand in Your Courts, I by faith prophesy my Jubilee.
As I walk in the Spirit of the fear of the Lord, I declare my Jubilee
is set in motion. There is a resetting of all the original intent of
God concerning my life. I ask that from Your Courts a decision is
rendered that allows complete restoration of all that has been lost
to be brought back to my life. In Jesus's name, amen.

THE CROSS AND JUBILEE

Then you shall cause the trumpet of the Jubilee to sound on the tenth day of the seventh month; on the Day of Atonement you shall make the trumpet to sound throughout all your land.
—Leviticus 25:9

The trumpet of Jubilee sounded on the Day of Atonement. The Day of Atonement is a prophetic picture of the cross of Jesus. The Day of Atonement was when the high priest would kill the Passover lamb. The blood of this lamb was then taken behind the veil in the holiest of holies and poured out and sprinkled. This activity gave God the legal right to roll the sins off Israel for a year so they could be blessed rather than cursed. Of course, the cross of Jesus and His blood forever secured forgiveness and cleansing from our sins. The trumpet of Jubilee sounding on this day, signifies that this activity allows the restoration of all things to be set into place. This is why we do not have to wait for a fifty-year period to pass for our Jubilee. As a result of what Jesus did for us, we have access into Jubilee perpetually. The cross and sacrifice of Jesus for us has set things in place for the prophetic announcement of Jubilee to be available to whoever will secure it through faith in Jesus and what He has done. Reach out today and accept your Jubilee and all that Jesus has made available to us.

Lord, as I stand in Your Courts, I thank You for the sacrifice of Jesus on the cross. Thank You, Lord, that what You have done allows my Jubilee to now be set into place. I receive fully from Your cross and believe that Jubilee is now mine. Lord, please allow a decision to be rendered in agreement with my faith and restoration to now come to me. In Jesus's name, amen.

LIBERTY FOR ALL

And you shall consecrate the fiftieth year, and proclaim liberty
throughout all the land to all its inhabitants. It shall be a
Jubilee for you; and each of you shall return to his possession,
and each of you shall return to his family. —Leviticus 25:10

Liberty was proclaimed on the day of Jubilee. The word *liberty* in the Hebrew is *derowr,* and it means *to move rapidly, a spontaneity of outflow.* In other words, it can speak of the moving of the Spirit of God. That which has been dammed up and restricted is now free. Perhaps in your life there seems to be a resistance of the free flow of God's Holy Spirit in you and through you. Jesus promised that from out of our innermost being rivers of living water would flow (John 7:38). There is to be an unrestricted move of God that brings life to us and to others. As the free-flowing rivers of God move, they produce a return of possessions and family to our life. As is the case of most things, everything begins from inside of us. Our outer world will always be a result of our inner world. As we come to liberty and God's presence is unrestricted in us, all other things will line up. We must ask the Lord for the experience of Jubilee to begin inside of us. The result will be the ordering of our life outside as well.

> *Lord, as I stand in Your Courts, I ask for the free flow of Your*
> *Spirit to move through me. Let every restriction be removed.*
> *Lord, allow the rapid moving sense of Your presence and the*
> *spontaneity of who You are take over my life. Let it influence and*
> *control me from the inside out. Thank You, Lord, that Jubilee*
> *begins first inside me and then orders my life outside. In Jesus's*
> *name, amen.*

KINGS AND PRIEST TO OUR GOD

...and from Jesus Christ, the faithful witness, the firstborn from the dead, and the ruler over the kings of the earth. To Him who loved us and washed us from our sins in His own blood, and has made us kings and priests to His God and Father, to Him be glory and dominion forever and ever. Amen.
—Revelation 1:5–6

Through Jesus's washing us from our sins in His own blood, we have been elevated to kings and priests to our God. Jesus's blood doesn't just cleanse us so we can get to Heaven. His blood changes our nature from one that has no standing before God, to one that is highly regarded before God. We are now kings and priests to our God because of His love and cleansing in our life. Priests are those who intercede and function legally before the Lord. Kings are those who decree and set things in place as a result of the priest function. These two positions that we have been granted because of Jesus's work for us are imperative to God's purposes being done. Our function as kings and priests cause His glory and dominion to be established forever. As we will see, these operations allow the increase of His government and peace to always be increasing and enlarging in the earth and its cultures. Let's take up the place granted us and see the passion of the Lord in nations prevail!

Lord, as we come and stand before Your Courts, we thank You for the power of Your love and cleansing. Thank You for the place You have positioned us as kings and priests to our God. Help us, Lord, to function in this place legally, judicially, and authoritatively as those set by You for Your purposes. Allow cultures to shift and nations to be divinely ordered as we are positioned by You. In Jesus's name, amen.

REIGNING ON THE EARTH

You...have made us kings and priests to our God; and
we shall reign on the earth. —Revelation 5:9–10

As kings and priests set by God we are to reign from this position on the earth. This means we are to be a part of arranging life on the planet into that which expresses God's will. The earth is to be our domain. We are told that God gave the earth to the children of men (Ps. 115:16). We are also told that from the beginning God put His works (the earth) under the authority of man (Ps. 8:6). Of course Jesus came to restore to us this reality that Adam lost through his transgression. Functioning as kings and priests before our God is critical to this. Our power to reign on the earth and dictate life in this sphere is connected to our function as kings and priests. As we learn how to stand as priests and judicially order things, we can also then stand as kings and decree with authority things into God's divine order. This is why kings in the Old Testament would never go to battle until the priest had first offered a sacrifice in their behalf. They understood the need for something to speak in their behalf as they marched against the enemy. We will find that the offering of Jesus does this for us. Also, however, God gives us the right to bring our own offerings that speak as well. When we learn to function in the judicial dimension as priests, we can then win on the battlefield as kings.

> *Lord, as I stand before You in Your Courts as a priest, I thank*
> *You that Your blood and sacrifice does speak for me. Any right the*
> *devil would claim to resist me or fight against me is silenced by*
> *Your offering. I also thank You that my offerings I have brought*
> *before You also speak. Thank You that this is judicially setting*
> *things in place for my victory before You. In Jesus's name, amen.*

HIS INCREASING RULE

Of the increase of His government and peace there will be no end, upon the throne of David and over His kingdom, to order it and establish it with judgment and justice from that time forward, even forever. The zeal of the Lord of hosts will perform this. —Isaiah 9:7

We are prophetically promised that the government of God will progressively take over more and more of the earth. This is not a promise that begins at the second coming of the Lord. This is a promise that started when Jesus came into the earth and announced the Kingdom (Matt. 4:17). This means that since that day things have gotten better and better on the earth. Many would want us to believe that things have gotten worse and worse. But even a casual investigation of history reveals just the opposite. Life is better in the planet today than ever before. This is because of the rule of God that Jesus announced. Two thousand years later we have advantages, benefits, and luxuries never known to man before. Life today is better than ever. However, we are to still be active in the expansion of the government of God in the earth. This requires our function as kings and priests. The more we step into this place of authority, the more the advancement of His rule will manifest.

> *As I come before Your Courts as king and priest, I thank You that the increase of Your government and peace will continue. Thank You that You allow me the right to function as Your instrument to see this glorious manifestation. Lord, I say come in all Your power and majesty and establish Your rule, in Jesus's name, amen.*

THE MELCHIZEDEK ORDER

So also Christ did not glorify Himself to become High Priest,
but it was He who said to Him: "You are My Son, today I have
begotten You." As He also says in another place: "You are a
priest forever according to the order of Melchizedek."
—Hebrews 5:5–6

When we speak of ourselves as priests, we must realize what order we are from. We are not priests connected to the Levitical priesthood. Even though from this priesthood we can learn valuable lessons about what a priest does. However, we are of the priesthood of Melchizedek. This is the order of priest that Jesus as our High Priest is from. The Bible is explicit that Jesus could not be a priest after the Levitical order because He was from the tribe of Judah (Heb. 7:14). God therefore made Him the High Priest after the order of Melchizedek. This was the priest that Abraham met when returning from the battle with the kings. This priesthood allows Him to continue forever. Just like Aaron's sons were priests in the priesthood of their father, so we are priest in the priesthood granted to Jesus. Our priesthood is after the Melchizedek order. We are functioning together with Jesus in this order set by God.

> *Lord, as I come before Your Courts as a priest after the order*
> *of Melchizedek, I thank You for this positioning. With boldness*
> *and yet humility I take my place as a part of the Melchizedek*
> *order of priest that Jesus has been granted. As a part of who Jesus*
> *is, I now function in this placement before You after this order*
> *granted and given to me. In Jesus's name, amen.*

A GREATER PLACE

Now it happened, as soon as he had finished presenting the burnt offering, that Samuel came; and Saul went out to meet him, that he might greet him. And Samuel said, "What have you done?" Saul said, "When I saw that the people were scattered from me, and that you did not come within the days appointed, and that the Philistines gathered together at Michmash." —1 Samuel 13:10–11

In the Old Testament people were forbidden to be both king and priest. When King Saul allowed the circumstance to press him to act presumptuously, it cost him greatly before God. He stepped into the function as a priest, which was forbidden of God. Only in the New Testament and those who had revelation of the New Testament order were allowed to function as both priest and king. The prophet declared that Saul's kingdom would not continue because he had transgressed the word of the Lord. We can learn two lessons from this. First, we have been granted a great privilege as New Testament believers of operating as kings and priests. Secondly, God is looking for those whose hearts are perfect toward Him and who will obey Him explicitly. May we learn from both of these.

Lord, as I come before Your Courts, thank You so much for the privilege to be both king and priest before You. With gratefulness and boldness I step into the places granted me. I also seek to fully obey You in all things. May I be one whose heart is perfect before You that I might please You well. In Jesus's name, amen.

THE PRIDE OF KINGS

But when he was strong his heart was lifted up, to his destruction, for he transgressed against the Lord his God by entering the temple of the Lord to burn incense on the altar of incense. So Azariah the priest went in after him, and with him were eighty priests of the Lord—valiant men. And they withstood King Uzziah, and said to him, "It is not for you, Uzziah, to burn incense to the Lord, but for the priests, the sons of Aaron, who are consecrated to burn incense. Get out of the sanctuary, for you have trespassed! You shall have no honor from the Lord God." —2 Chronicles 26:16–18

In his arrogance King Uzziah sought to operate as both king and priest. God judged him, and he died a leper because of this transgression. We must always guard our heart from pride, especially when God has blessed us with success and favor. Because Uzziah did not keep a watch on his heart, he found himself in deception. He ceased to operate in the fear of the Lord. The result was activity that brought the displeasure of the Lord. As New Testament believers we are granted the function of both king and priest. However, in this function we must guard our hearts with all diligence (Prov. 4:23). We must be careful to never think more highly of ourselves than we ought (Rom. 12:3). The result can be a loss of the place we have been granted. This is the condemnation the devil suffered (1 Tim. 3:6). A place that had been given was lost. May we guard our heart with all diligence.

Lord, as I stand before Your Courts, let the words of my mouth and the meditation of my heart be acceptable before You. I repent of pride, arrogance, and haughtiness before You. May I always walk in humility and surrender before You. May I guard my heart and keep it free from any sense of superiority, in Jesus's name, amen.

THE POWER OF REVELATION

*And so it was, when those bearing the ark of the Lord had gone
six paces, that he sacrificed oxen and fatted sheep. Then David
danced before the Lord with all his might; and David was
wearing a linen ephod.* —2 Samuel 6:13–14

David wore the garments that only priests were to wear, the linen ephod. This was because David as an Old Testament man lived from New Testament revelation. He understood God's heart for all His people to be priests before Him. He reached into what was yet to be fully manifest and pulled it into his present time. This is what revelation allows us to do. Just as David functioned both as a priest and king, so can we too, from revelation, live in a power others aren't touching. When we walk in intimacy with the Lord, as David did, revelation that empowers us outside the time we are living in can come. Time ceases to have restrictions on us because revelation has unlocked a new dimension for us. The key is intimacy that allows these secrets to be unveiled. David functioned in secrets outside his time. So can we.

Lord, I ask before Your Courts that I might walk in intimacy with You. Lord, from this intimacy, can I know secrets that birth revelation. Would You allow this revelation to propel me outside the time I am living in into new places of function and life without the present-day restrictions. Thank You, Lord, for birthing this in me and through me. In Jesus's name, amen.

MELCHIZEDEK: PRIEST OF GOD, KING OF SALEM

For this Melchizedek, king of Salem, priest of the Most High God, who met Abraham returning from the slaughter of the kings and blessed him, to whom also Abraham gave a tenth part of all, first being translated "king of righteousness," and then also king of Salem, meaning "king of peace," without father, without mother, without genealogy, having neither beginning of days nor end of life, but made like the Son of God, remains a priest continually. —Hebrews 7:1–3

This Melchizedek was not a *normal* human. He had neither beginning nor end. He had no earthly father or mother. There was no genealogy that could be traced. He was like the Son of God. In my opinion this would mean that Melchizedek, who met Abraham, was a preincarnate revelation of Jesus Christ. In other words, this was Jesus revealing Himself in another form before He appeared in earth as the baby in the manger. This is why Jesus is now High Priest in our behalf after the order of Melchizedek. This Melchizedek was one of only two allowed to operate as both king and priest in the Old Testament. David was the other one. As our High Priest after the order of Melchizedek, Jesus is our King of Righteousness and our King of Peace. As both King and Priest, Jesus ushers in righteousness and brings great peace. When we operate as both king and priest before our God, we take on these same characteristics as well. As He is, so are we in this present world (1 John 4:17).

Lord, I come and honor You as my High Priest and King of Righteousness and King of Peace. As Abraham honored

Melchizedek, Lord, I honor You. I thank You for who You are and what You are doing in the Courts of Heaven in my behalf. Thank You, Lord, for making me a king and priest to my God. I bless You and honor You, in Jesus's name, amen.

REVELATION YET TO BE SEEN

And having been perfected, He became the author of eternal salvation to all who obey Him, called by God as High Priest "according to the order of Melchizedek," of whom we have much to say, and hard to explain, since you have become dull of hearing. —Hebrews 5:9–11

The writer of Hebrews declares that there are things about the Melchizedek order that are yet to be explained. This means there are things God would desire us to know that we haven't come to the capacity to receive. Jesus even spoke of this when He said the Holy Spirit would have to guide His disciples into truth yet to be revealed (John 16:12–13). He said this would happen because there were things He wanted to speak of, but they couldn't handle them. May the Lord unlock our hearts to perceive the things from Heaven. May we not be so tied to the earth that we cannot receive what would be revealed from there. There are things that the Lord longs to impart to us. May the dullness of hearing be lifted from our spirits that we might perceive what belongs to us. The Lord desires to reveal secrets that belong to us and to our children (Deut. 29:29).

Lord, as I come before Your Courts, I petition You to lift the dullness from my heart and spirit. May my understanding be unlocked that I can perceive the weightier things that You would esteem belong to me and even my children. Would You even unlock what concerns the Melchizedek order that I am part of as a king and priest to our God. Thank You so much, Lord. In Jesus's name, amen.

SONS THAT ARE PRIESTS

So also Christ did not glorify Himself to become High Priest,
but it was He who said to Him: "You are My Son, today I have
begotten You." As He also says in another place: "You are a
priest forever according to the order of Melchizedek."
—Hebrews 5:5–6

Notice that Jesus is proclaimed to be God's Son and then declared to be a Priest forever. The function as a priest is born out of being a son. Sonship as opposed to a slavery mindset is essential to operating in our priesthood. So often we are striving from a mindset of seeking acceptance. As sons of God, we are accepted in the Beloved. The Scripture speaks of the manner of love that has been bestowed on us that has made us to be His sons (1 John 3:1). When we by revelation understand who we are as sons of God, we are now rightly positioned to move in our priestly role. God secured Jesus as His Son before He operated as a priest in the Melchizedek order. The secured place as sons before the Lord is an empowering place for us to function as His priest in the Courts of Heaven. As we are settled before Him in sonship, a great place of authority becomes ours as His priest.

> *Lord, as I stand before You, I accept my place of acceptance before*
> *You as Your son/daughter. From this place as Your child, I boldly*
> *take my position as a priest of the Most High God. Thank You*
> *that in this place I can move in judicial authority to see Your*
> *will accomplished in me and through me. In Jesus's name, amen.*

AN ANCHOR OF OUR SOUL

This hope we have as an anchor of the soul, both sure and steadfast, and which enters the Presence behind the veil, where the forerunner has entered for us, even Jesus, having become High Priest forever according to the order of Melchizedek.
—Hebrews 6:19–20

Jesus has entered behind the veil *for us*. This is the Holiest of Holies where He is functioning as our High Priest after the order of Melchizedek. This gives us an anchor for our souls and stills all doubts and fear because of what He is doing in our behalf. Any question concerning our salvation or God's heart and posture toward us is answered because of Jesus and what He presently is doing for us now. As our High Priest, He is going before us and standing in our behalf taking the sacrifice of Himself and using it to obtain atonement for us and our sins. The presence behind the veil speaks of the holiness of who God is. In this place Jesus is providing all that God needs to accept us and bless us. Jesus's ministry as High Priest after the order of Melchizedek secures the full salvation provided for us. This doesn't mean *just* what His death purchased, but also what His present-day life is doing for us. He ever lives to make intercession for us (Heb. 7:25). As a result of this activity for us, we are *prayed* into the fullness of all Jesus died for us to have. Salvation, healing, prosperity, peace, and all other benefits are ours because of Jesus's death, burial, and resurrection, plus His present-day life of prayer as our High Priest. Let these truths anchor your soul during any times of turbulence or storms.

> *Lord, as we stand in Your Courts, I thank You that You are my High Priest. You stand in the presence of God for me. Thank You that You take Your own body and blood and remind the*

Courts of that sacrifice. Because of this, the courts are moved to render decisions for my good and in my behalf. I declare that I am anchored because of that which You have done and are doing for me. Thanks so much Jesus for Your work in my behalf.

THE POWER OF AN ENDLESS LIFE

And it is yet far more evident if, in the likeness of Melchizedek,
there arises another priest who has come, not according to the
law of a fleshly commandment, but according to the power of an
endless life. —Hebrews 7:15–16

Jesus as our High Priest will never die. The priest of the Levitical tribe changed every few decades because of death. Jesus, however, continues forever as our High Priest because of the power of an endless life. He died once for our sins. He will never die again. There is an inexhaustible source of life that He now lives in our behalf. As a people part of this Melchizedek order, we also have access into this endless life. We too will live forever because of Jesus's life in us. In this life we can function from the power and authority of this *endless life.* This source of endless life will empower us in our function. It cannot be snuffed out or shut down. There is an inexhaustible source of power in us. For instance, we are told that our youth will be renewed (Ps. 103:5). We are told we will be made alive if the same Spirit that raised Jesus from the dead is in us (Rom. 8:11). Caleb was *kept alive* by the power of God when all around him died (Josh. 14:10). Abraham was empowered to father children at an advanced age (Gen. 25:1–2). All these and others functioned in this life in the power of an endless life. So can we as a part of the same priesthood.

> *Lord, as I come before Your Courts, I thank You for the power of*
> *an endless life. Even as You function as my High Priest according*
> *to this power, allow this power to flow in me. Allow, Lord, new*
> *strength, might, authority, and life to flow in me and through*
> *me for the function You have called me too. Thank You so much,*
> *Lord, for this divine empowerment from the Courts of Heaven.*
> *In Jesus's name, amen.*

PLACES OF INTERCESSION

As He also says in another place: "You are a priest forever according to the order of Melchizedek"; who, in the days of His flesh, when He had offered up prayers and supplications, with vehement cries and tears to Him who was able to save Him from death, and was heard because of His godly fear.
—Hebrews 5:6–7

When Jesus lived on the earth as a human being, He functioned already in His divine Priesthood. Part of this function was prayers and supplications before God, filled with cries, tears, and godly fear. This allowed Him to be heard by God. This depicts a place of travail and anguish in the Spirit that empowered Jesus's prayer life as One sent from God to intercede. As a part of this same priesthood we are to also experience these places of intercession and travail. The Holy Spirit will birth in us vehement cries and even tears out of the fear of the Lord. Please note that it isn't a terrorizing fear but the godly fear that produced this kind of praying. From a deep place of worship, adoration, and love for God, we intercede out of His heart. God hears us when we pray. We are used by Him to give birth to His purpose and passions in the earth. May we surrender ourselves to this piece of operating as a part of the Melchizedek order.

> *Lord, as we approach Your Courts, I ask that the same spirit of intercession that Jesus walked in would come upon me. Allow me, Lord, to walk in such godly fear that my vehement cries and even tears will move things in the spirit world. Lord, I surrender to You and Your heart. Would You allow this empowerment to pray and intercede come now upon my life? In Jesus's name, amen.*

THE ORDERING OF JUDGMENT AND JUSTICE

The Lord has sworn and will not relent, "You are a priest forever according to the order of Melchizedek." The Lord is at Your right hand; He shall execute kings in the day of His wrath. —Psalm 110:4–5

Notice that Jesus being commissioned as High Priest after the order of Melchizedek initiates a judgment against those who oppose God. Sometimes we think that operating as a priest is a sedate activity. However, from the position as priest, judgments can be rendered against what is opposing God. Jesus as our High Priest has the authority to execute these judgments and therefore establish justice. Justice is the result of righteous judgment. We can be used by God to render judgment against that which opposes the intent and desire of the Lord. Remember that at its core prayer is judgment (Isa. 56:7). When we pray, we are to be setting in place the judgment of Heaven against that which resists the will of God in the earth. This is a part of the function of a priest. These judgments are necessary in the spirit world for God's will to be fleshed out in the earth. We must take our place as a part of the Melchizedek order of priest and render these judgments into place. As we do, justice will be established in the earth.

Lord, as I come before Your Courts as a part of the Melchizedek order of priest, I thank You that righteous judgment is set in place and executed. I yield my heart to You and ask that anything that is opposing Your will would be judged as illegal and unrighteous. Let judgment be executed against it that justice might be established before You. In Jesus's name, amen.

PRIEST AND JUDICIAL ORDER

But into the second part the high priest went alone once a year,
not without blood, which he offered for himself and for the
people's sins committed in ignorance. —Hebrews 9:7

When the high priest went into the holiest of holies on the Day of Atonement, he would sprinkle and pour out the blood of the Passover lamb. This blood would atone for the sins of the people and the priest that had been committed in ignorance in the previous year. This happened because the blood would give witness and testimony before the Courts of Heaven. On the basis of the slain animal's blood, God would roll the sins off the nation for a year. We are told that Jesus's blood is now speaking for us better things (Heb. 12:24). On the basis of Jesus's blood our sins are not just rolled off, but rather forgiven and cleansed away. Notice that the high priest did this *alone*. This means that Jesus *alone* has made atonement for us. He has taken His *own blood* and has entered into the holiest place in Heaven. In this place, Jesus has *alone* applied His blood to the mercy seat. We had nothing to do with it. We by faith simply accept what Jesus has *alone* done for us. His sacrifice and activity in our behalf is perfect. Accept it today and come into your full salvation.

> *Lord, as I stand before Your Courts, I thank You for all that Jesus*
> *by Himself has done for me. Even as the priest of old went alone*
> *into the holy place, so Jesus alone has entered for me. Thank You,*
> *Lord, that You have taken Your own blood and offered it in my*
> *behalf. You, Lord, by Yourself have secured salvation for me. I*
> *thank You for this and enter fully into all You have provided. In*
> *Jesus's name, amen.*

THE PRIEST'S BLESSING

Then Aaron lifted his hand toward the people, blessed them,
and came down from offering the sin offering, the burnt
offering, and peace offerings. —Leviticus 9:22

One of the duties of the priest was to *bless* the people. After the offering for sin and other offerings were presented, the priest would then bless the people with the favor of God. When we function as priest to our God, this is something we should practice as well. Not only should we intercede and secure the blessing, we should also impart the blessing as well. This impartation of the blessing can change the course of life for people. Instead of doors being locked, they can open. Instead of favor being denied, it can be given. Instead of lack being experienced, prosperity can come. Instead of disease touching, health can be secured. There is great power in one functioning as a priest before God. The impartation of the blessing can change everything. We can do this in our own personal time of prayer, but in the presence of others we can also literally initiate these blessings from God. This is the duty and job of us as priests. We give people the goodness and graciousness of God in their lives.

Lord, as I approach Your Courts, I thank You that Your heart
toward us is one of blessing and not cursing. As a priest unto my
God, I take the blessing of God and impart it to others. I thank
You that this blessing will alter the course of people's lives for
good. Thank You that You grant me the privilege of functioning
as one sent from You to others. In Jesus's name, amen.

APPROACHING THE HOLINESS OF GOD

*Do not cut off the tribe of the families of the Kohathites from
among the Levites; but do this in regard to them, that they
may live and not die when they approach the most holy things:
Aaron and his sons shall go in and appoint each of them to his
service and his task.* —Numbers 4:18–19

Great care had to be exercised regarding approaching God and handling the holy things of God. If *mistakes* were made, people died. Leviticus 10:1–3 chronicles two of Aaron's sons dying because they presumptuously offered *strange fire*. They did not treat as holy that which was required of the Lord. In the New Testament things are not as severe. Yet there is still a need to honor God in His holiness. Perhaps people will not die naturally, but if we don't walk in the reverence of who God is, we can forfeit the destiny that God has for us. Many times *dying* is symbolic of the forfeiture of destiny. There must be a fear of the Lord that we live in even under the new covenant. We are received by grace that we might serve God with reverence and godly fear as we approach Him (Heb. 12:28).

> *Lord as we approach You, we thank You that You are loving,
> kind, and good. We also know that we must approach You in
> the fear of the Lord, being empowered by Your grace. We honor
> You as the King of glory and the Most High God. Would You
> always allow me to have the right heart before You that I might
> be acceptable in Your sight? I submit myself to You and Your
> ways, in Jesus's name, amen.*

APPROACHING THE GOODNESS OF GOD

*Blessed is the man You choose, and cause to approach You, that
he may dwell in Your courts. We shall be satisfied with the
goodness of Your house, of Your holy temple.* —Psalm 65:4

Notice that it is the choosing of the Lord that allows us to approach Him. Coming into His presence is a privilege granted to us and a mark of His acceptance. Of course, we all have access into the presence of God through the blood of Jesus (Heb. 10:19). Not everyone, however, exercises this right and privilege. Whoever by faith will approach the Lord will be granted access before Him. When we come before the Lord and encounter His presence, it is because we have been acknowledged, accepted, and chosen of the Lord. The result of this is being satisfied with the goodness of His house and/or presence. Out of partaking of His goodness we are settled, secured, and established in Him. Fears are dismantled and removed from our lives. We can say with the psalmist, *"He... delivered me from all my fears"* (Ps. 34:4). As we dwell in the Courts of the Lord, it becomes our habitation and place of occupancy. It is a place we are familiar with. From this place we obtain a sense of safety and security that only His closeness brings.

> *Lord, as I approach Your Courts, I thank You that I am accepted
> through Your blood. I thank You that I enter Your Courts and
> dwell in this holy place. I ask, Lord, that Your favor, security,
> and safety would calm all my fears. I thank You that as I stand
> before You, You cause me to approach You with the awareness of
> Your love for me. Thank You, Lord, that I live my life in closeness
> to You. In Jesus's name, amen.*

ZADOK THE PRIEST

*Then he conferred with Joab the son of Zeruiah and with
Abiathar the priest, and they followed and helped Adonijah.
But Zadok the priest, Benaiah the son of Jehoiada, Nathan
the prophet, Shimei, Rei, and the mighty men who belonged to
David were not with Adonijah.* —1 Kings 1:7–8

Zadok was a Levitical priest who stayed true during the uprising against David.
Even when all the hierarchy of the kingdom rebelled, Zadok remained loyal.
This eventually brought great reward. He and his *descendants* are spoken of
in Ezekiel as those who will have a prominent place in the Kingdom of God
because of their loyalty (Ezek. 44:16–31). Notice that it is recorded that Zadok
and others *"were not with Adonijah."* Sometimes it is as important as who we are
not numbered among as those that we are. When all the leaders were forsaking
David and following a rebellious son, Zadok stayed true. This was in the occa-
sion when David was old, sick, and close to death. These others were seeking to
get themselves rightly positioned for the next king that was not the one chosen
of God. Zadok on the other hand was loyal, true, and committed to David, even
in his weakness. This can be a true test of loyalty. Will we remain true until the
end even when it would seem advantageous to jump ship? The result of Zadok's
loyalty was a promotion in the kingdom and a name synonymous with faithfulness. May we pass the test as well.

> Lord, as we stand before Your Courts, we ask for the faithfulness
> of Zadok to be in our lives. May we be found true even when it
> would seem advantageous to do otherwise. Lord, I ask that the
> spirit of Zadok would be in me that I might be found worthy of
> exaltation in Your Kingdom. Allow me, Lord, to pass the test. In
> Jesus's name, amen.

PRIEST AND SEER

The king also said to Zadok the priest, "Are you not a seer?
Return to the city in peace, and your two sons with you,
Ahimaaz your son, and Jonathan the son of Abiathar."
—2 Samuel 15:27

Zadok was prophetic as a priest. David had confidence in his prophetic abilities. As a result of Zadok's prophetic power he was able to discern in the midst of rebellion who the chosen of God was. Because of his prophetic perception he did not follow Absalom or Adonijah. He stayed with David while others joined the revolts. Zadok was faithful, yet his prophetic sense empowered him to know the seasons and times and what he should be doing. If we are to be rightly positioned, our decisions we make in the now should be prophetically motivated. We must be able to *see* what others are missing. The result will be a future that others might forfeit because of wrong decisions motivated out of self-survival rather that prophetic insight. May we learn to pay attention to what God is saying rather than what the circumstance seems to be demanding. The result will be right decisions setting the course for times to come.

> *Lord, as I come before Your Courts, I ask that I might see and understand prophetically Your will and passion. Forgive me for the times I have allowed the circumstances rather than Your voice to direct me. Allow me to be as Zadok, even during revolts, that I might choose the right ways of the Lord and secure the future You have for me. In Jesus's name, amen.*

ZADOK, CHOSEN OF THE LORD

"But the priests, the Levites, the sons of Zadok, who kept charge of My sanctuary when the children of Israel went astray from Me, they shall come near Me to minister to Me; and they shall stand before Me to offer to Me the fat and the blood," says the Lord God. —Ezekiel 44:15

Zadok was chosen of the Lord to stand before Him because when others went astray, Zadok stayed true. God desired Zadok to come near to Him and minister to Him. Many times the sign that someone is chosen of the Lord is seen in how near God is to them. We can look for outward signs of God's approval. However, it is the closeness of His presence with a person that many times is the seal of his or her union with God. Does our life carry this closeness with God? It is not necessary for power to be exhibited or for there to be success. It is not always the gifted or the one celebrated by others. It is the closeness and nearness of the Lord to this person's life. If we don't recognize this, we can miss the ones that God is actually choosing. They are the ones who have not gone astray but have stayed true when others forsook. May we be those that pass the test and be of the Zadok priesthood accepted and chosen by the Lord.

Lord, as we come before Your Courts, we thank You for gifting, success, and even celebration of others. However, Lord, we ask that it would be Your presence that would verify we are chosen by You. You desire to be close to those whose hearts are joined to You. May this be that which testifies of our approval by You. In Jesus's name, amen.

NO SWEATING

And it shall be, whenever they enter the gates of the inner court,
that they shall put on linen garments; no wool shall come upon
them while they minister within the gates of the inner court
or within the house. They shall have linen turbans on their
heads and linen trousers on their bodies; they shall not clothe
themselves with anything that causes sweat.
—Ezekiel 44:17–18

The garments worn by the Zadok priesthood were designed to prevent sweating. Sweating is symbolic of something being done from our own efforts and activity. We are told it is not by might nor power but by the Spirit of the Lord that things are accomplished (Zech. 4:6). This means that we are empowered by the anointing of God on our lives. We are not to wear ourselves out seeking to be successful or impacting. Our effectiveness comes from the gifting and empowerment of the Spirit of the Lord. We are not to seek to accomplish God's agenda out of our own strength. In essence we must be clothed with linen that will *breathe*. The flow of the Holy Spirit will keep us inspired, moved, and motivated from the innermost parts of our heart and life. The result will be greater works accomplished with less natural effort involved. This means that what we could never do out of our own strength, God does in us and through us by His Holy Spirit. Therefore, it is a partnership with Him through His Spirit that empowers our lives for life and service.

> *Lord, as I come before Your Courts, I petition You that I would be clothed with the Spirit of the living God resting on me. Help me, Lord, not to depend on my own efforts but to partner with You and Your Holy Spirit. I ask that anything that makes me sweat would be disconnected from me. Let my life be a demonstration of dependence on You and Your precious Spirit. In Jesus's name, amen.*

DIFFERENT ANOINTING/CLOTHES

When they go out to the outer court, to the outer court to the people, they shall take off their garments in which they have ministered, leave them in the holy chambers, and put on other garments; and in their holy garments they shall not sanctify the people. —Ezekiel 44:19

The priests were forbidden to wear the clothes they ministered to the Lord in when they went outside among the people. Clothes can speak of different anointings that we can carry. Therefore, the clothes we wear while we minister to the Lord in intimacy and prayer are different from what we wear when we minister to the people. Of course, I am speaking in spiritual terms and not natural ones. In intimacy with the Father we can be broken and very vulnerable. When we are among the people and releasing the anointing of God, it can be different. We can be bold, assertive, and fearless. So often to try and wear the same anointing while ministering to the people will not be understood. It can be misinterpreted. They so often know nothing of that place where we have been with God. However, they can get the benefit of the anointing that is for them that we carry as a result of the *clothes* we have on. We must know how to *change our clothes,* as we move from one function to the other.

> *Lord, thank You for the different anointings that we are to carry. One can be for ministry to You, while another is ministry to the people. As I stand before Your Courts, I ask for the grace necessary to "change" clothes as I move from my ministry before You to impartation for the people. Thank You for this ability. In Jesus's name, amen.*

COVERED, ALIGNED, AND NO LAWLESSNESS

*They shall neither shave their heads, nor let their hair grow
long, but they shall keep their hair well trimmed.*
—Ezekiel 44:20

The priests were required to have proper hairstyles and haircuts. Why is this? Hair speaks of being under proper authority (1 Cor. 11:15). In that it had to be well trimmed, it also speaks of there being no insubordination or lawlessness. As we function as priests before our God, we must examine ourselves to make sure we are properly aligned with God and others in authority God has placed in our lives. This is essential to functioning as priests before Him. The more we surrender to proper authority, the more authority we can carry. This authority will make us more effective as we seek the face of God and operate as those who would represent Him. Every form of rebellion in us would allow the devil the legal right to contend against us. He would build cases against us to deny our rights to carry the authority of God into our spheres. We should repent for any and every place we would be in rebellion against God or those set by God to represent Him in our lives. We must denounce all lawlessness and walk in proper alignment and covering as priests to our God.

> *Lord, as we come before Your Courts, we surrender as best we
> know how to You. We ask that we have the proper "hairstyle" in
> the Spirit before You. Help me, Lord, to denounce all rebellion,
> insubordination, and lawlessness connected to my life. Let me
> reflect one who is truly submitted and yielded to You. In Jesus's
> name, amen.*

CONTROLLED ONLY BY THE HOLY SPIRIT

No priest shall drink wine when he enters the inner court.
—Ezekiel 44:21

God forbade priests drinking wine as they ministered to Him in the innermost court. This tells us that the only influence we are to be under is the influence of the Holy Spirit of God. Paul spoke of this in Ephesians 5:18 when he admonished them to not be drunk with wine but to be filled with the Spirit of God. His exhortation was to allow only the intoxication of the Spirit of God to rule our lives. There was to be no counterfeit or substitute to the real Holy Spirit and His function over and through us. We are not to allow any other influence to rule us. Whether it be substances such as alcohol, anger, moodiness, another person's ideas, or other forms of influence. We are to be ruled only by the Spirit of God and His leadership. If we allow other influences, they can mimic the Spirit of God and make us think we are *hearing* Him when we are not. Therefore, we should be submitted only to the presence of the Lord as we seek His face and stand before Him in His holy place.

> *Lord, I ask that You help me to come only under Your influence and power. Please, Lord, allow only who You are through the Holy Spirit to control my life, decisions, and choices. I ask before Your Courts that You would strengthen me to always serve You from this place. In Jesus's name, amen.*

MARRIED IN THE LORD

They shall not take as wife a widow or a divorced woman,
but take virgins of the descendants of the house of Israel,
or widows of priests. —Ezekiel 44:22

Priests were forbidden to *marry* widows who had not been formerly the wife of a priest. They were also forbidden to marry divorced women, who were therefore not virgins. These ideas go far beyond the idea of natural marriage. We must be careful who and what we *marry*. In other words, who and what we give our heart, desires, and loyalty to in covenant. This can be people, ideas, movements, and other things that can take control of our lives and pull us away from our first love of Jesus. Whatever we are married to will bring an influence into our lives that can defile. This is one of the main reasons why God forbade the marrying of women who had already been married outside the priesthood. He understood that they could bring ideas in the life of the one called to be priest that would not be healthy or right. We must make sure we are equally yoked together in all things (2 Cor. 6:14). We must not join ourselves to that which will defile us; we should join ourselves to that which will enhance our walk and function as priests to our God.

> *Lord, I ask that You help me to be wise in any and every covenant*
> *I make. Would You help me to not allow anything to possess my*
> *heart that doesn't press me to You. As I stand before Your Courts,*
> *please, Lord, allow this to be true and established. I yield my life*
> *to You, in Jesus's name, amen.*

DISCERNING WHAT IS HOLY AND UNCLEAN

*And they shall teach My people the difference between the holy
and the unholy, and cause them to discern between the
unclean and the clean.* —Ezekiel 44:23

Priests are to have a sense of the holiness and cleanness of the Lord. They are to live in such a way that they can help others discern what God approves of and what He doesn't in this present world. This is what Romans 12:1–2 implores us to do. We are to so present ourselves as living sacrifices before God that we understand and manifest what is pleasing and acceptable to Him. This is part of what we do as priests. There is such a confusion today in what is acceptable before the Lord. We need a people who are so walking with their God that they can reveal the difference between holy and unholy, clean and unclean. These are not legalistic requirements but rather revelation of the Holy Spirit through the Word of God. We must not reject what God approves, and we must not approve what God rejects. We are to function as priests before our God and help people discern from our own lives what God blesses and what allows curses to light.

> *Lord, as we come before Your Courts, we yield to You. We repent
> for every place we have breached Your standard and partaken
> of that which is unholy or unclean. We want to live as a holy
> people set apart to You. Allow us, Lord, to so demonstrate what is
> acceptable to You that others might be moved and motivated to
> walk in this way. In Jesus's name, amen.*

JULY 13

THE RENDERING OF JUDGMENTS

*In controversy they shall stand as judges, and judge it according
to My judgments. They shall keep My laws and My statutes in
all My appointed meetings, and they shall hallow My Sabbaths.*
—Ezekiel 44:24

Priests were the appointed *judges* of God in society. They had the wisdom according the law and Word of God to settle controversy between people. As we walk as priests before our God, may His wisdom so be in us that we too can be the *peacemakers* of God. We are told that these are called the sons of God (Matt. 5: 9). So those who carry the nature of the Father as His children, know how to put an end to controversy. They know how to diffuse a situation rather than detonate it. They do this by judging righteously in given situations. This doesn't require that we have a recognized position in society. People will search out those with wisdom when they are known as those who can end controversy. As we stand as the priests of the Lord in the realm of the spirit, may we too render judgments that end controversy so that peace might come into otherwise volatile circumstances.

> *As we come into Your Courts, Lord, we as priests stand before
> You as Judge. We thank You that You grant us the wisdom to
> judge righteously. May we render decisions that will put an end
> to controversy and establish Your peace in situations. May we be
> used to diffuse rather than detonate explosive circumstances. In
> Jesus's name, amen.*

TOUCHING NOTHING DEAD

*They shall not defile themselves by coming near a dead person.
Only for father or mother, for son or daughter, for brother or
unmarried sister may they defile themselves.* —Ezekiel 44:25

Priests were forbidden to touch anything dead. They were only allowed to touch the dead if it was related to them. This means that God made room for natural human affection when it came to this ordinance. Otherwise things that were dead brought defilement to the priests. This is because the priests were to carry life. Dead things defile. They corrupt. This is why we are commanded to *repent of dead works* (Heb. 6:1). Dead works produce death in those who do them. We are told in Romans 8: 6 that carnal or fleshly mindedness brings death. So we as priests to our God are to separate ourselves from anything associated with death and not life in the Spirit. Defilement is when we have a sense of uncleanness and guilt associated with a certain activity or attitude. This defilement must be dealt with through repentance and the blood of Jesus cleansing us. It washes away the consciousness of guilt associated with the activity. As priests to our God we must stay pure and clean from that which carries death. When we do, we are then free to minister life.

> *Lord, as I come before Your Courts, I repent of any accusation against me of defilement through associating with dead works. I ask that Your blood would cleanse every defilement and I would be free from it in Jesus's name. Thank You, Lord, for Your faithfulness to me. Amen.*

THE PRIEST INHERITANCE

It shall be, in regard to their inheritance, that I am their inheritance. You shall give them no possession in Israel, for I am their possession. —Ezekiel 44:28

God proclaimed that the priests would get no inheritance of land as the rest of Israel did. He Himself would be their inheritance. If you examine further, as their livelihood priests were given the offering the people brought to the Lord. However, whoever will step into their function as a priest to their God will be rewarded with a special sense of His presence over their life. God will be near those who dedicate themselves to be His priest and minister to Him. The Lord Himself will be their inheritance. Hebrews 11:6 tells us that *"He is a rewarder of those who diligently seek Him."* In other words, God rewards those who seek *Him* with *Himself.* This isn't to say that He doesn't meet our needs and such as well. However the real *reward* or inheritance is the Lord and the closeness of His presence over our lives. May we truly serve Him as priest that we might be found worthy to be His inheritance. This alone satisfies like nothing else.

Lord, as I come into Your Courts, I ask that You, Lord, would be my inheritance. Out of this, You will meet my needs. However, Lord, let it be known in Your Courts that my passion is You and Your presence. May You be close to me and may I be Your servant and friend forever. In Jesus's name, amen.

OPERATING AS KINGS

But you are a chosen generation, a royal priesthood, a holy
nation, His own special people, that you may proclaim
the praises of Him who called you out of darkness into His
marvelous light. —1 Peter 2:9

We are called a royal priesthood. When royalty is spoken of, it is in regard to kingship. So Peter is declaring that we are a kingly order of priests. We have looked extensively over many days at our function as priests. This is our legal activity in the spirit world. Once, however, we have fulfilled our function as priests, we must step into our kingship and decree a thing into place. As we do, things begin to move into divine order. The reason is because the legal rights that had resisted it have been removed through priestly activity. Kingly decrees are now able to move things to where God intended them to be. This is the joint venture of us functioning as kings and priests to our God. One of the major reason people do not see breakthroughs from the Courts of Heaven is passivity after they have functioned as priests. Getting things legally in order is of great necessity. However, we must with aggression step into kingship and with boldness and authority set things in place through our words, decrees, declarations, and announcements. As we do, the final and complete breakthroughs will come.

> *Lord, as I come before Your Courts, I thank You that You have*
> *heard me as priest. Thank You for this place of function. I now*
> *step into my place as a king and with boldness utter decrees,*
> *declarations, words, and announcements that shift things to the*
> *desired and intended place. In Jesus's name breakthrough now*
> *comes. Amen.*

STANDING AS KINGS

(As it is written, "I have made you a father of many nations")
in the presence of Him whom he believed—God, who gives life
to the dead and calls those things which do not exist as though
they did. —Romans 4:17

Kings are those who decree a thing and see it happen. We as kings actually get to operate even as God Himself operates. He called things that didn't exist as if they did. Abraham's revelation of who God is was that He gave life to the dead and called into reality those things that did not exist. Having been made in His image and likeness, we are to walk in portions of this same power (Gen. 1:26). This means that our words have creative power, even as God through His words created the visible world from what was invisible (Heb. 11:3). We also through spoken words and decrees can see things materialize from what is invisible. Just because something is invisible doesn't mean it doesn't exist. Many things we cannot see exist. Through our words, we call out of the invisible realm that which exists into the visible dimension. This is the power of operating as a king in the spirit world. Once things have been legally set in order as priest, we then decree as kings. The result will be physical manifestations of answers to prayers and requests before God.

> *As I come before Your Courts, Lord, I stand here as a king. I*
> *thank You that we are kings and priests before our God. From*
> *this position, I now call into place in the natural what already*
> *exists in the spiritual. Thank You, Lord, that all things are*
> *legally set, and I can now put this in place from my kingship. In*
> *Jesus's name, amen.*

FAITH-FILLED WORDS

So Jesus answered and said to them, "Have faith in God. For assuredly, I say to you, whoever says to this mountain, 'Be removed and be cast into the sea,' and does not doubt in his heart, but believes that those things he says will be done, he will have whatever he says." —Mark 11:22–23

When Peter marveled that the fig tree Jesus cursed so quickly withered away, this was Jesus's response. He was endeavoring to teach His disciples how to use their words as kings. They were to recognize the authority their words could carry in the spirit world. This would result in natural manifestations coming into agreement with God's will. Jesus was emphasizing that their words must be without doubt and filled with faith. In other words, they couldn't just *mouth* words from an unbelieving heart; they had to first have faith in their heart to empower the words of their mouth. From this, things would be set in motion that would produce supernatural happenings. We too are to use our words from the realm of faith. Paul spoke of faith-filled words in Second Corinthians 4:13. He declared that the *spirit of faith* in him caused him to speak in a certain way. Faith has a way of talking. We must allow the Holy Spirit to fashion this dimension in our hearts. We will begin to speak with faith that sets the right things in motion over our lives and situations.

> *As I come before Your Courts, Lord, I humble my heart and ask that the spirit of faith be formed in me. Let doubt and unbelief be extracted from my life, I pray. Produce in me, Lord, the spirit of faith that will allow me to walk as a king in boldness and authority. Use my words to set in motion that which is necessary for Your will to be done. In Jesus's name, amen.*

BOLDNESS OF KINGS

Now when they saw the boldness of Peter and John, and
perceived that they were uneducated and untrained men, they
marveled. And they realized that they had been with Jesus.
—Acts 4:13

One of the attributes of functioning as kings is boldness. The religious leaders marveled at the boldness of men who would otherwise have been petrified before them. This was because of the confidence and security that came from knowing Jesus. Uneducated and untrained individuals would normally have been greatly intimidated by the supposed prestige and authority of the Jewish leaders. This was not the case of Peter and John. In the natural they may have been uneducated and untrained, but in the spiritual realm they were kings, and they knew it! They knew they actually outranked in the spirit realm they stood before. Wow! This produced a boldness laced with humility. The presence of humility in the midst of boldness is what keeps us from brashness. This form of boldness will allow a release of faith with our words that produces the supernatural. This is the reason Peter and John were standing before these men. The miracle at the Beautiful Gate of the lame man being healed had brought them there (Acts 3:2–9). The man had been healed because Peter and John had made a bold decree of faith from their kingship. This release of authority through boldness healed the man. Kings function with boldness.

> *Lord, I come boldly before Your Courts. By faith I take my place*
> *before You that Your blood has granted. As I stand in this place, I*
> *ask that You help me to move in true boldness and not brashness.*
> *May I without fear or doubt through faith operate in an amazing*
> *boldness that brings the supernatural. In Jesus's name, amen.*

COMMANDING ANGELS

*Bless the Lord, you His angels, who excel in strength, who do
His word, heeding the voice of His word. Bless the Lord, all you
His hosts, you ministers of His, who do His pleasure.*
—Psalm 103:20–21

Angelic presence responds to the *"voice of His word."* They also are here to *"do His pleasure."* The voice of His word can come through our voice. It is His word, not necessarily the voice that is carrying it that angels respond to. When the Holy Spirit uses our voice to declare His word, this can initiate angelic activity and movement. Sometimes the lack of angelic involvement in the earth is because there has been *no voice* to carry His word. Our words as kings can arouse the movement of angels from the heavenly realm. This is important because angels are sent to be ministers to the heirs of salvation (Heb. 1:14). Could the lack of angelic help in our lives be because we haven't motivated them through the lack of speaking His word? We must learn to be the voice of His word. Angels move and heed the voice of His word. This requires we fill ourselves with the word of the Lord that the Holy Spirit might draw from it. As we speak His word under the unction of the Spirit of God, angels are aroused to pursue the doing of His word in our behalf. Let's boldly speak the word of the Lord and see angelic presence move for us and with us. The result will be supernatural help for us as the heirs of salvation.

> *Lord, as I come before the Courts of Heaven, I thank You that
> angels are present to move in my behalf. Forgive me, Lord, for
> the times I haven't activated this help. Forgive me for the times
> I have not been a voice that could speak Your word. May I step
> into this place as a king and see angels aroused for me and with
> me. In Jesus's name, amen.*

CHARACTER FITTING A KING

And whenever you stand praying, if you have anything against anyone, forgive him, that your Father in heaven may also forgive you your trespasses. But if you do not forgive, neither will your Father in heaven forgive your trespasses.
—Mark 11:25–26

As Jesus instructed His disciples how to use their words and mouth to move the heavenly realm as kings, He spoke of the necessity of forgiveness. Clearly forgiveness is necessary to walk in spiritual authority. This means that unwillingness to forgive will cause our spiritual authority to be diminished and even vanish. Our prayers will become ineffective. Jesus said *whenever we stand praying,* we should forgive. There is something about engaging in the spiritual activity of prayer that causes issues of the heart to be revealed. As we engage in prayer, we move into a dimension of the spirit where everything becomes open and manifest. Hebrews 4:13 tells us that all things are naked and open before the Lord. He sees and knows all things. As we pray, however, what God already sees, He can cause to come to the forefront, so we become aware of something we are harboring in our heart toward someone else. It can be something we are completely justified to feel. In this moment of prayer, however, we become aware of the wickedness of this thing before the Lord. We then repent and find freedom from it. Our spiritual authority as kings is restored as we stand before the Lord.

Lord, as I stand in Your Courts, I allow You the right to search my hidden and even stubborn place of unforgiveness. I realize this is displeasing to You and will result in the diminishment and even the vanishing of the spiritual authority I am to carry. Forgive me, Lord, even as I forgive those who have wounded me. Thank You for the grace to forgive even as You forgive me. In Jesus's name, amen.

A RESTRAINED TONGUE GRANTS AUTHORITY

*Now Joshua had commanded the people, saying, "You shall
not shout or make any noise with your voice, nor shall a word
proceed out of your mouth, until the day I say to you, 'Shout!'
Then you shall shout." —Joshua 6:10*

As the people circled Jericho for six days, they were forbidden to say a word
or make a sound. On the seventh day they encompassed the city seven times.
On the seventh time they shouted. When they did, the walls of the city came
down (Josh. 6:20). This required restraint for them to walk around the walls
of this city and not say a word. I'm sure the walls of this city seemed insur-
mountable and unconquerable. As they walked around the city, if they had said
something, it probably would have been statements of fear and doubt. After
seven days, however, perhaps faith had begun to arise in their hearts. Maybe the
walls no longer looked as large as they had at the beginning. Perhaps something
had begun to change because of the lack of the negative report. When it came
time to shout on the seventh trip around the walls on the seventh day, there was
now a supernatural development of faith. The shout was from a deep well of
expectancy that something was about to happen. From this place in the spirit
of a restrained tongue, a shout erupted that shook things in the spiritual world.
The walls fell flat, and the city was conquered. So will the strongholds of our
lives fall as well.

*Lord, as I come into Your Courts, I ask for the grace of a restrained
tongue that I may speak no evil. Forgive me for all the evil reports
I have brought in negativity. Help me have a guard over my
mouth that my words as a king may carry divine authority. In
Jesus's name, amen.*

BRIDLING THE TONGUE

For we all stumble in many things. If anyone does not stumble
in word, he is a perfect man, able also to bridle the whole body.
—James 3:2

The ability to not offend with the tongue grants authority to control our whole being. If we struggle with areas that are out of control in our lives and are not able to exercise authority there, the answer might be in learning to control the tongue. This Scripture seems to indicate that the power to control our tongue will give us authority over other unruly areas of our life. As we control what comes from our mouth, we grow in authority to rule our entire being. Other rebellious places of our life will become easier to subdue because we are exercising His authority. This Scripture seems to be clear. If we don't stumble or trip with our tongue, we are *able* to bridle every other appetite and desire. Wow! This means that we must set a guard over our mouth and let no corrupt speech come from our mouth. We must not be negative, arrogant, judgmental, or even hateful toward others. We must ask the Lord to empower us from His Courts to subdue the unruly member called the tongue. This will result in new levels of authority to operate as kings before Him and the purposes of His Kingdom.

> *Lord, I come and approach Your Courts. I ask, Lord, that I might have grace to subdue my tongue under Your authority. Forgive me for all the places where I have used my tongue for evil. I repent. Grant me, Lord, the grace I need to exercise the authority of the Lord to restrain the words of my mouth and speak only right things. In Jesus's name, amen.*

SMALL THINGS NEW OBEDIENCE

*For we all stumble in many things. If anyone does not stumble
in word, he is a perfect man, able also to bridle the whole body.
Indeed, we put bits in horses' mouths that they may obey us,
and we turn their whole body.* —James 3:2–3

Bits cause horses to obey. A bit is small, yet it produces obedience. The whole body of the horse gets turned in the direction that it needs to go. We must allow the Lord to *sit* upon us and turn us as well. We must allow the bit of the Holy Spirit to be in our mouth. If our mouth is controlled, every other part of us comes into obedience. This is what it means to be meek. Matthew 5:5 calls the meek blessed. One of the main definitions of *meek* is to be bridlewise. In other words, meekness is *power under control* as a result of allowing the Lord to bridle our tongue. The more my mouth lines up with the Word of the Lord, the more power under control I can walk in. I am able to function as a king in the earth in behalf of the Lord. I can be trusted with newer levels of authority and power. The result will be new dimensions of the Kingdom of God being realized. Jesus will be glorified, and His domain extended.

> *Lord, as I approach Your Courts, let my tongue come under Your power and control. Make me bridlewise that I might walk in power under control. Thank You that even as a horse is controlled with a bit, Holy Spirit, You cause a restraint to be on me and in my mouth. In Jesus's name, amen.*

DIRECTION GRANTED

*Look also at ships: although they are so large and are driven by
fierce winds, they are turned by a very small rudder wherever
the pilot desires.* —James 3:4

The rudder of a ship in comparison to the size of a ship is little. Even though the power source of a ship is the result of something else, it is the rudder that determines the direction and destination. What a powerful analogy. Perhaps we are motivated and even propelled forward by the wind of the Holy Spirit. It is, however, the rudder of our life, which is our tongue, that will determine where we end up and land. This means we can have a great anointing, tremendous gifting, and even wonderful authority, but if our tongue is setting the wrong course, we will not get to where we are supposed to go. The tongue, mouth, and speech will set a direction toward a place we are not intended to go. What a powerful truth to grasp. It is the *pilot* who sets the rudder and determines the direction of the ship. This means that whoever the pilot is must be under the guidance of the Lord Himself. We as the pilot of our ship must set our rudder or our tongue in agreement with the ways of God. Otherwise the force of the wind will not drive us to our destination but to a place we don't want to go. May God help us as the pilot to set the right course with the words of our mouth.

> *Lord, as I seek to walk as a king in the authority of who You are,
> may I set the rudder of my life. May I set my tongue to speak right
> things. May I before Your Courts petition that the Courts render
> a decision of grace to empower me to obey You in these things. I
> petition the Courts for Your help. In Jesus's name, amen.*

THE FIRE OF THE TONGUE

Even so the tongue is a little member and boasts great things.
See how great a forest a little fire kindles! And the tongue
is a fire, a world of iniquity. The tongue is so set among our
members that it defiles the whole body, and sets on fire the
course of nature; and it is set on fire by hell. —James 3:5–6

James gives us further insight into the power of the tongue. He speaks of the tongue as a force that can devour and destroy. He speaks of its ability to start a *fire* that consumes whole forests that have taken decades and even centuries to grow. This fire can consume and destroy in moments what it has taken years to grow and build. This is the destructive nature of the tongue. We are told it is because the tongue can become a demonic accomplice. Hell itself sets it on fire. This is why we have all seen situations that exploded into absolute annihilation as a result of words spoken in heat and rage. Relationships that have been built over years are destroyed in minutes. This is not just the words of humans, but words of humans set ablaze by demonic impulse. Divorces occur, estrangement takes place, lifelong wounds are inflicted, and families are annihilated because of the demonic savagery attached to the tongue. We must submit our tongue to the authority of the Lord. Yes, so we can function as kings, but also so we can preserve that which has been built and grown for years.

> *Lord, as I come before Your Courts, I beseech that You help*
> *me set a guard on my tongue that would quench any fire. I am*
> *asking, Lord, that every tendency toward demonic savagery*
> *with my tongue would be thwarted. Let me walk in peace with*
> *those I love. I am asking for help from Your Courts. Any place*
> *destruction has occurred, would You help me rebuild? In Jesus's*
> *name, amen.*

TAMING THE BEAST

For every kind of beast and bird, of reptile and creature of the
sea, is tamed and has been tamed by mankind. But no man can
tame the tongue. It is an unruly evil, full of deadly poison.
—James 3:7–8

The tongue is a beast to be tamed. Left to its natural tendency the tongue is a devouring beast. We are told that any and every other kind of beast has been tamed or at least captured. Without exercising spiritual authority over the natural tongue, it is an untamed beast. However, through the power of the Holy Spirit this beast can be tamed. When taming a beast, that animal must become convinced that you are more powerful and in control. You are able then to domesticate the creature. The same is true with the tongue. We must use the spiritual authority granted to us as children of God to bring the tongue into submission. John 1:12 tells us that as many as received the Lord they were given authority to *become* children of God. This means that when we accepted Jesus, we were granted the necessary authority to subdue anything under His feet that would be in opposition to Him and His purposes. This includes our tongue. As we ourselves submit ourselves to Jesus's Lordship, this authority is enacted to bring the beast of our tongue under His power. This beast of our tongue then becomes something that serves us rather than us serving it.

> *Lord, I come before Your Courts and ask that my unruly tongue come under Your authority. I surrender this member and all its rebellious intent to You. Let the beast of my tongue be domesticated and surrendered to You. Let it no more expect to be served, but let it now serve You and Your purposes. In Jesus's name, amen.*

THE CONSECRATION
OF THE TONGUE

With it we bless our God and Father, and with it we curse men,
who have been made in the similitude of God. Out of the same
mouth proceed blessing and cursing. My brethren, these things
ought not to be so. —James 3:9–10

James bemoans the fact that we use our tongue for dualistic reasons. We bless God with our tongue as believers, yet curse men in our speech with it as well. This means we are not consecrating our tongue for the reason it was created. The main purpose of the tongue is to bless, worship, and honor God and others. We are told to let the sacrifice of praise come from our lips to the Lord (Heb. 13:15). We are also to bless humans who are made in the image, likeness, and similitude of God. We are to have an awareness of the honor that all men are worth simply because they were made in God's likeness. This means that no matter how vile we might think someone is, they are worthy of honor from our tongue. This is why we are told to *"honor all people"* (1 Pet. 2:17). This can be a real challenge, but if we make it our practice to speak well and not evil of people, we are using our tongue as a consecrated instrument to God. We should choose whether our tongue is going to be an instrument of blessing or cursing. If we choose blessing, then we are aligning with God's purpose for our tongue and its power. However, if we choose cursing, we are choosing destructive powers to be loosed. May we choose wisely!

> *Lord, as I approach Your Courts, I bring my tongue and surrender it as one called to operate as a king in Your Kingdom. I choose this day to consecrate my tongue as an instrument of blessing and not cursing. May my tongue be Your vehicle to bless others and not to curse them. In Jesus's name, amen.*

SWEET OR BITTER SPRING

Does a spring send forth fresh water and bitter from the same opening? Can a fig tree, my brethren, bear olives, or a grapevine bear figs? Thus no spring yields both salt water and fresh.
—James 3:11–12

Our tongue is either bringing forth fresh water or poison/bitter water. James also speaks to the fact that the *kind* of tree or plant determines its fruit. In other words the *nature* of the plant determines the *kind* of fruit it will bear. We as believers have received the new nature of who Jesus is (2 Pet. 1:3). We have the divine nature of God in us through the new birth of the Holy Spirit. This means our tongues should reflect this new nature. We should speak out of the heart and passion of God. From *this opening,* fresh water should flow for others to drink from. Are our words producing fruit consistent with the nature of God we claim is in us that people might eat and be healthy? Is the *water* coming from the *opening/mouth* refreshing and edifying people or defiling them? Our words are to be as fresh water quenching the thirst of those who would drink from our lives. May they replenish the people who hear what proceeds from this opening. May our words be used to bring life. May people not come expecting to drink of that which is fresh only to take a big gulp of salt water and actually be sickened or made even more thirsty. Let the spring coming from our lives be filled with the freshness of the Lord. Let words that edify spring forth from us (Eph. 4:29).

As I come before Your Courts, Lord, I thank You that You have called me to be a king and priest before You. May my tongue be under Your authority that it might be a spring bringing forth life-giving flow. May people drink from the opening of my mouth and be refreshed and blessed. I yield myself and my mouth to You. In Jesus's name, amen.

OPENING DOUBLE DOORS

Thus says the Lord to His anointed, to Cyrus, whose right hand
I have held—to subdue nations before him and loose the armor
of kings, to open before him the double doors, so that the gates
will not be shut. —Isaiah 45:1

Opened doors are essential for success and purpose in life to be fulfilled. So often the enemy is using legal action against us to keep these doors of favor, opportunity, and privilege shut. When we know how to come before the Courts and discern what the devil might be using, we can see the promises we have waited on become a reality. In this Scripture, God promises to open *double doors*. This means unprecedented opportunities are made available to us, perhaps even what eye hasn't seen, ear hasn't heard, and even what the heart hasn't imagined (1 Cor. 2:9). One of the main things we have to contend against in regard to embracing and moving through these double doors is the disappointment of the past season. If we aren't careful, we can allow the troubles and tribulations of the past form a mentality that is more about doubt than it is faith. The Lord will heal us of this so that as the doors open we will have the necessary belief to move through them and into the future God has for us. We must repent before the Courts for any unbelief we have allowed to be formed in us so that we can embrace the double doors that are opening for us.

> *As I approach Your Courts, Lord, I thank You for the open doors*
> *that You have set before me. I repent and shake free from the past*
> *season of trouble that would have fashioned me with a thinking*
> *more in agreement with unbelief than faith. I ask, Lord, that*
> *real faith might arise in my heart that I can move through the*
> *opened double doors. In Jesus's name, amen.*

OPEN DOORS AND ADVERSARIES

For a great and effective door has opened to me, and there are many adversaries. —1 Corinthians 16:9

As we approach the Courts of Heaven, we should believe God for great and effective doors to open. When doors open, we have great opportunities for success and influence. Notice that the Apostle Paul said that in the midst of the excitement of these doors opening, there were adversaries. Not just adversaries but *many* adversaries. Some people allow the presence of adversaries to convince them that the doors that are open are not from God. Or they completely cannot *see* the open doors because of the trouble. They wrongly believe that anything God does wouldn't have challenge, hardship, or difficulties attached to it. How wrong they are! In fact, it can be just the opposite. When doors of great favor open, the devil will seek to thwart our taking advantage of it by raising up adversity. If these doors are set by God, any adversary we face will be overcome through our faith and obedience (1 John 5:4). Many times when doors open, it looks like *crisis*, but in every crisis there can be an opportunity. Yes, there can be danger as well. However, we mustn't allow the *danger* to overwhelm the *opportunity*. We should be aware of the danger and move cautiously, yet also see the opportunity and take advantage of it. When we do, we step through open doors and into the destiny of God.

> *As I approach Your Courts, Lord, I ask that I have eyes to see the open doors and not just the adversaries. Lord, place in my heart a faith that would realize the adversaries will be conquered and the destiny embraced. Thank You, Lord, that from Your Court there is a rendering of judgment against every adversary that would seek to stop my embracing and moving through these open doors. In Jesus's name, amen.*

GREAT AND EFFECTIVE DOORS

For a great and effective door has opened to me, and there are
many adversaries. —1 Corinthians 16:9

The word *great* in this Scripture is the word *megas* in the Greek. Obviously, most know the term *mega*. It means and implies something that is enormous and super large. So a *great* door being opened meant huge opportunities were made available. With every opened door there is a great sense of responsibility that goes with it. When God grants opportunity to us, we are required to be faithful with the privilege He is granting. It necessitates that we move in the fear of the Lord to make full use of what we are being granted. When these doors open, we must be aware they may never open again. We must treat them with a sense of urgency and even sacredness. These doors are also said to be *effective*. This is the Greek word *energēs*. It means "to be active, operative, and powerful." This speaks of the activity in the spirit realm connected to open doors. In other words, there is much moving and active in our behalf. As we step through the open doors, we are coming into agreement with the activity of Heaven. We are not producing something ourselves. On the contrary, we are connecting and moving with the spiritual dimension to see what human effort could never produce. It's not by might nor power, but by His Spirit (Zech. 4:6).

> *Thank You, Lord, that I have access by Your blood to the Courts of Heaven. As I come before Your Courts, I ask that great and effective doors would now open. Let mega doors open for me now. Allow the forces of Heaven to move and produce what my own efforts never can. I thank You, Lord, for this from Your Courts. In Jesus's name, amen.*

A SET OPEN DOOR

*I know your works. See, I have set before you an open door, and
no one can shut it; for you have a little strength, have kept My
word, and have not denied My name.* —Revelation 3:8

Open doors of favor, privilege, and opportunity are not something we pry open.
They are *set before us.* Sometimes we think it is our responsibility to open these
doors. However, we are told these open doors are *set before us.* This means that
it isn't necessarily my business to *open* the door. It is my business to be faithful
with the open door. I must recognize it is something that is available to me. I
then must move through it and engage that which is connected to it. David, as
one ordained by God to be king, had to steward faithfully the open door. The
people loved him, and he was granted great favor in the palaces of the kingdom. However, Saul had an agenda against him. We are told that in the midst
of this scenario, *"David behaved wisely"* (1 Sam. 18:14). David knew how to
steward the place he had been granted. So often we walk through doors God has
opened. However, if we don't know how to behave wisely, these open doors can
shut. God is not shutting the doors; we cause them to close when we are unwise.
May we have the wisdom of God to manage faithfully the doors God open for
us. May we walk in His wisdom and secure the divine purpose for which these
open doors were entrusted to us.

> *As I approach Your Courts, Lord, I thank You for "setting" before
> me opened doors. Help me Lord to have the necessary wisdom
> to steward these places You have granted. I desire to be faithful
> and see Your will done through these doors of privilege and
> opportunity. In Jesus's name, amen.*

MEASURED BY GOD

I know your works. See, I have set before you an open door, and no one can shut it; for you have a little strength, have kept My word, and have not denied My name. —Revelation 3:8

Notice that opened doors are preceded by God *knowing our works.* In other words, there has been an investigation of our life. The opened doors are a result of God evaluating our lives, and we pass the test. Opened doors have now been set for us because we have been proved and found faithful. We are told that we are to grow up into the full measure of Christ (Eph. 4:13). We are being measured by the stature of who Jesus is. Of course, Jesus is perfect in all His ways. He is our measuring rod. We are not measured by what someone else is doing. We are told these comparisons are unwise (2 Cor. 10:12). Our measurement is to the Lord Himself and His grace in our lives. God looks at all our works. He knows the secrets of our lives. He sees what others see. However, more importantly, He sees what others don't see. When the Lord sets before us an open door, it is because we have been proven faithful to Him. He esteems that we can be trusted with that which is valuable and precious to Him. This is why these doors are opened. Have we been found faithful? When we have, it speaks great things in the Courts of Heaven in our behalf. It grants the Lord as Judge the right to render decisions for doors of favor to open to us.

> *As we come before Your Courts, Lord, I ask that I might be found faithful. As You would measure me, may I measure up in Your grace. May I be one that can be entrusted with open doors that Your purposes would be accomplished and I might fulfill what is written in my book in Heaven. In Jesus's name, amen.*

FAITHFULNESS TESTIMONY IN THE COURTS

He who is faithful in what is least is faithful also in much; and
he who is unjust in what is least is unjust also in much.
—Luke 16:10

Remember that opened doors for our life and purpose are a result of God *knowing our works* (Rev. 3:8). In other words, we have been proven and found faithful. God proves faithfulness in the *little things.* Many times people falsely believe that if they had big responsibility that really mattered, lots of money or a great position, then they would be faithful. The Lord declared that the test of faithfulness is in the *small things.* If we know how to take care of little things, then we will be faithful and just in the larger things. Before God will entrust us with the great things of life, we must pass the test of the small things and places. This is why we are told not to despise the day of small beginnings (Zech. 4:10). How we handle small things is evidence of the character we have or do not have. Faithfulness is not about just what we do. Faithfulness is about who we are. When the character trait of faithfulness has been formed in us, we will be faithful no matter what situation we are in. What God is looking for is not momentary acts. He is looking for a heart that will always obey and be true to Him. When this is located, He will move in our behalf and show Himself strong (2 Chron.16:9). Open doors will be set before us that no one can shut.

> *As I approach Your Courts, my Lord, I ask that I might be found*
> *faithful. May I be one who is true in small things, that You might*
> *trust me with the big things. As You evaluate my life, please,*
> *Lord, let Your grace form faithfulness in me that it might speak*
> *before Your Courts. In Jesus's name, amen.*

AUGUST 5

FAITHFUL WITH MONEY

Therefore if you have not been faithful in the unrighteous
mammon, who will commit to your trust the true riches?
—Luke 16:11

One of the main proving grounds that Jesus spoke about was money. *Mammon* is a term for wealth. Unrighteous mammon is Jesus referring to natural finances. So we are being told that the Lord's willingness to trust us with *true riches* can be dependent on how we handle natural riches. The Lord watches our activities as it relates to natural wealth to see if we are ready to handle what He considers really valuable. The true riches can be anointing, authority, favor, open doors, and influence. There are others, but these are some of the things that would qualify as true riches. As we steward our natural money, not only is God watching, but He is using it to teach us how to handle the really valuable stuff. The disciplines that are necessary to be successful with *unrighteous mammon* are the same disciplines necessary to use the true riches effectively. I must be willing to come under the scrutiny of the Lord in my finances and the way I handle them if I desire to be entrusted with the realms important to God. Our faithfulness with money can release a testimony in the Courts of Heaven for us that will cause doors of great and effective opportunity to open. May God's grace empower our obedience.

> *As I approach the Courts of Heaven, I allow, Lord, Your scrutiny*
> *over the way I manage money. Help me, Lord, to be faithful with*
> *this world's wealth that I might be trusted with the heavenly*
> *wealth. May my faithfulness with money allow a testimony in*
> *my behalf before Your Courts. Let the double doors open for me*
> *now, in Jesus's name, amen.*

FAITHFUL IN WHAT BELONGS TO ANOTHER

And if you have not been faithful in what is another man's, who will give you what is your own? —Luke 16:12

As the Lord looks at our lives and measures us to determine if double doors may be open to us (Isa. 45:1), He looks at how we handle what belongs to someone else. This is a test of faithfulness. Not only are we to take care of what is ours and what we have a stake in, but we are to care for what belongs to someone else. Serving another person's interest and calling is one of the main ways we become qualified before God to have our own. It would seem many would never consider it to be advantageous to serve another person. Yet this is one of the ways that God prepares us for our own destiny and purpose. As He evaluates and judges our readiness to steward our own callings, the Lord looks at how we have served someone else. David served his father by taking care of his father's sheep. He also served Saul as the king of Israel through first ministering to him through music and then being his chief warrior. Timothy was a beloved son to the Apostle Paul (2 Tim. 1:2). Joshua served Moses (Num. 11:28), while Elisha *poured water* over the hands of Elijah (2 Kings 3:11). Those who were used to impact the world first had their faithfulness proved through the service to others. God's ways have not changed. This is still true today.

Lord, let it be recorded before Your Courts that I have faithfully served another. I have been willing to humble myself before You as I helped what You had called another to do. As this speaks before You, please open for me the double doors. Let Your glory be known, in Jesus's name, amen.

GRASPING THE MOMENT

...redeeming the time, because the days are evil.
—Ephesians 5:16

There are two main words for *time* in the New Testament: *chronos* and *kairos. Chronos* basically means a *span of time,* while *kairos* means a *moment in time.* We live our life in *chronos.* We get up, go to work, pay our bills, raise our kids, and other seemingly significant and insignificant tasks that we do. Then there is *kairos,* those moments in time where our decisions and activities are going to produce a new future and destiny. *Kairos* are those moments when doors and even double doors are open to us and we step through them. Suddenly, from this activity a new dimension of operation is set into place. Jesus spoke of the Jewish people having missed their time of visitation or *kairos* moment (Luke 19:44). As a result, instead of the future God had for them, they came under judgment. This can happen when people miss the moment that God has meticulously prepared for them. At the least, the destiny that He had arranged is lost. This is why we are told in our Scripture to *redeem the kairos. Redeem* means "to buy back." We are to buy back the *kairos* moment. In other words, we are to fully invest ourselves in these moments that God grants to us. The result will be that we walk through the double doors and into the future God planned for us. As we prophetically sense and *buy back* the moment of our visitation, we will garner the future prepared for us by God.

> Lord, as I approach Your Courts, I ask that I might be faithful in chronos. However, Lord, would You allow me to recognize the kairos time prepared for me. Let me with faithfulness buy back this moment and step into the destiny You have arranged. Please, Lord, I ask and would petition the Courts that I wouldn't miss it, in Jesus's name, amen.

JESUS THE DOOR OPENER

I know your works. See, I have set before you an open door, and
no one can shut it; for you have a little strength, have kept My
word, and have not denied My name. —Revelation 3:8

Jesus declares that He Himself has set before them an open door. Open doors are not a result of circumstances just being arranged. Open doors are the result of Jesus Himself having ordered things for certain opportunities to be presented. This is the Lord's doings. If we don't recognize this, then we will not value and treat with holiness these privileges that would seem to be presented to us. We can actually feel that we have a *choice* in the matter rather than seeing it as a place of *obedience*. Even though in one sense we always have a choice, we must choose to obey. With open doors goes a sense of responsibility that we must care for. Every open door that Jesus opens for us has an assignment attached to it. We must with great diligence and precision seek to obey and fulfill the assignment connected to this open door. To do this we must first *see*. Jesus declares that we must *see* the open door that He has set. May the Lord open our eyes to *see* the open door set before us by the Lord. As we *see,* may we move through it with fear and trembling to fulfill every assignment given us by the Lord.

> *Lord, I recognize You as the door opener. I thank You that open*
> *doors are not just a result of circumstances being arranged. Lord,*
> *You personally have prepared these opportunities and presented*
> *them to me. As I stand before Your Courts, may I be judged*
> *faithful in the way I see and steward these open doors. May I*
> *walk in the fear of the Lord to fulfill every assignment connected*
> *to these open doors. In Jesus's name, amen.*

OVERCOMING WEARINESS

When Gideon came to the Jordan, he and the three hundred
men who were with him crossed over, exhausted but
still in pursuit. —Judges 8:4

As Gideon pursued the kings that he had defeated to finish the job so they wouldn't regroup, he and his men were exhausted, yet pursuing. We all get tired and weary at times. In regard to open doors, the devil will use our weariness to distract us from entering the doors that Jesus has actually opened for us. Revelation 3:8 speaks of having a *little strength* in the midst of the doors opened by Jesus. Our little strength can be a result of the fight we were in during the last season. We cannot allow this fatigue to stop and hinder us from seeing and walking into the doors Jesus opened for us. There is a time where we must draw from the grace and strength of who the Lord is to keep pursuing even when we are weak and exhausted. There is too much at stake in this time to not move through the open doors. We must gird up our loins and move forward even in our frailty (1 Pet. 1:13). The effort we expend in these moments will pay great reward in the days to come as we move through the open doors prepared for us by the Lord. We will gain a new breath in the aftermath and be so glad that we did not allow our weariness to overcome us.

> *Lord, as I move through the open doors You have prepared for*
> *me, I may be exhausted, but I choose to still pursue. I will not*
> *become weary in well doing. I gird up the loins of my mind and*
> *set my gaze on You. May it be recorded before Your Courts that*
> *I have chosen to be faithful and move into the doors You have*
> *opened for me. In Jesus's name, amen.*

OPEN DOORS AND WORK

*I must work the works of Him who sent Me while it is day; the
night is coming when no one can work.* —John 9:4

Open doors can seem like exciting things. We can get exhilarated because of
the new opportunities and privileges being granted to us. However, open doors
almost always mean more work. Jesus spoke of having a season where He could
work. He had an awareness that the *night was coming.* In this time no one could
work. In other words, the doors and opportunities He presently had would
no longer be available. We too must recognize that the open doors we may be
enjoying may not last forever. Therefore, we must work *while it is day.* We must
take full advantage of the advantages we have been granted in this season and
persevere and endure during this time. We must extract from this season all that
we can to get the fullness out of what has been afforded us. If we take advantage
of the doors opened to us now, we can gain a harvest that we can still enjoy even
after the doors are shut. This, however, requires that we work. Open doors are
times of busyness. There is much activity during seasons of open doors. It is not
the season of rest and relaxation. It is the season where we with great diligence
steward the doors that have been open to us that we might gain all that we can
for ourselves and the Kingdom of God.

> *Lord, I ask that You grant me the heart and mind to work. Let
> me take full advantage of these open doors provided for me. Allow
> me, Lord, to work while it is day and not lose the fullness of what
> You have given me access into. May the Courts of Heaven record
> that I am seeking with all my heart to be faithful and diligent in
> what has been afforded me. In Jesus's name, amen.*

OPEN DOORS GLORIFY THE LORD

I know your works. See, I have set before you an open door, and
no one can shut it; for you have a little strength, have kept My
word, and have not denied My name. —Revelation 3:8

Open doors are to be used to bring glory to the Lord. Even though open doors benefit us, and we gain from them, the ultimate purpose is to see the Lord glorified. Notice that open doors are connected to *not denying the name of the Lord.* Obviously, this can be a reference to not faltering under persecution and wavering in our faith of who the Lord is. However, it can also speak that we are jealous for the Lord to receive the glory due His name. Jesus's prayer in John 17:1 was that the Father would glorify the Son that the Son might glorify the Father. In other words, that the Lord would allow us a place of influence that would give us the ability to lift the name of Jesus and see His majesty manifest. This is one of the purposes of open doors. They are to position us to see the Lord magnified on another level. This is so that more people can come to the awareness of who the Lord really is and see Him in His trueness. There is much misconception about who God is. Open doors grant us the ability to unveil the nature of God on a greater level. The devil has always sought to misconstrue the true nature of God from the earliest time (Gen. 3:1–4). Satan, through the serpent, implied that God was not good and was lying to Adam and Eve. When Eve believed the lie, the fall occurred. Since this time, God has been looking for vessels that He can glorify that they might glorify and give a true representation of His name.

> *Lord, I ask that I might never deny Your name. I am asking that I*
> *would stay true to You and who You are. Would You open doors for*
> *me that I can more powerfully and effectively bring glory to Your*
> *name? I am asking for the Courts of Heaven to render a decision*
> *that would cause these doors to open. In Jesus's name, amen.*

LIES EXPOSED

Indeed I will make those of the synagogue of Satan, who say they are Jews and are not, but lie—indeed I will make them come and worship before your feet, and to know that I have loved you. —Revelation 3:9

As doors that are set open are manifest and moved through, lies that have been believed are exposed. Jesus says that those who have masqueraded as something they are not will be revealed. Many people suffer from lies that have been told about them. There is probably not a whole lot more injurious than people believing lies and reputations being damaged and destroyed. Jesus promises that as doors open there will be a pulling back of every veil of darkness. What has been believed will change as truth becomes known and lies are debunked. This happened in Joseph's life when the door opened, and he was set as the prime minister of Egypt under the rule of Pharaoh. As time progressed, the lies Joseph's brother had told about him being destroyed by a wild beast were uncovered (Gen. 37:31–35). Their jealousy and envious nature were revealed to all. It became known that Joseph had done nothing wrong but seek to fulfill the assignment and mission his father had sent him on. It took years, but there was a day when the doors were open and Joseph came out of the prison cell and lies began to be uncovered. Open the doors, Lord, that lies might be exposed!

> *I am asking You, Lord, that all lies that have shaped the attitude of people against me would now be exposed. As I stand before Your Courts, I petition You that doors would open, and the revelation of truth would come. Thank You, Lord, for exposing lies and restoring what was lost. In Jesus's name, amen.*

VINDICATED!

*Indeed I will make those of the synagogue of Satan, who say
they are Jews and are not, but lie—indeed I will make them
come and worship before your feet, and to know that I have
loved you.* —Revelation 3:9

The Lord promises that there will be vindication. Those who have persecuted
and defamed will be required to come and bow before you and to acknowledge
that you are the *loved* of God. They will have to admit that you were not rejected
by God, but on the other hand were actually one that He has chosen. Isaiah
says that those who looked on Jesus on the cross actually considered Him to
have been rejected by God (53:4). They esteemed Him to be stricken, smitten,
and afflicted by the Lord. However, three days later Jesus resurrected as a sign
for all generations that He was in fact chosen of the Lord. Resurrection is a
depiction that what we thought God thought about something was not true.
The Lord through resurrection manifested who He chooses and vindicates in
the process. Open doors many times are our resurrection. Through the favor of
opened doors the destiny that seemed to be lost is resurrected and restored. This
can produce vindication and a clear awareness that God has loved us. There is
nothing worse for our enemies than to see that God actually has chosen us. They
are forced to admit that what they believed and hoped about us is wrong and
vindication comes. They realize that if they fight against us, they fight against
the favor of God. Vindication and justification has now come.

> *Lord, as I approach Your Courts, may doors be set open that will
> cause vindication to come. I pray, Lord, that what they thought
> You thought about me was not true. Unveil Your love for me, O
> God, and cause vindication to come. In Jesus's name, amen.*

CONCERTED PRAYING

Again I say to you that if two of you agree on earth concerning anything that they ask, it will be done for them by My Father in heaven. For where two or three are gathered together in My name, I am there in the midst of them. —Matthew 18:19–20

The word *agree* is the Greek word *sumphōneō*. We get our word *symphony* from it. A symphony cannot occur unless there is a tuning of instruments together. So when we *agree* in prayer, we are coming under the same *burden* of prayer for a particular thing. I believe that we can only really *agree* under the unction and impetus of the Holy Spirit. He must create within each of us the same burden, passion, and desire in prayer for a given thing. When we pray from this place, the Bible promises that what we do on earth will move the Father in Heaven. Notice that Jesus promises to be a party to those who gather in this manner. In other words, wherever two or three gather in His name in agreement, Jesus is among us. We are not there with just natural people praying. Jesus comes to pray and agree with us and we with Him. We are told that He is our intercessor (Heb. 7:25). When the Scripture says He is in our midst, He is not there as a spectator; He participates with us. Through our coming in His name and agreement, we step into a supernatural realm with Him and see Heaven move the things of earth.

> *Lord, as I approach Your Courts, I thank You for the power of agreeing prayer. Would You cause an unction of the Holy Spirit to tune our hearts together that we might pray in Your name? Come, Lord, and be a part of this gathering as we seek Your passion. In Jesus's name, amen.*

CRYING IN AGREEMENT

And being let go, they went to their own companions and reported all that the chief priests and elders had said to them. So when they heard that, they raised their voice to God with one accord and said: "Lord, You are God, who made heaven and earth and the sea, and all that is in them."
—Acts 4:23–24

As Peter and John were threatened by the Jewish religious leaders because of the healing the lame man (Acts 3:6–8), they returned to their companions. The word *companion* is the Greek word *idios*. It means *one's own*. In other words, it is that which we are a part of. In the midst of these threats and attacks Peter and John had company they could retreat to. Do we? They ran to this company, and as a group began to beseech the God of Heaven. They began to cry out from their fears and insecurities, yet in faith in the midst of the threats of the Jewish religious leaders. They were in *one accord*. This means *unanimous*. It is the Greek word *homothymadon*. We all need a group we can run to in the pressures of life. We need those who will stand unanimously with us. They will not debate and argue over what should be. They will engage in prayer as we bombard Heaven with our plea. They will not question why something was done that precipitated the problem. They will instead set their face with us to request that God would answer us as sheep in the midst of wolves (Matt. 10:16). May we each have a company of people that we can run to and who will engage themselves with us in our times of trouble. Prayers from these people will cause answers from Heaven.

Lord, I ask that You might connect me to my own group. May I not be alone. May I have those I am a part of who know how to pray in agreement and see verdicts rendered out of Your Courts. Join me, Lord, to this kind of people I pray. In Jesus's name, amen.

RELEASING THE HAND OF GOD

Now, Lord, look on their threats, and grant to Your servants
that with all boldness they may speak Your word, by stretching
out Your hand to heal, and that signs and wonders may be done
through the name of Your holy Servant Jesus. —Acts 4:29–30

In the midst of threats and assaults from demons and demonized people we need the hand of God stretched forth. This means we need a manifestation of the supernatural seen in our behalf. This gives us boldness and causes our enemies to tremble. When they realize the God of Heaven is fighting for us, they will shrink from us in fear. Even our enemies do not want to be found to fight against God. They realize that they may prevail against us, but they cannot prevail against God. When the Jewish leaders were persecuting the early church, Gamaliel exhorted them to be careful not to war against the Lord (Acts 5:34–39). Gamaliel exhorted them that if what was occurring was from God, they could not overthrow it. We need desperately the hand of God stretched and manifest in our behalf. When the enemies see His hand, it may not change their attitude toward us, but it can diminish and even stop the attack, as it did in the days of the early church in this instance. We must have God arise and His enemies be scattered (Ps. 68:1). When God arises in behalf of us and His purposes through us, the enemy will scatter. They will see that God Himself has arisen to fight in our behalf.

> *I ask, Lord, that You might arise and let it be known that You are with us. Would You cause signs and wonders to be revealed that it might be known that we are Your people. Allow, I pray, the Courts of Heaven to decree into place Your persevering power concerning us. In Jesus's name, amen.*

SHAKING AND FILLING

And when they had prayed, the place where they were
assembled together was shaken; and they were all filled with
the Holy Spirit, and they spoke the word of God with boldness.
—Acts 4:31

As the church prayed in one accord, the power of God so came into their midst that the literal structure they were in was shaken. The shaking of God can cause things to be removed that are not of Him (Heb. 12:27). We are told that the shakings are to remove things but they also reveal the things that are unshakable and are to remain. No one enjoys the *shakings* of God. They make everything seem uncertain. Yet the shakings have a divine purpose. It is to manifest that which cannot be moved. This allows us to build with that and on that which is secure and steady. When the place was shaken, it was in a sense revealing those who were in this group as being unshakable. They could be trusted. There is nothing like building your life on those and with those who can be shaken and removed. This can bring devastation to families, churches, businesses, and other entities. God is His mercy will at times allow shakings to unveil those who can and will be shaken out. This will protect us against greater heartache in future times. Once the shakings are done, there is a *filling* of the Holy Spirit. Those who pass the test of the shakings always receive a new dimension of the fullness of the Holy Spirit and the boldness that accompanies this. May we endure and be filled to fullness and even overflowing!

> *Lord, as I stand in the holy place of Your Courts, I ask that I*
> *might be found worthy to endure all shakings and stay true,*
> *steadfast, and immovable. Would You also fill me with the power*
> *of Your Holy Spirit? Thank You that You are releasing judicial*
> *decrees for this to be so. In Jesus's name, amen.*

CONSTANT PRAYER

Peter was therefore kept in prison, but constant prayer was offered to God for him by the church. —Acts 12:5

Herod's intent was to kill Peter just like he had killed James with the sword. The devil always has an intent and a desire. Daniel 7:25 tells us that satan through his forces in the earth *intends* to do certain things. We as the people of God are God's wall of resistance. We are the ones commissioned and set by God to turn back the desire and intentions of the devil. We do this the same way the early church did. We must give ourselves to *constant prayer*. The word *constant* in the Greek is *ektenēs*. It means *without ceasing* and *fervent*. The prayer that the church was bringing to God in behalf of the deliverance of Peter didn't stop. It was being offered around the clock without ceasing. It was also fervent. In other words, they weren't just mouthing words. They were praying with passion from the depths of their heart. There was a cry of the Holy Spirit flowing in them and through them that was full of power. This kind of prayer from the church caused Peter to be saved from devilish intent. May we as the church recapture this fire of prayer that stops the hordes of hell's pleasure from being done. May we stand as a wall against demonic aggression and see it stopped in our day.

> *Lord, I thank You that there is being released from Your Courts a move of Your Spirit that will inspire the church to constant prayer. Thank You that You would use us to turn back the forces of darkness and see them negated. In Jesus's name, amen.*

SLEEPING PETER

And when Herod was about to bring him out, that night Peter was sleeping, bound with two chains between two soldiers; and the guards before the door were keeping the prison. —Acts 12:6

Peter is scheduled for execution the very next day. He is in a very uncomfortable place physically. He is between two guards with two chains attached to him. There are other guards keeping the prison secure. You would think that in the midst of the difficult and uncomfortable place he is in naturally, Peter would be worried, concerned, or even afraid. However, Peter is sleeping. He is at total rest in the midst of his situation. There would appear to be no apprehension at all. He is very much in the condition Paul described in Philippians 1:21. He declared that to *live was Christ and to die was gain.* In other words, if he continued in this life, it would be for the purpose of manifesting the Lord; however, if he died, then it would be great gain and reward for him. Therefore, there was no fear. This is where I'm sure Peter was—absolute confidence as he slept, on potentially his last night on earth. However, through the prayers of the saints, he was delivered by an angel. There is a place though where we can be at perfect peace. Where there is such a trust in God that regardless of the outcome, we believe Him. I'm sure this was a result of the deep faith Peter had developed, but also a result of the prayers of the church. Their prayers were creating an atmosphere around Peter that was heavenly in nature. In the middle of our greatest distress there is a peace that passes all understanding (Phil. 4:7).

Thank You, Lord, that regardless of where I am You are there. Even as Peter rested and had perfect peace, allow me Lord to be there was well. My confidence is in You. Would You render from Your Courts a decree of deliverance? However, if You choose something else, I trust You always. In Jesus's name, amen.

CHAINS FALLING AWAY

*Now behold, an angel of the Lord stood by him, and a light
shone in the prison; and he struck Peter on the side and raised
him up, saying, "Arise quickly!" And his chains
fell off his hands.* —Acts 12:7

As a result of the prayers of the church, an angel was dispatched to Peter in prison. This angel woke Peter up from his sleep and told him to, *"Arise, quickly!"* The moment that Peter moves in agreement with the angel's words, his chains fall off his hands. That which was holding him and constraining him was instantly and supernaturally removed. There may be that which seems to be restraining you. Perhaps you feel as if you are being held in a prison or some other form of incarceration. Maybe you wonder where the Lord is in all of this. The key to being freed is to move in agreement with the word of the Lord. Only when we take a step of faith in agreement with God's word does the supernatural activate. When the priest put their feet in the water, only then were the waters of the Jordan cut off (Josh. 3:13). Only when Moses stretched his rod over the Red Sea did the waters divide (Exod. 14:15–16). There is always an action needed from us connected to the word of the Lord. When we move in agreement with what God is saying, chains are removed, and we go free.

> *As I come before Your Courts, Lord, I ask that I might move in
> concert with You and Your word. As I do, Lord, allow the chains
> of bondage and imprisonment to please fall from me. Let me go
> free into all that You have made for me. In Jesus's name, amen.*

MINISTERING TO THE LORD

Now in the church that was at Antioch there were certain prophets and teachers: Barnabas, Simeon who was called Niger, Lucius of Cyrene, Manaen who had been brought up with Herod the tetrarch, and Saul. As they ministered to the Lord and fasted, the Holy Spirit said, "Now separate to Me Barnabas and Saul for the work to which I have called them." —Acts 13:1–2

There was a corporate gathering of prayer and worship to the Lord by the prophets and teachers at the church in Antioch. They obviously had set aside a time just to come before the Lord and love Him. It doesn't say there was some crisis to be handled or discussed. It seems to imply that they were just spending some dedicated time honoring and seeking to bless the heart of God. Psalm 103:1 says, *"Bless the Lord O my soul."* We are not told here to ask Him to bless us, but for us to *bless* Him. This is the heart to minister to the Lord. As they did this, the Lord spoke concerning Barnabas and Saul. They were to be apostolically sent out to the nations of the earth. They were to be commissioned for the work that God had called them to. They clearly knew what they were called to. However, in these moments of worship and ministry to God the timing of the Lord is discerned. They are now being launched forth into destiny and purpose. They are being separated to the Lord for this service. As we minister to the Lord, God can speak concerning our destiny, future, and timing. May we spend time separated to Him that we might be separated to His purpose for us.

Lord, I come before You and repent for all the times I haven't separated myself to You, in ministry to You. I ask that You help me to dedicate myself to these places and times. As I do, Lord, from Your Courts would You unlock purpose and timing to me? In Jesus's name, amen.

JUDGING IN THE SPIRIT

*For I indeed, as absent in body but present in spirit, have
already judged (as though I were present) him who has so done
this deed.* —1 Corinthians 5:3

When dealing with a serious issue of immorality in the Corinthian church, Paul said he had *already judged* it. The word *judged* is the Greek word *krinō*. It means "to decide, condemn, punish, sue at law, sentence." Paul makes an astonishing statement. He says that even though he isn't physically in Corinth, he has in the spirit realm *judged* the situation from his apostolic realm and authority. When he says *judge*, he doesn't mean he's just determined that something is right or wrong. He means he has legislated a judgment against this which is defiling the church and threatening the integrity of the work. He has released a spiritual force against the powers of darkness that are propagating this issue. Paul in the spirit world has taken legal action. We must know there is a place in the spirit world where we can render judgment against that which is opposing the purposes of God. We do not even have to be physically where this is occurring. If we have spiritual authority, which Paul had by virtue of his connection with the church, we can determine what the outcome of these things will be. We are not helpless or victims. Through the authority of the Lord, we can take the place granted us of God and *judge* that which would threaten purpose and destiny.

> *Lord, as I come before Your Courts, I thank You that I can judge
> what is within my spiritual realm. Give me wisdom to operate in
> these dimensions that I might set in place Your will and passion.
> I surrender before You and ask for Your name to be glorified. In
> Jesus's name, amen.*

THE POWER OF GATHERING

In the name of our Lord Jesus Christ, when you are gathered
together, along with my spirit, with the power of our Lord Jesus
Christ, deliver such a one to Satan for the destruction of the
flesh, that his spirit may be saved in the day of the Lord Jesus.
—1 Corinthians 5:4–5

Paul is urging the church at Corinth to gather together and set in place the apostolic judgment he has made in this situation. Remember that Paul had already *judged* this (1 Cor. 5:3). There has been legal transaction concerning this thing in the spirit world in the Courts of Heaven. Paul is exhorting the church to gather together to execute this judgment into place. Notice they are to be gathered as a corporate man, in agreement with the spirit of Paul and with the power of the Lord Jesus Christ. Apostles have the right to *judge.* However, it appears the church must execute or ratify that judgment into place for the effects of it to be seen. God sees His church as that which has the power. Through the activity of the apostle and the agreement of the church, that which was threatening this church and the individuals in it was judged and sentenced. The result was a cleansing and a breakthrough for this people because of the exercising of God's authority granted to us.

> *As we seek to be Your people, Lord, please help us to understand*
> *Your ways. May we walk in the apostolic authority You have*
> *granted us. May we learn how to render judgments into place*
> *from the Courts of Heaven that will allow Your will to be done.*
> *In Jesus's name, amen.*

SETTING BOUNDARIES

Deliver such a one to Satan for the destruction of the flesh, that
his spirit may be saved in the day of the Lord Jesus.
—1 Corinthians 5:5

Most of the church would know nothing of what this Scripture is declaring. However, Paul exhorted the church as a last resort to set in place his judgment that he has already rendered (1 Cor. 5:3). He urges this church to deal with the man who is having a sexual affair with his step-mother (not natural mother). This man is a part of the church. Paul tells them to *deliver this person to satan.* This is for the purpose of allowing the devouring process of satan to work against this man and bring him to repentance and back to the Lord. This says the church has a right to establish the boundaries in which satan can operate. So often we think the devil can do whatever he wants. This is not true. We should determine his boundaries with the authority that God has granted us. We must seek the Lord and know how to stand as those who occupy His judicial place in the earth. Perhaps we can render judgments, with the agreement of apostolic authority, and see the effects of satan broken and people returned to the Lord.

> *Thank You, Lord, for allowing us to learn how to operate in the judicial realms of setting boundaries. Would You help us to know how to determine what satan can and cannot do? Would You help us in seeing people turned again to You and freed from demonic holds? In Jesus's name, amen.*

THE YEARNING FATHER'S HEART

For out of much affliction and anguish of heart I wrote to you,
with many tears, not that you should be grieved, but that you
might know the love which I have so abundantly for you.
—2 Corinthians 2:4

It grieved Paul as a true father in the faith to have to correct the Corinthian church in what it was allowing. The absence of real "fathers" has caused the church to not really know what a father does. In this instance where the church was allowing things even the world would frown on, Paul had sternly corrected them (1 Cor. 5:1). He had announced to them how serious their tolerance was in this situation. We must know that our God is a holy God. Even in New Testament order, we are to walk in holiness before Him and not condone or allow outright sin to persist. God is loving and merciful, yet He must be honored in the fear of the Lord. As a father, Paul is pressing this church and people to repent and deal with this, which is awkward and uncomfortable. They cannot turn a blind eye to it. The father heart of Paul is pushing them to confront this situation and purify themselves as a people. This takes a courage and a love born out of the fear of the Lord. May this heart again be in the church.

> *Lord, would You allow us as Your church to recognize the true*
> *heart of a father. Even as Paul was afflicted and in anguish over*
> *this church's sin, would You help us to honor fathers who carry*
> *Your heart as our Heavenly Father? Raise up these fathers, I*
> *pray, to help bring Your people into maturity. Do this even from*
> *the Courts of Heaven, in Jesus's name, amen.*

FATHERS AND THE KINGDOM OF GOD

But if anyone has caused grief, he has not grieved me, but all of you to some extent—not to be too severe. —2 Corinthians 2:5

Paul sought to bring correction to the Corinthian church because of what they were allowing, but he didn't want them to be overcome with sorrow of having disappointed him. Paul understood that everyone desires the approval of a father. The sense of disappointing our father works greatly against us. It will fashion an idea about ourselves that is not good. The image we have of ourselves can be warped. Paul is seeking to straddle middle ground between holding them accountable but also approving them with his love. We desperately need this kind of fathering in the Body of Christ. We must petition the Courts of Heaven to again release into the church fathers who can bring us to maturity. Maturity in the church is not attainable without the influence and heart of fathers. We must have those who affirm but also know the need to confront us in our sin and shortcoming. This will produce a new kind of believer that can establish the rule of the Kingdom of God.

> *Lord, we petition the Courts of Heaven. We ask that there would be a producing of fathers who can bring us to maturity. Raise them up we pray, God, that we might become the kind of people necessary to Your purpose. In Jesus's name, amen.*

THE PAIN OF LOVE

For out of much affliction and anguish of heart I wrote to you,
with many tears, not that you should be grieved, but that you
might know the love which I have so abundantly for you.
— 2 Corinthians 2:4

Paul speaks of the anguish within his heart that he feels toward this people. He speaks of the tears and pain that he has concerning them and the choices they had made. He doesn't want to make them feel bad but his concern for them has overwhelmed him. This is not Paul being selfish and accusing them concerning his own feelings. This is Paul with a legitimate and deep care for these as the people of God. He is seeking to communicate his motives for writing them in given matters. When the scripture speaks of the tears that have been cried, I am sure this included the weeping associated with intercession. We must learn to take the pain caused by our love for others and turn it into prayer. Pain turned into prayer is very effective intercession. This cry is heard in heaven and has great weight and authority in the Court of Heaven. All prayer is substantial. Prayer born out of pain however usually carries the desperation that grasps the attention of God.

> *Lord, as I come before Your Courts, may it be recorded that I have a great love for these lives. I am grieved over the choices that have been made. I am appealing to Your Court for intervention in the lives of these that I care for deeply, and know You care for more. I ask, Lord, that their lives not be destroyed by wrong decisions. Please Lord, let every deceptive thing be removed from their eyes and may they choose Your ways and live. In Jesus's name, amen.*

FORGIVE AND RESTORE

This punishment which was inflicted by the majority is sufficient for such a man, so that, on the contrary, you ought rather to forgive and comfort him, lest perhaps such a one be swallowed up with too much sorrow. —2 Corinthians 2:6–7

As Paul dealt with the sin problem in Corinth, the church went from tolerating to not forgiving when repentance was secured. The pendulum had swung from one extreme to the other. Paul is now as a father exhorting them to forgive, comfort, and restore this one that is now broken and repentant. He warns that if they don't respond correctly to him now, he could be swallowed up with much sorrow. This actually would work against the process. It could *drive* him back to his sin. We are promised in the Word of God that the *"scepter of the wicked will not rest on the righteous"* (Ps. 125:3). If this were to happen then the righteous would be tempted to put forth their hand to iniquity. This means they would see no reason to live holy and undefiled. In other words, there would seem to be no reward for righteous living. Paul is urging the Corinthians to receive the one who has repented back into the group. They should love him, forgive him, and fully accept him back without scandal or shame. Otherwise he could be tempted to slip away and never return. We as the church led by fathers must know how to bring restoration to the broken. This should be one of the times when we shine the brightest in the earth. We should manifest to the world how to love without compromising the holiness of God. This can only occur when fathers are restored to their rightful function.

As we approach Your Courts, O God, we ask that fathers might be restored to Your church. We petition the Court that people who carry the DNA of You as the heavenly Father might be placed by You. Allow those who need restoration to be restored and set again. In Jesus's name, amen.

PUT TO THE TEST

*Therefore I urge you to reaffirm your love to him. For to this end
I also wrote, that I might put you to the test, whether you are
obedient in all things. —2 Corinthians 2:8–9*

Paul declared as the father of the Corinthian church that how they handled the fall and the restoration of this one had actually been a test. Could this be true today? Is this still a test being administered in the church by the Lord? Do we know how to strike the right balance between the love of God and the holiness of the Lord? This takes the very wisdom and leadership of the Holy Spirit. Otherwise we tend toward legalism or lawlessness. Both of these actually produce death. We must be able to recognize the heart of God in these matters. In John 16:8–10 we see Jesus telling us the Holy Spirit will now help us understand the righteous standards of the Lord, because Jesus Himself has now gone to the Father. From the revelation of the Holy Spirit, we are able to obey and secure the right verdict in these matters. We are able to uphold the holiness of God while seeing those who have fallen be restored and healed. This is the heart of God in these places.

> *Lord, as I approach Your Courts, I ask for the wisdom of God
> for the church and its leaders to pass this test. Lord, we ask from
> Your Courts that You would grant the right heart to discern how
> to uphold Your righteousness while bringing restoration to those
> who are broken. In Jesus's name, amen.*

HOLDING NO GRUDGES

Now whom you forgive anything, I also forgive. For if indeed I have forgiven anything, I have forgiven that one for your sakes in the presence of Christ. —2 Corinthians 2:10

The giving of forgiveness is essential to releasing someone into their destiny. Paul shows that as the Corinthian church had forgiven the man who had caused the trouble, Paul himself had forgiven him as well. Remember that Paul had judged him (1 Cor. 5:3). He had legally set a judgment against him. Therefore, Paul had to forgive him so that he could legally be free. Jesus said in John 20:23 that if those who are granted authority *remit* sins, they are *remitted*. If, however, they *retain* sins they are *retained*. This is speaking of the authority granted to deal with issues in the church. This authority is to never be operated with a personal vendetta. It is to be operated in as Paul and the Corinthian church did in this scenario. It was for the purpose of keeping defilement out of the church *and* seeing those who had backslidden return to the Lord (1 Cor. 5:6–8; 5:5). When Paul says he did this *"in the presence of Christ,"* he means that as he has stood before the Lord, he has set this forgiveness in place so this man can be freed. This is an apostolic legal operation in the Courts of Heaven.

> *Lord, we thank You that You are restoring to the church the apostolic power to function in Your Courts. We thank You that from this place before You order will come, grudges will be dismissed, and freedom will be established for all. In Jesus's name, amen.*

THE LIVES OF FATHERS

You are witnesses, and God also, how devoutly and justly and blamelessly we behaved ourselves among you who believe; as you know how we exhorted, and comforted, and charged every one of you, as a father does his own children.
—1 Thessalonians 2:10–11

Paul is claiming that the Thessalonians and God Himself have a good testimony of him and his apostolic team. The word *witness* is the Greek word *martys*. It means "a judicial witness and to go on record." This is important in functioning in the Courts of Heaven. We need the testimony of those in the earth to speak good of us. However, when God Himself speaks and testifies in our behalf, this grants us authority in His Courts. Hebrews 11:39 speaks of those *who have a good report*. This means they have status in Heaven. When God testifies of us, this gives us this place as well. Apostle Paul's devoutness, just life, and blameless living allowed God to testify of Him in this way. This is our challenge, to live in such a way that the testimony in the earth and the testimony in Heaven speaks of us as devoted, just, and blameless. This is my passion. We must repent for any place where this would not be true of us. We must ask that our lives depict these things, that earth and Heaven might give witness concerning us.

> *I ask, Lord, that my life might reflect these things. May I be devout, just, and blameless before You. May You be able to testify in my behalf that I might be granted status in Your Courts. I humble my heart before You and request this in Jesus's name, amen.*

DEVOTED TO THE LORD

*You are witnesses, and God also, how devoutly and justly and
blamelessly we behaved ourselves among you who believe.*
—1 Thessalonians 2:10

The word *devoutly* is the Greek word *hosiōs*. It has the idea of having *divine character*. When something is devout, it means it has been *devoted* to the Lord. If God is to testify of us and our devoutness, it will be because His divine character is in us and we are *behaving* like God because we are *devoted* to Him. When we were born-again, we received God's divine nature. This should create in us an ability and power to live devoted and devout lives. We are no longer mortal men and mere humans. We have been empowered to live beyond that which is human. Devotion also carries with it a sense of being restrained by a great love. Devotion is not something we do from a legalistic place. Devotion is a display of a love relationship with the Lord. The more we love Him, the more devoted we will be to Him. The Lord is committed to bringing us to this place of ultimate devotion and a display of His character in the earth. Even as He promised Peter, so He will do it for us (John 21:17–19). He will perfect in us a devotion to Him that will empower us to give ourselves completely. So be it, Lord Jesus.

> *Lord, as I come before You, I ask that I might live a devoted and
> devout life. Allow, Lord, Your character to be fashioned in me.
> Let this speak before You in Your Courts that You might testify
> in my behalf. In Jesus's name, amen.*

BEHAVING JUSTLY

You are witnesses, and God also, how devoutly and justly and
blamelessly we behaved ourselves among you who believe.
—1 Thessalonians 2:10

As we seek to have the Lord testify of us, we must also behave justly. Whereas being devoted is about having divine character, being *just* is about our interaction with others. Behaving justly is about treating others with respect, honor, and fairness. It is about not taking advantage of another but seeking their welfare as well as our own. If we expect justice to be rendered to us from the Courts of Heaven, we must have a history of treating others with justice. This will speak volumes in the Court. This can actually be presented in the Courts as evidence concerning us. However, if we have manipulated, controlled, or sought to dominate others, this can speak against us. We must repent and ask for the Lord to forgive us. We must break off this kind of perspective and seek to do good to others rather than to *use them*. This is actually the fulfilling of the *royal law* of love: to love our neighbor as ourselves (James 2:8). When we live this way, we are operating out of a kingly nature that is of the Lord Himself. This will allow the Lord and others to testify of us for good.

> *Lord, as I come before Your Courts, I ask that I might behave*
> *justly toward others. I ask, Lord, that I would be forgiven where*
> *I have ever taken advantage of someone else. I repent. I ask that*
> *Your blood would speak for me. I break off my sins and set my*
> *heart to do justly. In Jesus's name, amen.*

FINDING NO FAULT

You are witnesses, and God also, how devoutly and justly and
blamelessly we behaved ourselves among you who believe.
—1 Thessalonians 2:10

The other thing Paul mentions that allows God to testify and bear witness to us about is being *blameless*. It is the Greek word *amemptōs*. It means "to be fault-less." If you search it out to its root, it doesn't just mean to be *faultless*; it is connected to finding fault. We are to live lives that will not allow others to point a finger at us and to blame us. However we are also not to be *fault-finding people*. This is not easy to do. We can develop a critical spirit out of the wounds of our own heart. There can be something in us that wants to tear others down that we might feel better about ourselves. This is not the nature of God. The nature of the Lord is to love, affirm, and confirm. The key to changing any *fault-finding* tendency in us is to allow the Lord to confirm us in His love. When we are *loved* by God, we are empowered to therefore love. This is the nature of who God is as our heavenly Father (Matt. 5:43–48). As we are perfect as He is perfect, we love with His love through us.

> *As I approach Your Courts, Lord, I ask that I might be delivered*
> *from fault-finding. I ask that Your nature might be in me to*
> *empower me to love. May You be able to bear witness to me in*
> *Your own Courts. In Jesus's name, amen.*

A FATHER'S EXHORTATION

*As you know how we exhorted, and comforted, and charged
every one of you, as a father does his own children.*
—1 Thessalonians 2:11

As God testified of Paul, he could take his place as a father in the church. We need fathers who have the witness of God speaking for them. From this place Paul *exhorted*. This is the Greek word *parakaleō*. It means "to call near." One of the main functions of a father is to *heal rejection*. Rejection is a part of life. Not that it was meant to be, but in this fallen world we will experience it. The pain and even fear of rejection can fashion and mold us into something that God never intended. Through the love and acceptance of a father this can be healed. The pain and fear of rejection destroys lives, families, destinies, and futures. God's plan for dealing with this is *a father*. This is a person who is sent by God to manifest the heavenly Father's heart toward you. Through the affirmation and confirmation of one who carries the heavenly Father's heart, destiny can be reestablished. Lives, families, and futures that were lost through the fear and pain of rejection are recovered. We petition the Courts of Heaven for these fathers to be established in the House of God, His church.

> *As we approach Your Courts, O God, we ask that fathers be reestablished in Your church. May the fear and pain of rejection be healed in us through these fathers set by You. May Heaven testify of them that Your heart might manifest. In Jesus's name, amen.*

HEALING TRAUMA

As you know how we exhorted, and comforted, and charged
every one of you, as a father does his own children.
—1 Thessalonians 2:11

One of the things a father does that God has testified of is bring comfort. Comfort is not just soothing and convincing someone things will be OK. Comfort is the healing of trauma that could otherwise thwart destiny. We as people can go through traumatic events in our life. We can experience loss, pain, trouble, and grief. This can paralyze and neutralize our movement toward the destiny of God for our lives. Fathers are used by God to heal that trauma so that futures might be recovered. The word *comforted* in this Scripture is the Greek word *paramytheomai.* Part of this word means *tale* or *myth*. When someone is in pain, the idea that they have a future can seem untrue, even a myth or a *tall tale*. A father, however, will convince this one that God's purposes have not been destroyed. The father's influence will bring comfort until the one who is traumatized begins to believe again. That which seems impossible will again be believed. This is the power of a father to bring comfort to God's people. Restore, O Lord, fathers in the faith.

> *Lord, we petition Your Courts for fathers to be set in Your*
> *church. Bring those who can comfort and cause a faith to arise*
> *that otherwise might be lost. Heal our hearts to believe again*
> *through Your comfort. In Jesus's name, amen.*

THE EVIDENCE OF FATHERS

As you know how we exhorted, and comforted, and charged
every one of you, as a father does his own children.
—1 Thessalonians 2:11

Fathers that God testifies of are those who *charge* their children in the Lord. The word *charge* is the Greek word *martyreō*. It means "to be a witness." The job of fathers is not to make decisions for their children. It is to give them the needed information so they can make their own decisions. They grant *evidence* that allows their children to learn how to operate in a proper decision-making process. This is what judges do. They hear evidence, then based on that evidence, they render a decision. Good fathers allow their children to operate as *judges*. They grant them the honor to hear the information or evidence and then make decisions or choices. So many "fathers" never allow their children the privilege of developing decision-making abilities. They constantly tell them what to do rather than presenting them evidence and allowing them the opportunity to succeed or fail. As difficult as it might be, if fathers do not allow their children the right to choose and decide, they are not preparing them for life. Fathers are not doing their children a favor by never allowing them this privilege. Good fathers know how to *charge* their children and allow them the joy of choosing rightly or even the pain of choosing wrongly. Either way, their children learn and grow into mature people as a result.

> *As we approach Your Courts, Lord, we petition You that good*
> *fathers would be established in the family, church, and society.*
> *We pray that there would be fathers that would prepare the*
> *coming generations for their destiny and futures. Lord, set in*
> *place wise fathers who can help the coming generations mature*
> *in their decision-making process. In Jesus's name, amen.*

ALIGNMENT AND RANK

*And He Himself gave some to be apostles, some prophets, some
evangelists, and some pastors and teachers, for the equipping of
the saints for the work of ministry, for the edifying of the
body of Christ,* —Ephesians 4:11–12

The word *equipping* is the Greek word *katartismos*. One of its best definitions is "to align." Through the fivefold ministry gifts that God gave to the church, *alignment* is produced. The purpose of alignment is to grant empowerment and authority. Alignment is about *who* we are connected with in our spiritual journey. Alignment is a legal thing. How we are aligned speaks either for us or against us in the spirit realm. When we are *aligned* properly, we can be granted a new dimension in the spirit world that gives us a new place of authority to operate from. How we are recognized in the spirit world determines our rank and what we are allowed to do. This rank can be the result of faithfulness, battles fought and won, and other realms of responsible living. However, *alignment* is a deciding factor as well when it comes to rank and authority in the spirit world. When we are aligned, connected, and joined in the spirit dimension with those who God has approved, we can be brought into the same dimension they themselves move in. We get the benefit of the battles they have fought and won even though we might not have had those same victories. As far as the spirit world is concerned, we carry the same rank because of how we are aligned.

*As I come before Your Courts, O God, I ask that I might be
aligned properly. Allow my alignment with those You have
connected me with to produce new realms of authority in my life.
May the Courts of Heaven recognize this alignment. In Jesus's
name, amen.*

THE POWER OF ALIGNMENT

He who receives you receives Me, and he who receives Me
receives Him who sent Me. —Matthew 10:40

Jesus unveils the principle of alignment in this Scripture. He shows that who-ever receives us, receives Him, and whoever receives Him receives the One who sent Him. In other words, when they *received* us, they got not only the effect of what we carry but also the effect of who the Son and the Father are. The idea here is that the alignment we operate in produces new levels of authority and power that we could never operate in by ourselves. This is true in our connec-tion with other people. For instance, how I am connected in life and ministry can determine what I carry in the spirit world. When I go forward to minister or function, the breakthrough others receive is not just dependent on who I am and what I carry myself. They can glean from the anointing of others that I am joined to. This allows new realms of authority to be functioned in because of the principle of alignment. The connections I have and the relationships I honor can give me realms of empowerment for myself and others. The align-ments allow the anointing and authority the legal right to function through me.

> *As I approach Your Courts, Lord, I boldly ask that new places*
> *of power and authority flow through me because of alignment. I*
> *claim the legal right for the authority others have gained in You*
> *to flow through me because of my connection with them and my*
> *honor of who they are in You. In Jesus's name, amen.*

AUTHORITY AND ALIGNMENT

For I also am a man under authority, having soldiers under me. And I say to this one, "Go," and he goes; and to another, "Come," and he comes; and to my servant, "Do this," and he does it. —Matthew 8:9

The centurion soldier understood the principle of alignment. As He spoke to Jesus about healing his servant, he reiterated this idea. He espoused the concept that his authority as a commander was a result of his alignment with the Roman government. Therefore, when he issued a command, others in the natural moved and responded. This reality caused him to recognize the authority Jesus carried. He realized that Jesus was one under the authority of Heaven, just like he was under the authority of Rome. The result would be that as his words moved things and people in the natural, Jesus's words moved things in the spiritual. This would cause his servant to be made whole. This is in fact what happened. Jesus was amazed that this Roman soldier understood this principle that others were not seeing. They were missing this idea and therefore forfeiting their faith. Tapping the unseen world can be connected to the revelation of the principle of alignment.

As we approach Your Courts, Lord, we ask that we might understand the connection of alignment with Heaven and the power of God. Let us surrender ourselves in absolute submission to You that we might be properly aligned and carry the authority of Heaven. In Jesus's name, amen.

ALIGNMENT AND RELATIONSHIP

Many will say to Me in that day, "Lord, Lord, have we not prophesied in Your name, cast out demons in Your name, and done many wonders in Your name?" And then I will declare to them, "I never knew you; depart from Me, you who practice lawlessness!" —Matthew 7:22–23

Signs and wonders can be done from several different arenas. They can be the result of a gift having been received and operated in. The problem is that once God gives a gift, He doesn't take it away, even if the person becomes defiled (Rom. 11:29). This gift can give people a false sense of the approval of God. This can result in people ending up eternally lost because they lived immoral lives, yet the gift kept operating. If, however, the signs and wonders are being done out of a deep relationship with the Lord, then the power is flowing from alignment and not just the gift. This is actually a protective means of functioning in the power of God. When the demonstration is a result of alignment and intimacy with God, the Lord is consistently judging our hearts and keeping us pure. While the miraculous is occurring, the Holy Spirit is testing our hearts and causing us to walk in the fear of the Lord. We endeavor to keep ourselves in the love for God while we demonstrate His power and authority from alignment in the earth.

As I approach Your Courts, Lord, I ask that I might function in Your power not just from a gift, but out of loving alignment with You. Deliver me from any self-deception I ask. Let me walk holy and humbly before You in alignment that produces authority and power. In Jesus's name, amen.

ALIGNMENT AND SUCCESS

So Abram said to Lot, "Please let there be no strife between you and me, and between my herdsmen and your herdsmen; for we are brethren. Is not the whole land before you? Please separate from me. If you take the left, then I will go to the right; or, if you go to the right, then I will go to the left." —Genesis 13:8–9

The blessing of the Lord had come on Abraham and Lot so much that the land where they were feeding their flocks couldn't sustain them. Abraham suggested that Lot separate from him so they wouldn't have conflict with each other. We know this is what happened. The problem was that when Lot broke alignment with Abraham, the blessing lifted off his life. His life began a downward spiral that saw him end up losing everything. His family was lost, his wealth was destroyed, and his destiny was forfeited (Gen. 19:31–38). This all occurred after he *left* Abraham. Lot made a deadly miscalculation. He believed the success he was having was a result of his own wisdom. He didn't understand it was his connection with Abraham that was allowing it. His alignment with Abraham caused him to partake of the blessing that God had placed on him. When Lot didn't factor this in, he removed himself from alignment and suffered loss. We must be very careful. Where is the source of our success? Is the blessing on us or on the one we are joined to? This must be discerned or we can make miscalculations that can cost us dearly. We are to honor the alignments that God has set us in.

> *Lord, I ask that I might have wisdom and discernment to know Your ways. May I never be arrogant and consider that I have created success You have granted me through alignment. I ask that the Courts of Heaven might judge my heart and cause me to stay joined. In Jesus's name, amen.*

WHO ARE WE WITH?

But Peter, standing up with the eleven, raised his voice and said to them, "Men of Judea and all who dwell in Jerusalem, let this be known to you, and heed my words." —Acts 2:14

When Peter stood up on the Day of Pentecost after the outpouring of the Holy Spirit, he stood up *with* the eleven. The word *with* is a word that depicts alignment. When Peter began to preach, the release of the anointing was a result of the entire group and not just Peter as one man. The power that flowed from them corporately was what caused the multitude to respond and three thousand to be born again. This was the principle of alignment at work. Peter's was the voice that was used, but the authority that flowed was from the whole group. For ten days they had been together in the upper room. We are told that they were all in *one accord* (Acts 2:1). This is the Greek word *homothymadon*. It means *to be in fierce unity*. In other words, they were not tolerating each other. They were bound together in a passionate alignment with each other. Therefore, they spoke as *one* as the word of the Lord was proclaimed. When Peter opened his mouth, the very power of the Lord flowing through all of them moved in and through Peter. A manifestation of God caused the church to be born with great power.

> *As we approach Your Courts, Lord, we ask that the power of alignment would make us as one. We ask that we might be in fierce unity, full of the power of God. May we stand, not tolerating each other, but standing with each other in alignment with You. In Jesus's name, amen.*

PARTNERS TOGETHER

And when they had done this, they caught a great number
of fish, and their net was breaking. So they signaled to their
partners in the other boat to come and help them. And they
came and filled both the boats, so that they began to sink.
—Luke 5:6–7

As Peter launched out into the deep at the word of the Lord and let down his nets, he secured a great catch of fish. The catch was so much that they signaled to their *partners* for help. They were partners because they were *aligned*. The result of this alignment was that James and John got the *same* blessing and results that Peter received. Jesus was in Peter's boat, not James and John's. Peter had heard the word of the Lord to launch out into the deep, not James and John. However, because they were partners and aligned, they received the same blessing and enrichment that Peter got. This is the power of alignment. When we are aligned with the one in whom Jesus is *in their boat,* we can get the same thing they get. This is why we should practice alignment. It positions us to receive from the Lord in the same way that those we are aligned with do. Both *boats* were filled. We must know how to *partner* with the ones God has called us to in the spirit realm. When we do, we experience supernatural results that come through the principle of alignment.

As I stand in Your Courts, Lord, I ask that You allow me to be
rightly aligned. I ask that I might partner with the ones You have
ordained me to partner with. Let the power of alignment work
in and through me, I pray in Jesus's name, amen.

THE YIELDING EARTH

For the earth yields crops by itself: first the blade, then the head, after that the full grain in the head. But when the grain ripens, immediately he puts in the sickle, because the harvest has come.
—Mark 4:28–29

Usually when we talk about a harvest, the Bible seems to emphasize the *seed*. However, in this parable Jesus places an emphasis on the *earth or ground* yielding the crops. This is because as powerful as a seed is to produce a harvest, it cannot happen without being *connected and aligned* with the ground. The seed has to be joined to the ground to bring forth a harvest. In other words, we can only get the power that is in the ground by connecting to it with a seed. When we take our money, which is a seed (2 Cor.9:6–7) and sow it into the Kingdom of God and its approved ministries, we are connecting to good ground. Through our seed we are aligning with these ministries and making a connection. This connection allows us to draw from what is in this *ground* to see a harvest produced. Our seed in the right ground creates an alignment that allows a harvest of blessing, life, prosperity, and enrichment to come into our lives, families, ministries, and businesses. May we practice the power of alignment and receive the yielding power of the earth!

> *As I come before Your Courts, Lord, I ask that my seed might connect me to the right ground. I thank You that what is in this earth will cause a harvest to flow into my life through the principle of alignment. In Jesus's name, amen.*

ALIGNMENT CREATED THROUGH FAITH AND HONOR

And Elijah said to her, "Do not fear; go and do as you have said, but make me a small cake from it first, and bring it to me; and afterward make some for yourself and your son. For thus says the Lord God of Israel: 'The bin of flour shall not be used up, nor shall the jar of oil run dry, until the day the Lord sends rain on the earth.'" —1 Kings 17:13–14

When the widow of Zarephath by faith honored Elijah with the last that she had, a miracle occurred at the word of the Lord. She and her family were sustained during the famine because of the principle of alignment. Her sacrificial offering into this prophet's life created an alignment with him and the anointing he carried. The result was supernatural life and sustenance for the duration of the famine. We must realize that the seed that we sow creates alignment in the spirit world. Whether it is in churches, ministries, or organizations, our money makes connections in the realm of the spirit. This allows us the right to legally draw from this that we are connected to. We therefore should be very strategic in *where* we put our money. Notice that the prophet declares that *afterward* she would make a cake for her and her son. She had already told the prophet that she only had enough for one. They would eat it and die. However, when alignment was created, this granted the woman and her house an *afterward* or a *future*. This can be the power of alignment when stepped into though faith and honor. Our seed can create a connection in the spirit that allow this drawing rights.

Thank You, Lord, for the power of alignment. Thank You that as a result of my financial sowing, even in hard places, an alignment

---

is created. From this alignment I exercise my legal rights and ask that from the Courts of Heaven breakthrough would now come to me and my family. In Jesus's name, amen.

ALIGNMENT AND IMPARTATION

Now Joshua the son of Nun was full of the spirit of wisdom,
for Moses had laid his hands on him; so the children of Israel
heeded him, and did as the Lord had commanded Moses.
—Deuteronomy 34:9

Moses imparted wisdom that Joshua led Israel with. This impartation was a result of the alignment that Joshua had with Moses. Joshua had served Moses (Exod. 24:13). Joshua's connection and alignment with Moses had come through his ministry and service to him. Real impartation usually comes through an investment we have made of honor into another's life. Joshua had honored Moses. This created a joining that in the spirit realm allowed impartation. Many times we desire impartation but don't have a connection that will allow it to occur. Have we *invested* out of a spirit of honor? Have we sown seed? Have we served? Is there a connection we can claim in the Courts of Heaven that would allow impartation to occur? If there is, we can stand in the Courts and ask that what someone else carried might be imparted and invested into us. Can we make a case before the Courts that we have a right to receive impartation that would empower our lives? May we walk in such a way that through honor, we have a right in the spirit world to make a claim on what God has entrusted to someone else. When we do, the Courts of Heaven will allow an impartation that will empower us for the future ordained by God.

> *Lord, I ask for impartation through the principle of alignment. I*
> *thank You that I am rightly connected. I thank You that because*
> *of this alignment I petition Your Courts to allow impartation*
> *into my life. Let my honor for this one speak before You and cause*
> *empowerment to come. In Jesus's name, amen.*

HONOR-PRODUCING ALIGNMENT

For this Melchizedek, king of Salem, priest of the Most High God,
who met Abraham returning from the slaughter of the kings and
blessed him, to whom also Abraham gave a tenth part of all, first
being translated "king of righteousness," and then also king of
Salem, meaning "king of peace." —Hebrews 7:1–2

Abraham in honor gave a tithe to Melchizedek. This created an alignment with him and his priesthood and kingship. The result was that Melchizedek could now impart a blessing. The connection was created through the tithe. When we bring our tithe, we are connecting to the Melchizedek priesthood that Jesus is now High Priest of. We have a right based on our tithe to call for a blessing from this New Testament priestly order. Jesus is our High Priest after the order of Melchizedek (Heb. 5:6). My tithe in honor of this priesthood creates a connection that allows the impartation of a blessing. We can stand in the Courts of Heaven and petition the Courts. On the basis of our tithe we can request for a blessing to be imparted to us. Abraham was the one who had the promises (Heb. 7:6). When Melchizedek blessed Abraham, he was empowering him to see the promises he carried be fulfilled. Many times the promises we carry seem to frustrate us rather than us seeing them fulfilled. We could need the blessing that comes from alignment. Let us approach the Courts of Heaven and petition them for blessings from the Melchizedek order of Heaven. We have a right based on our tithe and the alignment it creates through honor.

> *On the basis of my tithe, I declare that I honor Jesus as my High Priest after the order of Melchizedek. I request the Courts that there would be a blessing come on the promises I carry. May they be fulfilled because of my alignment with this priesthood. In Jesus's name, amen.*

TWO ALIGNMENTS

And so it was, when they had crossed over, that Elijah said to
Elisha, "Ask! What may I do for you, before I am taken away
from you?" Elisha said, "Please let a double portion of your
spirit be upon me." So he said, "You have asked a hard thing.
Nevertheless, if you see me when I am taken from you, it shall be
so for you; but if not, it shall not be so." —2 Kings 2:9–10

Elijah had served Elisha. The result was that he had a claim on the mantle that Elijah carried. So often we want things we don't have a legal claim to. We haven't met the stipulations or requirements in the spirit realm to legitimately make a claim. Elisha had faithfully served Elijah. Therefore, when the day of impartation was upon him, he made his bold request. Elijah assured him that if he saw him go, he would have it. Elisha was already rightly positioned to see this happen. Through a commitment to God, he and Elijah had made sure he was where he needed to be. Elisha's alignment was twofold, as ours must be. He had declared to Elijah, *"As the Lord lives, and as your soul lives, I will not leave you!"* (2 Kings 2:4). When we are first aligned with the Lord and then with those who represent the Lord, we can expect impartation for our calling and future. Elisha's faithfulness to his two alignments rightly positioned him to *see* when Elijah left. The result was a reception of the mantle he had served. May our alignments with God and those who represent God, produce this as well.

As we contend before Your Courts for the mantles of the Lord for
our lives, we ask that we might be true to these two alignments.
May we serve You, Lord, with all our hearts. Also, may we honor
those You have set in our lives. We ask, therefore, that we might
receive the mantle of the Lord over our lives. Even the double
portion and measure. In Jesus's name, amen.

LAYING ON OF HANDS
AND IMPARTATION

Therefore I remind you to stir up the gift of God which is in you
through the laying on of my hands. —2 Timothy 1:6

Paul told Timothy as a son in the faith to him to be faithful with the gifts he had. He had these gifts because Paul had imparted them through the laying of his hands. It was no accident that this impartation came at the expense of Timothy being a son and in relationship with Paul. This allowed the hands of Paul to bless Timothy with a gift or gifts. Many times we desire hands to be laid on us so we can receive a gift. I'm not debating that this can and does happen. I would say, however, that deep impartation of gifts through the act of laying on of hands comes as a result of intimate relationships. When there is a joining of hearts and spirits, the laying on of hands is simply a vehicle that allows the transmission of a gift into another's life. We are imparting through the hands what we carry in our spirit to one that is joined to us. It is not a cheap thing, but something that is actually quite costly. From a heart-to-heart connection a transaction in the spirit is commenced. The result is an empowering through the principle of alignment. This allows for a generational enlargement of the Kingdom of God as gifts pass from fathers to sons/daughters.

> *I ask, Lord, that as a result of the legality of alignment, there*
> *would be an impartation into my life of gifts. I ask that from*
> *Your Courts this one be allowed, that Your Kingdom might*
> *advance from generation to generation. In Jesus's name, amen.*

ALIGNMENT AND PROVEN CHARACTER

Do not lay hands on anyone hastily, nor share in other people's sins; keep yourself pure. —1 Timothy 5:22

Timothy is being exhorted to *not* lay hands on someone quickly. This is Paul urging him to not place his *endorsement* on someone prematurely. When someone aligns with us and we publicly display this, we are endorsing them. If they don't have maturity or have ungodly traits in their life, it is not just a reflection on them, but also on the one they are aligned with. This is why Paul is imploring Timothy to *not share in other people's sin.* Paul was not saying that Timothy was sinning. He was saying that if he endorsed someone and publicly declared his alignment with them, if they sinned, Timothy would then be drawn into the scandal. Timothy is being encouraged to make sure of the character of whoever he publicly endorses, commissions, and aligns. This means that with real alignment there is accountability. When I am aligned with someone, I am accountable to them. They have a right and privilege to require of me explanations concerning my conduct and life. My alignment should propel me to new levels of holiness and godliness, knowing that it's not just my reputation but the reputation of the one I am aligned with and who has sent me.

As I align, I bring myself into accountability before You and Your Courts; Lord, I ask that I never bring reproach on You of those I am aligned with. Cleanse me, O God, that I would never be a source of scandal or treachery. In Jesus's name, amen.

ALIGNMENT AND REPRESENTATION

*So Jesus said to them again, "Peace to you! As the Father has
sent Me, I also send you."* —John 20:21

Sending is an act of alignment. When someone is *sent,* it doesn't just mean they are going somewhere. It means they are now authorized to represent. Jesus is telling His apostles that just like He came to represent the Father, they are now being sent to represent Him. This is one of the main purposes of alignment. When we are aligned and sent, we are being endorsed to represent not just ourselves, not just the Lord, but also those who *sent* us. We are representations of who they are. This is what Jesus said He did as being sent as God's Son. He declared that whoever had seen Him had seen the Father (John 14:9). Jesus came into the world as the sent Son. His main objective was to manifest and represent the Father who had sent Him. When we are *sent* as those aligned with God, but also by those who represent God in our lives (those we are aligned with and under the authority of), we are to manifest their heart and their integrity in a matter. Paul spoke of this concerning Titus, his spiritual son, when he declared they walked in the same spirit (2 Cor. 12:18). One of the greatest honors is to be allowed to represent another. They are trusting us with their reputations.

*As we come before You, Lord, may we represent You and Your
heart. May we also walk in such integrity that we might represent
the others we are aligned with and sent from as well. May it be
recorded in Your Courts that we are faithful in this and true to
You and those we serve. In Jesus's name, amen.*

MENDING THE NETS

Going on from there, He saw two other brothers, James the son
of Zebedee, and John his brother, in the boat with Zebedee
their father, mending their nets. —Matthew 4:21

As Jesus called these to be his first disciples, they were mending their nets. In the natural these were fishermen. Jesus promised to make them fishers of men (Matt. 4:19). The word *mending* is *katartizō*. It means *to repair*. Again it is the word that would most clearly relate to *alignment*. This is what they were doing when they were *mending* the nets. They were tying together the broken strands. This would allow the fish to be caught and not swim away through the holes created by the broken and torn places. Jesus calling them as they were involved in this process was a prophetic statement. They would be used by Him to *mend* the nets of the church that would be able to contain the catch of men. This would happen through the principle of alignment. When we are aligned properly, there is a *net* that is created that will allow the catch to be kept. Otherwise, we can have the best evangelistic efforts and still not see a *catch* occur. This can be because there are holes in the net. We must allow *alignment* to set us together. This will ensure that the catch of men will happen, and the Kingdom of God will advance. Are we aligned? May we each find our place in the *net* as we are strategically joined with one another.

> *Lord, as we approach Your Courts, allow me to be aligned in*
> *Your Body as it pleases You. May I be connected and joined in*
> *such a way that I become a part of Your net to contain the catch*
> *of fish for Your Kingdom. In Jesus's name, amen.*

CONNECTED AND RESTORED

Brethren, if a man is overtaken in any trespass, you who are spiritual restore such a one in a spirit of gentleness, considering yourself lest you also be tempted. —Galatians 6:1

The word *restore* is the Greek word *katartizō*. This again is the word concerning *alignment*. Notice that *alignment* is important to seeing one who has been overtaken in a fault or a sin healed and renewed. This means that when we are a part of bringing restoration to people, it is seeing them realigned with God and His church. The reestablishing of their connection with God and His people is critical to their being healed and made new. This *alignment* is designed to empower them and remind them of who they really are. We are told that when someone is overtaken in a fault, it is because they have forgotten who they really are (2 Pet. 1:9). The alignment with the Lord and with His people will bring the healing and awareness that is necessary to help them become free. They will remember and find again the joy of their salvation because of the connection with the Lord and with His people. Alignment and the acceptance that goes with it has the power to free a broken heart and bring it back into a union with the Lord.

> *Lord, we ask that through the power of alignment that those who are overtaken will be freed. Even in my own heart, any place I am in bondage, would You from Your Courts render a decision that would allow my connection to You to be reestablished? Lord, forgive me and heal me that I might be realigned. In Jesus's name, amen.*

WALKING AS SPIRITUAL

Brethren, if a man is overtaken in any trespass, you who are spiritual restore such a one in a spirit of gentleness, considering yourself lest you also be tempted. —Galatians 6:1

Notice that it is those who are *spiritual* who can be used to bring people who need help back into alignment with God and His people. This is in contrast to those who would be *carnal*. When someone is spiritual, it speaks of the perspective with which they see life. They are aware of the true nature of things. They do not react to situations from a carnal perspective. They understand that there is a spiritual, unseen realm that is influencing and affecting things. They are willing to look deeper and help people discover *why* this is a struggle in their life. As spiritual people they are able to help these deal with past wounds and trauma that may have allowed certain ideas to be in their life that led them into these bondages. This can result in even demonic control and influence that becomes a part of their struggle. These who are spiritual have the patience and ability to help these who are overtaken to really find freedom. Those who desire to be loosed from what is dominating them can be liberated.

> *Lord, thank You that You have those who are spiritual that can help bring us to freedom. Would You allow every legal thing the devil might be using to hold me in bondage to be revoked. Allow spiritual discernment to come that I might be freed. In Jesus's name, amen.*

THE SPIRIT OF GENTLENESS

Brethren, if a man is overtaken in any trespass, you who are spiritual restore such a one in a spirit of gentleness, considering yourself lest you also be tempted. —Galatians 6:1

The power of being restored and aligned comes out of the ministry from gentleness. This word *gentleness* is the Greek word praotēs. It means *humility* and *meekness*. The idea being communicated here is that when we are dealing with one who is overtaken, we are not judgmental of them. We do not approach them with a self-righteous mentality. We recognize our own weakness and therefore minister to them out of a spirit of gentleness and humility. Paul warned us about thinking too highly of ourselves and thinking we could never fall. We are told that as those who stand, we should take heed lest we fall (1 Cor.10:12). This births within us a right perspective when seeking to bring another back into alignment with God and His people. We become ministers of His grace, imparting to those who are in need that which can set them free. We are told that ministering from this spirit is a safeguard for us. Otherwise the devil finds a legal right from our arrogance to tempt us into the same sin we are seeking to free others from. Being judgmental actually grants satan a legal right to lure us into sin and compromise (Rom. 2:21–22). May the Spirit of the Lord Himself be in us as we seek to help others.

> Lord, as we stand before Your Courts, we ask for the spirit of gentleness and humility to be in us. May all arrogance and criticalness be removed from me. Set me free that I might set others free and not be consumed myself. In Jesus's name, amen.

HEALING HISTORY

By faith we understand that the worlds were framed by the word of God, so that the things which are seen were not made of things which are visible. —Hebrews 11:3

The word *framed* is also katartizō, which again means *alignment*. The word *worlds* is the Greek word *aiōn*. It means *an age* or *period of time*. So the Lord is declaring that through the word of God, the ages are aligned. In other words, history is healed that it will not be used to pollute and defile the future. The devil uses things in the past as a legal right to defile the present and the future. When we repent in behalf of what occurred in the past, we grant Jesus, through His blood, the right to revoke the claims of the devil. The claims satan is making to pervert present-day issues are annulled. Through our repentance in behalf of the past we activate the blood of Jesus (Dan. 9:16–17). This allows a realigning of the ages. The invisible forces being empowered through issues in the past that would work against our future are silenced. Instead the word of God will fashion and form the future that God has for us. The invisible realm is set in order through God's word. The result will be a future aligned with the healed history that allows God's purposes to be done. Our future is created through the word of God spoken from His lips and ours. The ages are aligned, and history is healed.

> *Lord, as I come before Your Courts, I ask that any rights satan is claiming to defile our future from our past would be revoked. I ask that history would be healed. Thank You that Your blood is speaking for us as we repent. In Jesus's name, amen.*

ALIGNED TO BEAR FRUIT

*For if the firstfruit is holy, the lump is also holy; and if the root
is holy, so are the branches. And if some of the branches were
broken off, and you, being a wild olive tree, were grafted in
among them, and with them became a partaker of the root
and fatness of the olive tree.* —Romans 11:16–17

The grafting in of branches to a vine is a picture of alignment. We as Gentiles are grafted into the Jewish vine. As a result of them rejecting Jesus, God graciously grafted us in. The reason for grafting a branch into a vine or tree is to create a new kind of grape or olive. The tree or vine that was grafted into supplies the life and power that allows the grafted-in branch to live. However, the branch doesn't lose its identity because it is grafted in. In fact, it maintains its integrity that it might produce a new kind of fruit and harvest. It is significant that we were *wild*. God is not looking for a religious expression or that which is tame and domesticated. He is looking for that which is full of life and even undefiled with religion. This does not mean we don't have the new nature of Jesus in us. We do. We are born again. We just have an aspect of who He is that a religious people can never manifest. May we not allow the religious to tame us and remove our wildness. It is that which God loves.

*Lord, thank You that You love wildness that is not defiled by
a religious spirit. May You grant us wisdom to discern between
Your divine nature and that which is the rebellion of man. We
want to walk before Your Courts in such a way that we bring joy
to Your heart. In Jesus's name, amen.*

REARRANGING TERRAIN

Every valley shall be exalted and every mountain and hill brought low; the crooked places shall be made straight and the rough places smooth; the glory of the Lord shall be revealed, and all flesh shall see it together; for the mouth of the Lord has spoken. —Isaiah 40:4–5

As God brings mountains down, exalts valleys, makes rough places smooth and crooked places straight, alignment occurs. This is the process of aligning the nations for the purposes of the Kingdom. The result will be the manifestation of the glory of God on a level not seen until now. All flesh together shall see His glory. Mountains being brought low can be those who are in authority yet use their place to hinder God's purposes. They will be lowered. Valleys can be those disregarded that are esteemed by God. They will be lifted. Crooked places can be that which is perverted and twisted giving a wrong idea of who God is. They will be straightened. Rough places is the idea of peaks being joined. False alignment will be dismantled. God will cause an alignment of His people and the nations to be established. The result will be a vehicle to propagate the glory of God into nations. The Lord in a jealousy for His glory will order and do this thing. The nations will be touched, and those who have been cut off from the glory will see it and encounter it. This will result in a worldwide harvest. God is arising in His passion to do this thing.

> *As we approach Your Courts, Lord, we stand in agreement with Your global alignment. May Your passion be seen. May all that has hindered the glory of God from being encountered now be removed. Let the manifestation of You be known in the earth. In Jesus's name, amen.*

APOSTOLIC AGENDA

And God has appointed these in the church: first apostles,
second prophets, third teachers, after that miracles, then gifts of
healings, helps, administrations, varieties of tongues.
—1 Corinthians 12:28

Apostles are set first in the church. This is their place and rank. The word *first* is the Greek word *prōton*. It means "first in time, place, order, or importance." This is why Jesus spent three and a half years producing apostles. They had to be set first so the church that would be produced could reflect His order and purpose. As a result of who they are by rank in the spirit world, they carry authority in the Courts of Heaven for the sphere they are called to. When we align with these apostles, which is the order of God (Eph. 4:11–12), we can become a part of the apostolic agenda of God. This agenda is to shift nations, territories, and regions into a Kingdom expression. Our alignment with apostles gives us a sphere of authority in prayer, activity, and function that we might not otherwise have. In regard to the Courts of Heaven, we must recognize our *jurisdiction* or *measurement of rule* (2 Cor. 10:15–16). When we function in our measure or jurisdiction, we get the privilege of helping fulfill His passion and see His enemies be placed under His footstool (Heb. 10:13). There is no higher call or placement of the Lord. May the apostolic agenda of God be fulfilled and satisfied.

> *As I come before Your Courts, I ask that I might be joined and*
> *aligned apostolically. I desire that my prayers and other spiritual*
> *activities might have impact beyond my own life and interest.*
> *May they affect nations and other regions for Your Kingdom*
> *desire. In Jesus's name, amen.*

APOSTLES AS GENERALS

*For the weapons of our warfare are not carnal but mighty in
God for pulling down strongholds.* —2 Corinthians 10:4

The word *warfare* in the Greek is the word *strateia*. This word means *apostolic
career*. It is also where *strategy* comes from. It is the idea of a *general* developing
strategy for war and then overseeing those plans and strategies being carried
out. This is what apostles do. Through divine wisdom connected to their call as
apostles they have understanding of how to route the enemy. We see this in the
days of Joshua; he had strategy to know how to take each city of Canaan. There
were different strategies for each city they faced. They took the entire land. At
Jericho they marched around the city seven days and then shouted. The walls
came down and they took the city (Josh. 6:1–5). Ai, another city, was taken
by feigning defeat with an ambush set (Josh. 7:4–8). In the next battle God
rained hailstones down on the adversaries, and Joshua spoke to the sun, and it
stood still for a day so victory could be completely secured (Josh 6). All of this
was different strategies for different cities. There must be apostolic strategies
from apostolic generals to see cities and have them become an expression of the
Kingdom of God. That which rules and influences cities will change as apostles
as generals take their place. We must pray for these to arise.

> *Lord, as we approach Your Courts, we ask that all that has
> hindered the arising and setting of apostles as generals would
> be revoked. Allow those who are called and assigned by You to
> take their place so that cities and others realms might become
> expressions of Your Kingdom. In Jesus's name, amen.*

APOSTOLIC FATHERS

*For though you might have ten thousand instructors in Christ,
yet you do not have many fathers; for in Christ Jesus I have
begotten you through the gospel.* —1 Corinthians 4:15

Apostles are fathers. This is the statement of the Apostle Paul. Even though there might be many, many teachers, by comparison there are not many apostolic fathers. This is true today. Many would claim to be *apostles.* However, as it was in the days of Paul, there is confusion concerning the different ministry functions. The Corinthian church was clearly a highly gifted group of people. The gifts of the Holy Spirit operated in them (1 Cor. 12). The church seemed to be enjoying the good life of serving Jesus and reigning in life (1 Cor. 4:8). Paul speaks of them as reigning as kings. He actually says this is a good thing. However, in the midst of this it appears they were allowing other ministry gifts to have an influence over them that Paul himself was claiming as their father. It is a good thing to drink deeply from the gifting God places in His body. However, we must know who our father is. The honor of apostolic fatherhood is essential to maturity and longevity. Yes, we should drink of the anointing of those set by God in His church. We must, however, recognize who our apostolic father is. This will empower us for function in the spirit world and stabilize us during good times and bad ones. It is essential to identity and purpose as we recognize our apostles and honor them as being sent from God into our lives.

As I approach Your Courts, Lord, I ask for the ability to recognize my apostolic joining. Help me honor those who have sacrificially laid their lives down for my progress. May I honor this. May this be recorded in Your Courts in testimony concerning me. In Jesus's name, amen.

FAKE APOSTLES

I know your works, your labor, your patience, and that you
cannot bear those who are evil. And you have tested those who
say they are apostles and are not, and have found them liars.
—Revelation 2:2

If we are to recognize true apostles, we must also be aware there are those who will masquerade as apostles! They do this to manipulate and try to gain from the Body of Christ acknowledgement, places of authority, and money. We need the spirit of discernment to be able to recognize those who desire to use and abuse us. The Bible says there are those who will exploit and seek to make gain from you by these claims (2 Pet. 2:3) This can produce the introduction of heresies and untruths into the Body of Christ. These will be used by the devil to lead people astray and do damage to the cause of the Lord. It is imperative that we have the discerning of the Lord to recognize who is really an apostle and who is not. There are many defining points of real apostles. One of the most prevalent is the sacrifice they have made. Any real apostle will have suffered on some level. This is at least partially because the devil hates the apostolic. He understands that it is this gifting of grace that has the power and authority to break his rule over regions. This results in demonic attacks against the apostolic. This doesn't mean apostles don't live blessed lives. However, if you gaze deep enough, you will find those who have stayed true through testing and trials because of their apostolic mandate.

> *Lord, help me to discern the real apostles. Let this be that I might*
> *align properly and gain new realms of authority before Your*
> *Courts. Help me value the sacrifice that real apostles have made*
> *for the mandate on their life. In Jesus's name, amen.*

APOSTLES AND AUTHORITY

And when He had called His twelve disciples to Him, He gave them power over unclean spirits, to cast them out, and to heal all kinds of sickness and all kinds of disease. Now the names of the twelve apostles are these: first, Simon, who is called Peter, and Andrew his brother; James the son of Zebedee, and John his brother; Philip and Bartholomew; Thomas and Matthew the tax collector; James the son of Alphaeus, and Lebbaeus, whose surname was Thaddaeus; Simon the Cananite, and Judas Iscariot, who also betrayed Him. —Matthew 10:1–4

Notice that Jesus called His disciples and gave them power and authority. The very next verse then declares them to be apostles. The main thing that determines if someone is an apostle is the authority they carry in the spirit world. The transition from being a disciple to having a rank in the spirit world that is apostolic comes when Jesus invests *authority* in us. The word *power* in this verse is the Greek word *exousia*. It means "delegated influence, authority, jurisdiction." Apostles are not necessarily apostles to everyone; they have a jurisdiction. Peter was an apostle to the Jews, while Paul was an apostle to the Gentiles (Gal. 2:8). This was their primary jurisdiction as apostles. When they functioned in these realms, the authority they carried brought significant breakthroughs. Real apostles are mindful of where their jurisdiction begins and ends. They know that functioning within these realms will produce greater results and create a safeguard over them, their families, and those joined to them. Boundaries are important in the spirit world. Apostles are aware of these and walk in the fear of the Lord to stay in them.

As I come into Your Courts, Lord, help me to recognize apostolic authority. Help me to perceive boundaries in the spirit world and stay in them. As I do, allow the Courts of Heaven to recognize my function before You, I pray. In Jesus's name, amen.

APOSTOLIC BUILDER

Am I not an apostle? Am I not free? Have I not seen Jesus
Christ our Lord? Are you not my work in the Lord?
—1 Corinthians 9:1

Paul recognized that his claim as an apostle was connected to a church that had been built and was in existence. He saw the Corinthian church as a seal of his apostleship. Real apostolic authority always *builds* something. Many would claim to be apostles yet can't point to anything they have built. Whether churches, networks, businesses, or other organizations. Anyone who really carries the apostolic authority will have as a proof of their apostleship that which has been built. We must only be connected and aligned with real apostles. Is the supposed authority they carry producing something tangible? Any real spiritual authority will cause things to be arranged in the unseen world, that something is established in the seen realm. We cannot see what is happening in the spiritual realm necessarily. We can however see the results of what is happening in the unseen dimension in the natural. Any true apostle will be a builder. They will be able to build in the natural realm what is seen in the spirit world. The result will be that which carries apostolic authority and influences the earth.

> *Lord, as I stand before Your Courts, I thank You that You allow me to connect with real apostles who build from the authority You have granted them. May the Kingdom of God have a natural expression because of the authority of apostles in the unseen realm. In Jesus's name, amen.*

MOTHERING APOSTLES

*But we were gentle among you, just as a nursing mother
cherishes her own children. So, affectionately longing for you,
we were well pleased to impart to you not only the gospel of God,
but also our own lives, because you had become dear to us.*
—1 Thessalonians 2:7–8

The Apostle Paul and his apostolic team pictured themselves as those who mother. We hear very little, if anything, about the mothering influence of apostles. Cleary there is to be one. Paul said they were as *nursing mothers* to this church. When a mother nurses her child, a bond is created that can last a lifetime. Nursing isn't just about the child receiving nutrition; it is also about the mother and child creating a connection that can be unbreakable. Paul said they imparted their own lives. They didn't just preach the gospel; they also gave themselves. Apostles are not just to be the hierarchy of the church. They are not to be the untouchables that no one can reach. They are to be relational in nature and relatable to the people of God. When this is in place, a lot of the criticism of the apostolic movement will cease. Relationship does wonders for demolishing false concepts and ideas. May the people of God be *nursed* and *cherished* by the apostolic of the church. This will create a sense of security and importance in the people of God that will allow destiny to be fulfilled.

*Lord, thank You that from Your Courts apostles who can both
mother and father are being established. Thank You that because
of this, Your church is coming to greater levels of maturity and
power. In Jesus's name, amen.*

JUSTICE RENDERED

A bruised reed He will not break, and smoking flax He will not quench, till He sends forth justice to victory. —Matthew 12:20

There is a cry for justice in the hearts of God's people. There is much loss that has been suffered and much pain that has been inflicted. The cry is that this would be acknowledged and repaid with good. This is actually the hope that is in the heart of God's family. It is promised that *justice will be sent forth.* In other words, there will be a rendering of justice that brings God's people out of defeat and into victory. There will be a returning of fortunes that cause the pain of the last seasons to be forgotten. Whether the loss that has been suffered is the result of human action or completely the activity of the demonic, the word of God promises justice to victims. From the Courts of Heaven, we can expect and endure until this verdict is set into place. There are times when it seems that no one is actually aware. Please realize that God knows. We can approach His courts and petition Him for justice to be set for us and what concerns us.

As I come before Your Courts, Lord, I ask for justice. I have experienced loss and pain. Would You take up my case and hear my petition, that righteous judgment might be established for me? In Jesus's name, amen.

ANOINTED TO JUDGE

*Behold! My Servant whom I have chosen, my Beloved in whom
My soul is well pleased! I will put My Spirit upon Him, and He
will declare justice to the Gentiles.* —Matthew 12:18

Jesus has been granted the Holy Spirit without measure (John 3:34). One of the
main reasons for this anointing is to *declare justice*. Justice is always the result
of righteous judgments. There can be no justice without righteous judgment.
Jesus has been granted the authority and power to judge so that justice might
be established for all. This means all wrongs will be righted. All suffering will be
rewarded. All loss with be restored. This is justice. Notice that there is a require-
ment of being anointed with the Holy Spirit that will allow judgment to establish justice. From the Holy Spirit the wisdom that is necessary to render right
verdicts to this end is granted. In the days of Moses, God took some of the Spirit
that was on Moses and put it on seventy others. This was so they could judge
rightly the cases and disputes of the people (Num. 11:16–17). They had to be
anointed with the Spirit that was upon Moses. They received an impartation
to stand as judges and establish justice among the people. We must have the
anointing to underwrite judgments for justice.

> *As we come before Your Courts, Lord, we ask for the anointing
> of Your Spirit. May we be empowered to see the judgments of the
> Lord set so that justice might be revealed. Move by Your Spirit,
> we pray, and cause Your name to be glorified and justice to come.
> In Jesus's name, amen.*

THE CHOSEN SERVANT

Behold! My Servant whom I have chosen, my Beloved in whom My soul is well pleased! I will put My Spirit upon Him, and He will declare justice to the Gentiles. —Matthew 12:18

The *chosen servant* is the one who will render justice into place. He is the one who will be anointed for such activity. Being chosen speaks of having passed the test of being a *servant*. God loves to exalt those who in secret have served to places of extreme importance and influence. He loves to take those others have disregarded and even condemned and establish them in the eyes of all as those He has chosen. This in itself is justice. We are told that the Lord takes people from the dust and the ash heap and sits them with the princes of His people (Ps. 113:7–8). This happened to David. When the prophet came to the house of Jesse to look for a king, David wasn't even called. However, through the Holy Spirit on Samuel the Lord searched him out. He couldn't be hidden or disregarded always. He was the chosen one who was in the sheepfolds serving. He was set as king to judge God's people and to bring forth equity. So it will always be in the Kingdom of God! The chosen of the Lord to administer justice will be a servant at heart. This is so they will not mistreat the people of God from the place of authority they've been granted.

> *Lord, thank You that You establish judges and kings that are servants at heart. They are Your chosen ones to execute justice. May this spirit be in me that the Courts of Heaven might regard me as one who can serve in this capacity. In Jesus's name, amen.*

THE BELOVED OF GOD

Behold! My Servant whom I have chosen, my Beloved in whom My soul is well pleased! I will put My Spirit upon Him, and He will declare justice to the Gentiles. —Matthew 12:18

Notice that the one who is to declare *justice* is the *Beloved who pleases God.* Whoever walks in the authority to render judgments that produce justice must have the heart of God. The beloved is one who is intimate with the heart of God. Therefore, they know what God desires and wants. From this place they are able to render judgments that satisfy God's heart and soul well. For those who are granted a place of rendering judgments, they must treasure the heart of God above the cry of the people. There must be a commitment beyond what people would yearn for. There must be an intense intention to never violate the standards set by God Himself. It is so very easy to allow the persons of men to sway away from righteous judgment. This is why only those who cannot be manipulated by money or other means are allowed to judge. Justice must never be perverted. The thing that possesses the heart of one granted authority to judge is a passion for God's will. They walk in the fear of the Lord, knowing they themselves will give an account of their judgments rendered. They are the beloved of God that the Lord takes delight in.

Lord, as I would approach Your Courts and cry for justice, please allow me to be Your beloved that pleases You. Let there be no injustice in me. I humble my heart before You and say my heart is to obey You fully. In Jesus's name, amen.

OCTOBER 10

FIREPROOF

The sinners in Zion are afraid; fearfulness has seized the hypocrites: "Who among us shall dwell with the devouring fire? Who among us shall dwell with everlasting burnings?" He who walks righteously and speaks uprightly, he who despises the gain of oppressions, who gestures with his hands, refusing bribes, who stops his ears from hearing of bloodshed, and shuts his eyes from seeing evil. —Isaiah 33:14–15

Notice that those who love righteousness and administer it to others have nothing to fear before the Lord. Only hypocrites and sinners should fear the devouring fire of God's judgments. Sinners and hypocrites in Zion speak of the church. These were God's people. We are told that *judgment* begins at the house of God (1 Pet. 4:17). God is a rewarder of those who walk in justice with others. When we walk righteously and speak rightly, God sustains us. We are fireproof from His judgments. When we despise gain and won't sell out, we are fireproof. When we aggressively refuse to be bought, we are fireproof. When we will not be party to bloodshed, we are fireproof. When we shut our eyes from seeing evil and have nothing to do with it, we are fireproof. We are set so that the judgments of God will be in our favor. May we walk in the fear of the Lord and depart from evil, that His name might be glorified.

Lord, as I stand in Your Courts, I ask that I might be fireproofed. Let me make the decisions that are in agreement with You and Your word that will allow for Your judgments to be in my favor. Help me to serve You with a true heart that I might be acceptable before You. I yield my life to Your scrutiny and examinations. In Jesus's name, amen.

TRUE JUDGMENTS

His delight is in the fear of the Lord, and He shall not judge by
the sight of His eyes, nor decide by the hearing of His ears.
—Isaiah 11:3

This Scripture is prophetic of Jesus and His ministry in the earth. He did not *judge* by the sight of His eyes or the hearing of the ears. In other words, He wasn't able to be manipulated and fooled. This is good news. Some face the scrutiny of others because lies have been believed about them. Jesus can't be deceived. His judgment is not based on any natural senses. His judgment is pure and true. Judgment will be rendered from His Courts based on the reality of things, not perceived realities. The Lord looks deep into our lives and ponders the ways of man (Prov. 5:21). His judgments are always based on truth. The Holy Spirit is called the Spirit of truth (John 14:17). In other words, He will always speak the truth, even if it is painful. Yet when this truth is embraced, it will set the captive free (John 8:32). We must allow the truth of the Lord to penetrate our lives. As we embrace this truth, we free the Lord to unveil truth concerning our situations, that righteous judgments might be enforced.

> *Lord, as I come before Your Courts and petition You for righteous judgments, I ask in the fear of the Lord for my life to be aligned with truth. Thank You that You judge pure judgments. They are not based on what eyes see or ears hear; they are based on the deep reality of all things. In Jesus's name, amen.*

JUDGED OF THE LORD

*For I know of nothing against myself, yet I am not justified by
this; but He who judges me is the Lord.* —1 Corinthians 4:4

The Apostle Paul declared that he was not critical of himself. He understood
that most of us, if we judge ourselves, would be overly critical or lenient. He
had committed the judgment of himself to the Lord. In other words, he was
allowing the Holy Spirit the right to speak into his life on a momentary basis.
If we will allow the Lord this place, as His possession we will be judged, and
things will be set in order. Judgment is not the activity of an angry God. Judgment is God having the right to unveil heart issues that we might not be aware
of. We are told that the human heart can be deceptive (Jer. 17:9). However,
when we allow the Lord to judge us, He uncovers this deception and causes
us to know truth. In the Book of James it is called looking in the perfect law
of liberty (James 1:23–25). It is the idea of beholding our face in a mirror and
taking stock of what we see. The Lord will use His Word and law to show us any
discrepancies in what we say we believe and how we really walk. We must invite
the Lord who judges to show us places where we need repentance and cleansing.
We don't fall prey to navel-gazing or paralysis of self-analysis. We do, however,
allow the Lord to judge our lives and bring divine order to every place.

> *Lord, as I stand and petition You for Your judgments in my
> behalf, I ask that You might be my judge. That You, Lord, would
> judge me and not myself. I know Your judgments are true and
> pure. Set me free from Your Courts, Lord, that Your righteousness
> might be seen. In Jesus's name, amen.*

JUDGED AND SET AS A BONDSLAVE

But if the servant plainly says, "I love my master, my wife, and
my children; I will not go out free," then his master shall bring
him to the judges. He shall also bring him to the door, or to the
doorpost, and his master shall pierce his ear with an awl; and
he shall serve him forever. —Exodus 21:5–6

In Hebrew order, when a man was sold into slavery to another Hebrew to pay a debt, he would serve for six years and go free on the seventh. If, however, he had grown to love the master's house and all that he enjoyed there, he could choose to remain there forever and be a bondslave. This is what should happen to us with Jesus. We first encountered Jesus so His sacrifice could pay our debt. However, the longer we serve Him, the more we never want to go "free." In other words, our relationship with the Lord began because we needed our debt to be paid. It became, however, a love relationship. To consummate this transaction with the master and the slave, the man would be taken to the *judges,* and his choice to become a bondslave would be publicly announced. The *judges* speak to us of the evaluation of our heart in the process of becoming a bondslave. As we desire for the Lord to have more of us, we must allow the *judges* to look into our lives. The Holy Spirit, the Word of God, prophetic encounters, and others can be the *judges* that expose our hearts as we prepare to move from one whose debt needed to be paid to one who loves the Lord and will not go free. We will then be marked by having our ear pierced. This speaks of our ear being opened that we might ear. This is the mark of a bondslave, a hearing ear.

> *Lord, as I come before Your Courts, I announce and declare that*
> *I want to be Your bondslave. May it be recorded this is my desire.*
> *Would you allow the "judges" to lovingly examine my life as my*
> *ear is opened to hear Your voice. In Jesus's name, amen.*

EXPOSED AND PERFECTED

He said to him the third time, "Simon, son of Jonah, do you love Me?" Peter was grieved because He said to him the third time, "Do you love Me?" And he said to Him, "Lord, You know all things; You know that I love You." Jesus said to him, "Feed My sheep. Most assuredly, I say to you, when you were younger, you girded yourself and walked where you wished; but when you are old, you will stretch out your hands, and another will gird you and carry you where you do not wish."
—John 21:17–18

In questioning Peter, Jesus exposed Peter's heart. He asked him three times, *"Do you love Me?"* This meant, "Do you love Me so much that you will give everything for Me?" Having just walked through his denial of Jesus, Peter was painfully aware of his heart and its lack of devotion to Jesus. All Peter could do was tell Jesus that he loved Him as a friend. Peter was *grieved.* It hurts when the examination of the Lord reveals the true nature of our hearts. When Peter answered *honestly,* however, Jesus told him in essence, "I will bring you to where I'm asking you to be." In other words, as Peter walked with Jesus, he would become one who would die for the Lord and His purposes. Jesus would finish the work in Peter. A part of this work, however, is allowing the penetrating examination of the Lord to unveil our hearts. As Peter walked through his process, Jesus perfected what concerned him. He became one who was willing to die for the Lord and in fact did. The love of Jesus consumed Peter until he was willing to give all and *love* Jesus as the Lord had desired. The Lord is the author and finisher of our faith (Heb. 12:2).

Lord, I ask before Your Courts that I might love You and be devoted to You as You would desire and require. I do not have the ability in myself to love You this way. Lord, I give You the right to examine my heart and perfect all that would concern me. As I would stand in Your presence, before Your Courts, may I be found surrendered and yielded to You. In Jesus's name, amen.

MAKING OUR ADVERSARY PAY

Now there was a widow in that city; and she came to him,
saying, "Get justice for me from my adversary." —Luke 18:3

Jesus tells the story of the widow who approached an unjust judge and asked him to get *justice for her from her adversary.* She wanted the adversary to be made to pay for whatever she had lost. In other words, her adversary would be made to give back all that he had stolen. We know the devil is a thief and a robber (John 10:1). He comes to steal, kill, and destroy (John 10:10). When we come before the Courts of Heaven and make our case, we can request retribution from the devil and his forces. We can ask that all he has stolen be given back to us. All the pain, sorrow, finances, reputation, and other precious things can be restored. One verdict from the Courts of Heaven can set this in place. We are told we can have double what was lost (Job 42:10). We are also told that we can have sevenfold what was taken from us (Prov. 6:31). We can come before the Courts and remove any legal right the devil would claim against us as his right to consume. Once this is done, we can then petition the Courts of Heaven to have all that was lost restored and reinstated. The Lord delights in making the devil pay back what he has taken from His children.

> *As I approach Your Courts, O Lord, I ask that the adversary, my legal opponent, be made to repay all that he has taken. Let every precious thing be restored at least double if not sevenfold. I thank You, Lord, for justice from Your Courts. In Jesus's name, amen.*

PLUNDERING THE ENEMY'S HOUSE

*Or how can one enter a strong man's house and plunder his
goods, unless he first binds the strong man? And then he will
plunder his house.* —Matthew 12:29

We are told that when the strong man is bound, we can then plunder his house. *Bind* is the Greek word *deō*, and it is connected to something being arrested, which is a legal activity. When we *legally* have incapacitated the devil and his forces, we can then plunder his house. When satan was kicked out of Heaven, he was stripped of everything. Everything he has in his *house* today is a result of his stealing, killing, and destroying (John 10:10). As the people of God we are to take back all that satan has gained through these activities. We are to see revoked every legal right he is claiming through the history of sin that he claims has granted him these rights. When we repent in behalf of ourselves, our bloodlines, and our histories, the blood of Jesus has the power to silence his claims against us. We then have the right to ask for a judgment against satan and to require that all that is in his house be requisitioned to meet that judgment! We are allowed to plunder his house to pay off the judgment of Heaven against him. This means souls released for the Kingdom. Finances restored. Health reinstituted. Anything and everything that has been lost can be reclaimed from *his house!* This is the judgment from the Courts of Heaven.

> *Lord, as we come before Your Courts, we thank You that satan is bound. We thank You that any legal case against us is silenced and all that he has used to steal, kill, and destroy is revoked. Let the plundering of his house begin now. In Jesus's name, amen.*

PUNISHING DISOBEDIENCE

...and being ready to punish all disobedience when your obedience is fulfilled. —2 Corinthians 10:6

Paul exhorts us that there can and will be a punishing of all disobedience. The word *punish* is the Greek word *ekdikeō*, and it means "to vindicate, retaliate." When justice is rendered in our behalf, there is a vindication that can and will come. All lies, untruths, falsehoods, and wrong ideas about us will change because God has vindicated us. Notice, however, that this is connected to *fulfilled obedience.* In other words, as long as there are places of disobedience in us, the devil will use this as a legal right to deny our vindication. The vindicating of all disobedience means that the results and effects of my disobedience and the disobedience or others is thwarted. Any curses associated with it lose their rights to operate. Any reaping of wrong seeds sown is stopped. All legal rights the devil might claim to harass my life and hinder my future is revoked. We must embrace the grace of God to fully obey the Lord in every area. May He grant us the desire and strength to obey Him fully that all effects of disobedience will be removed, and my life can come into new places of blessing and breakthrough.

As I approach Your Courts, Lord, I repent for the places of disobedience in my life. Any place of willful rebellion in me or unintentional sin, would You please forgive? Would You allow Your blood to speak for me? Empower me, Lord, that I might fully obey. May all effects of disobedience now be revoked, and may vindication now come. In Jesus's name, amen.

OCTOBER 18

REPAYING WITH TRIBULATION

It is a righteous thing with God to repay with tribulation those
who trouble you. —2 Thessalonians 1:6

This Scripture would seem to not agree with the loving nature of who we know God is. However, this word is clear. Those who persecute and mistreat the righteous because they belong to Him will be repaid with trouble. The Bible actually says the awareness of this principle is where we as the people of God get strength to persevere. Revelation 13:10 unveils that whoever hurts and does wrong to others will themselves suffer. We are told this is the patience and faith of the saints. In other words, there is justice with God. The understanding that God is a just God who will defend the righteous but punish the wrongdoer is a source of empowerment as we seek to *keep the faith* and walk out our salvation. Without this assurance of the justice of God, life would be unbearable for some. However, because there is justice with the Judge of all the earth, we can prevail knowing that God is true. In the midst of the wounding, however, we must keep our hearts pure and free of anger, unforgiveness, and bitterness. Should we let these things reside in us they can short-circuit the Lord's ways. We must allow Him to seek vengeance in our behalf.

> *As we stand before Your Courts, Lord, I ask that I might have an*
> *awareness of Your justice. I know, Lord, that You will defend me.*
> *Help me to maintain a right heart that I would allow vengeance*
> *to belong to You. In Jesus's name, amen.*

VENGEANCE IS MINE, SAYS THE LORD

Beloved, do not avenge yourselves, but rather give place to wrath; for it is written, "Vengeance is Mine, I will repay," says the Lord. —Romans 12:19

We are admonished to not seek vengeance ourselves. We are told to *"give place to wrath."* In other words, we are not to respond in anger and try to hurt someone who has hurt us. When we do this, we take the situation out of the righteous hand of God. If we seek to defend ourselves, God will not defend us. Vengeance, or repayment for wrongs done, belongs to the Lord. If I try to do this myself, I seek to operate in a dimension that God says is His alone. If, however, I trust that He is just and righteous, I can leave it to the Lord. My challenge is to not allow anger and wrath to fester in my heart and make me bitter. Should I allow this, then a *root of bitterness* can develop (Heb. 12:15). Now I am guilty of not allowing the grace of God to rule my heart. Any wish for the hurt of another is not from God. I must place this in the hand of God and instead have a heart to bless. I must be like Jesus as much as possible. Even as they were crucifying Him, He cried, *"Father, forgive them, for they know not what they do"* (Luke 23:34). May my heart be so healed that this would be my cry. Remember, vengeance belongs to God.

Lord, I ask that my heart might be free from bitterness and anger. I trust You with any vengeance You see fit. Would You allow the very nature of Jesus to be in me, that I might reflect who You are? May it be recorded before Your Courts that this is my prayer. In Jesus's name, amen.

JUDGMENT NOT OPPRESSION

As for the Almighty, we cannot find Him; He is excellent in
power, in judgment and abundant justice; He does not oppress.
—Job 37:23

Oppression is a result of the lack of justice. Where there is judgment and justice there is no oppression. The word *oppress* in the Hebrew is the word `*anah*. It is the idea of "looking down or to browbeating." The Lord does not push us down or make us feel inferior. He doesn't take the life and spirit out of us so that we have no more heart to seek or to try. This is what the Egyptians did to the children of Israel. They caused them to serve with hard bondage and made their lives bitter (Exod. 1:14). Righteous judgment that brings justice delivers us from oppression. It is not God's heart for one to oppress another. Anyone with real authority is granted that authority to *serve with* not to *oppress from*. However, because of the perversion of man's heart without God, many consider the authority they have to allow them to abuse. The Lord in His justice actually declares whoever would use authority for this purpose would themselves be judged (Matt. 24:48–51). There is severe punishment for those who oppress others with their authority. Those who use authority correctly, use it to bless not oppress.

> *Lord, as I am aware that Heaven is watching, I choose to use*
> *any authority I have to bless and not oppress. Through judgment*
> *You relieve the oppressed. May righteous authority be set so that*
> *people are liberated. May it be recorded in Your Courts, Lord,*
> *that this is my heart and desire, and I have prayed this prayer. In*
> *Jesus's name, amen.*

THE FOUNDATION OF HIS THRONE

Righteousness and justice are the foundation of Your throne;
mercy and truth go before Your face. —Psalm 89:14

Righteousness and justice have founded and established the throne of God. This is the foundation from which God as the Judge of all the earth functions. This means that the judgments that come from the throne of God are righteous in nature. This means they are right and good based on the standards of who God is. They are also full of justice in that there is no preferential treatment for one above another. There is justice for all regardless of a person's social standing or position. This is why we are told God is no respecter of persons (Acts 10:34). Peter made this statement when he saw the Holy Spirit poured out on the Gentiles. Until this time, Peter was certain that God loved the Jews more than any other people group. He suddenly realized that whoever fears God and worked righteousness was accepted by Him. This is because God's throne is full of justice. Whoever will seek the face of God will find Him. His righteousness and justice demands it. Whoever will call on Him and His name will be saved and delivered.

> *Lord, as we approach Your Courts, I thank You that there is righteousness and justice in Your throne. In fact, this is the foundation of Your authority, rulership, and Court system. Thank You that because You are just, you hear me when I cry. There is no respect of persons with You. In Jesus's name, amen.*

SUFFERING IN THE FLESH

Therefore, since Christ suffered for us in the flesh, arm yourselves
also with the same mind, for he who has suffered in the flesh has
ceased from sin, that he no longer should live the rest of his time
in the flesh for the lusts of men, but for the will of God.
—1 Peter 4:1–2

Suffering is a part of life. We all go through it to one degree or another. In fact, when we are tempted and say no to sin, the Bible says this is suffering. Whoever has suffered in the flesh has ceased to sin. In other words, when we resist temptation our flesh is suffering. We are choosing to live the remainder of our days in the flesh, not to fulfill lust and desires, but to do the will of God. It can be easy at times to look at the persecuted church in parts of the world and to think of them as better Christians. We should honor them. However, anytime we choose the will of God over our own desires, we too are suffering according to the Word of God. This suffering actually speaks before the Courts of Heaven and is recorded in our behalf. It is being stated that we have chosen God's ways instead of the ways of the world. May we be granted grace that we might serve the Lord *"acceptably with reverence and godly fear"* (Heb. 12:28). May our suffering for His sake speak for us before the Courts and give testimony concerning us. May it grant us a status in His presence that will allow us to be heard before Him (Heb. 11:39). May we have a good report.

> *As I approach Your Courts, may I say no to my flesh and choose*
> *Your ways. May this be recorded in Heaven that I have chosen*
> *the ways of God. As for me and my house, let it be known that we*
> *shall serve the Lord. In Jesus's name, amen.*

SUFFERING AS A CHRISTIAN

But let none of you suffer as a murderer, a thief, an evildoer, or as a busybody in other people's matters. Yet if anyone suffers as a Christian, let him not be ashamed, but let him glorify God in this matter. —1 Peter 4:15–16

Just because we suffer doesn't mean we get any benefit from it. To gain from our suffering out of the justice of God, it must be for righteousness's sake. If my serving is a result of my own foolishness or rebellion, this produces nothing for me but heartache and pain. If, however, my suffering is because I am a believer, I don't have to be ashamed or reproached. There is a reward and justification that will come to me. Suffering as a believer can be because the devil has targeted you. In other words, his hatred for you is so great that he desires to inflict pain. When this is true, God in His justice will see to it that you are rewarded, either in this life or the one to come. Jesus said those who are persecuted for righteousness's sake will receive a great reward in Heaven (Matt. 5:11–12). When evil is spoken against us, we are granted a wonderful reward in Heaven out of the righteous judgments of God. Eye has not seen, ear has not heard the things that have been prepared for those who love Him (1 Cor. 2:9). May we be found faithful.

> *Lord, as I stand before Your Courts, I thank You that You are the righteous Judge. In every place I would be persecuted for righteousness's sake, there is laid up for me a reward in Heaven. I believe You, Lord, judge righteously. May I be found faithful. In Jesus's name, amen.*

THE CHURCH IS THE KEY TO DIVINE SOCIETAL ORDER

By faith Noah, being divinely warned of things not yet seen, moved with godly fear, prepared an ark for the saving of his household, by which he condemned the world and became heir of the righteousness which is according to faith.
—Hebrews 11:7

Noah *condemned* the world. The word *condemn* is the Greek word *katakrinō.* It means "judge against, sentence." Noah through his obedience to God built that which saved his family. He moved in faith when he was divinely warned. These activities released a judgment against the world and it inhabitants. God did not and could not render a judgment against the wickedness of the earth until Noah had fully obeyed. This is still true today. God must have a people who will obey Him. When this is in place, His judging hand that brings order can be released. If the Lord were to judge the earth prematurely, He would have to judge His people as well (1 Cor. 11:32). The Lord in His mercy *waits* for us to be perfected and obedient before His judgments can come. Some wonder why God will not intervene. This is why. We as the church are the key. When we are in full obedience, the order of God can and will come to the earth (2 Cor. 10:6).

Lord, as we come before Your Courts, may we have the same heart as Noah, who moved with fear and obeyed. May we fully yield and say yes to You. As we do, Lord, let judgments come that can set things in order in the earth. In Jesus's name, amen.

GOD AVENGES INNOCENT BLOODSHED

And they cried with a loud voice, saying, "How long, O Lord, holy and true, until You judge and avenge our blood on those who dwell on the earth?" —Revelation 6:10

Those who had been martyred are revealed to be crying out for judgment. They are from Heaven asking the Lord to avenge their blood that was shed because they belonged to Jesus. All blood has a voice (Heb. 12:24). The blood of the innocent, however, can be crying for judgment. We can actually set our cry in agreement with the cry of those whose blood was spilled for the cause of Christ. Why would we want judgment? Without judgment, there is no justice. When judgment comes, a true perspective of who God is in His holiness begins to be reestablished. Yes, the Lord is our gracious Father. He is, however, the supreme God of the universe who judges righteously. When the Lord stretches His hand to judge, society begins to once against return to the fear of the Lord. He is not an angry God to be appeased. He is a good Lord who is to be obeyed. May we never despise the goodness of His forbearance toward us, that we might receive of His mercy and kindness.

> *Lord, I stand before Your Courts and ask that You will help me balance who You are in Your goodness and severity, even as the Apostle Paul declared (Rom. 11:22). You are not an angry God, but You are the supreme ruler of all. May Your name be known in all the earth and Your judgments bring us to the fear of the Lord. In Jesus's name, amen.*

JUDGING ANOTHER WHILE GUILTY

*Therefore you are inexcusable, O man, whoever you are who
judge, for in whatever you judge another you condemn yourself;
for you who judge practice the same things. —Romans 2:1*

Contrary to popular belief, we as believers are to judge (1 Cor. 2:15). But we are not to judge when we are guilty of the same thing. When I judge another who is doing what I am doing, I set a judgment and condemnation over my own life. Paul said we were *inexcusable*. This word in the Greek is *anapologētos*. It means "without a defense." In other words, I have no legal footing to be defended when I condemn and judge someone for doing the thing I am guilty of. This is quite serious. Even though we are called to judge, we must be careful that we ourselves are free. If we aren't, we are setting ourselves us for condemnation and potentially devastating legal action against us. This is one of the reasons satan is so successful against us legally. He points out our hypocrisy before the Courts of Heaven. This allows him to claim a right to bring hardship, restrictions, and limits against us. We must repent for any and all judgmentalism. When we do, the legal right of our adversary can be revoked—we have a defense.

> *As I stand before Your Courts, Lord, I ask that all hypocrisy would be removed from me. Forgive me for being hard and without mercy. I repent. I ask that every double standard in my life be now removed. Cleanse me, Lord. In Jesus's name, amen.*

ESCAPING JUDGMENT

And do you think this, O man, you who judge those practicing such things, and doing the same, that you will escape the judgment of God? —Romans 2:3

It would appear that our violation of the standard of God is serious. When I judge others and am critical of them for what I am guilty of, I set myself up for severe judgment. In other words, we should repent for that which is offensive to God. We must not give ourselves room to live in sin. And I must be careful to not be judgmental of those who are in sin like mine or struggling. If I am, the Scripture says that because I gave them no mercy, I will not escape the judgment of God. If I have not given mercy, I will not receive mercy. Judgment is without mercy to those who have shown none (James 2:13). This appears to be a huge thing with God. Hypocrites who slam others for the very thing they are guilty of will be judged. I want mercy. I petition the Courts of Heaven to help me in my process to give others grace in theirs. This will work for my benefit as I stand before the Lord and give an account of my activities and life.

> *Lord, I thank You that You are perfecting what concerns me. Make me a merciful person. Draw me near to You that I might have Your heart toward others. I repent before Your Courts for any places of being judgmental. In Jesus's name, amen.*

THE GOODNESS OF GOD AND REPENTANCE

Or do you despise the riches of His goodness, forbearance, and longsuffering, not knowing that the goodness of God leads you to repentance? —Romans 2:4

When we judge others and are harsh with them, we despise the riches of God's goodness and long-suffering with us. We are failing to realize that the goodness of God is what can produce and lead us to repentance. God doesn't judge us quickly. He gives us space. In the days of Noah, He gave them time to repent (1 Pet. 3:20). Remember that the Lord takes no delight in the death and judgment of the wicked (Ezek. 18:32). He will give as much time as can possibly be granted for people to turn. He even did this for Jezebel. He gave her space to repent of her immoral and controlling issues, but she didn't (Rev. 2:21). Therefore, God legislated judgment against her. He was lenient for a long time in an effort to see repentance come that judgment would not result. When we realize this about God toward us and others, it should make us lenient as well. It should birth in us a heart to show mercy rather than to pronounce a sentence. When this is worked in us, we are moving away from judgment and into mercy.

> Lord, as I come before Your Courts, make me merciful. Help me see and recognize Your heart to show kindness. You actually send rain on the just and unjust and shine Your sun on the wicked and the righteous. May I walk in this same heart. In Jesus's name, amen.

DIVINE ORDER IN GOVERNMENT

*"They have grown fat, they are sleek; yes, they surpass the deeds
of the wicked; they do not plead the cause, the cause of the
fatherless; yet they prosper, and the right of the needy they do
not defend. Shall I not punish them for these things?" says the
Lord. "Shall I not avenge Myself on such a nation as this?"*
—Jeremiah 5:28–29

God promises to judge and avenge Himself upon governmental leaders that do not use their place and position appropriately. Instead of caring for the fatherless and needy, they are making themselves fat and prosperous. When people who have been granted places designed by God to minister to people, but instead use their position to prosper themselves, without helping these others, this is grievous to the Lord. If the church can come to a place of obedience that would allow us to call for judgment on these things, then we could see change. The problem is we haven't walked in a place of purity, holiness, and love that would allow us to cry for God's judgment on these things. The lack of obedience to the ways of the Lord have denied God the liberty to judge that which is out of order in our societies. Only when we have walked in fulfilled obedience can God judge and revenge all disobedience (2 Cor. 10:6). The Lord will be able to set in order that which is polluting society. Governmental officials will be brought under the scrutiny of Heaven and required to care for that which is on the heart of God.

> *Lord, as we come before Your Courts, we repent for ourselves
> and the church. We ask that we might walk in purity that would
> allow us to stand in Your Courts and ask for Your judgments on
> all that is in opposition to You. Let governmental leaders come
> into alignment that society might reflect Your heart and care. In
> Jesus's name, amen.*

AVENGING APOSTLES AND PROPHETS

Rejoice over her, O heaven, and you holy apostles and prophets,
for God has avenged you on her! —Revelation 18:20

We see the Lord judging that which has persecuted and hindered His servants who represented Him in the earth. In these days there seems to be little known of the God who is the *"Judge of all"* (Heb. 12:23). As much as He is the loving Father, He also functions as the supreme Judge of the universe. One of the things God will judge is those who have hindered, hurt, and damaged the apostles and prophets He sent to them. God promises to *avenge* them on those who worked against them, persecuted them, and even killed them. This will cause these men and women of God to rejoice, because God has taken up their cause in their behalf. Remember that vengeance belongs to the Lord; it is His to repay (Rom. 12:19). These will not have to defend themselves. The Lord will regard their case before Him and render decisions against those who attacked them and sought to hinder their call in God. True apostles and prophets will be defended by the Lord. Even though they might suffer for a season, it is only so God can legally avenge them upon those who sought to do them harm. Let God arise and His enemies be scattered (Ps. 68:1).

> *As we approach Your throne and Courts, we request that all that would hinder Your work through true apostles and prophets would be judged. Avenge them upon their captors and those who would persecute, in Jesus's name. Justify and vindicate them and Your cause in them. In Jesus's name, amen.*

AVENGING BROTHERS

*That no one should take advantage of and defraud his brother
in this matter, because the Lord is the avenger of all such, as we
also forewarned you and testified.* —1 Thessalonians 4:6

When you read the context of this Scripture, it is in regard to sexual immorality. In other words, if someone has used their place or influence to become sexually involved with someone who is not their spouse, God says He will judge the wrongdoers, and He will avenge the defrauded. The idea could involve someone who was not consenting, and sexual activity was forced upon them. This is a grievous thing before the Lord. It could also involve the spouse of one who was cheated on by another. God declares He will be the defender and avenger of this situation. Regardless, we must know that sexual activity outside of marriage can result in the judgment of God. In fact, Hebrews 13:4 declares that God will judge fornicators, adulterers, and whoremongers. In this age of sexual freedom, we have adopted standards that I fear will bring the judgment of God before it is all said and done. We must repent of sexual uncleanness and ask that the blood of Jesus speak for us. May we live clean lives that bring the blessings of God and do not cry for His avenging and judgment.

As we approach Your Courts, we bring our lives into Your inspection. We ask that any place of sexual uncleanness will be cleansed and purified. May the holiness of who You are possess our being and make us pure as You are pure. In Jesus's name, amen.

MISUSING AUTHORITY

Woe to those who devise iniquity, and work out evil on their beds! At morning light they practice it, because it is in the power of their hand. They covet fields and take them by violence, also houses, and seize them. So they oppress a man and his house, a man and his inheritance. Therefore thus says the Lord: "Behold, against this family I am devising disaster, from which you cannot remove your necks; nor shall you walk haughtily, for this is an evil time." —Micah 2:1–3

God promises to judge the *family* who is a part of misusing their place of authority to steal what belongs to another. They scheme and connive to take away what the Lord has trusted to someone else. We are told a disaster is fashioned and devised against them from which they will not be able to escape. If there has been anything like this in our family line where someone has stolen from another through deceitful means, we must repent. When the Bible speaks of a disaster against a family, it is speaking of a family line and its generations. The devil takes this word as a legal right to visit destruction upon families. We must repent for any place in our history where anyone coveted and by force and violence took something from another. When we repent in behalf of anything of this nature in our ancestral history, we remove the right of the devil to bring hurt and harm against us. The result can be that the blessing of the Lord is restored. We begin to see the goodness of the Lord rather than the destruction of the devil against us.

> *As we approach Your Courts, Lord, we repent for any place in our history where something has been stolen through deceitful and violent means. We ask for the blood of Jesus to speak for us. May the goodness of God be seen in our lives and future rather than the destruction of the devil. In Jesus's name, amen.*

JUDGING THE TONGUE OF DECEIT

"Their tongue is an arrow shot out; it speaks deceit; one speaks
peaceably to his neighbor with his mouth, but in his heart he
lies in wait. Shall I not punish them for these things?" says the
Lord. "Shall I not avenge Myself on such a nation as this?"
—Jeremiah 9:8–9

When there are unrighteous motives at work and deceitful tongues devised to hurt, harm, and steal from another, God says He will avenge Himself on such a people. Those who speak words that are deceitful and designed to entrap others, God says He will punish. Those who are positioned waiting on an opportunity to devour and steal, God is watching. We should ask that the Lord would deliver us from these tongues. That He would make us discerning to recognize that which others would intend to do. We must be wise as serpents and harmless as doves, as Jesus declared we should be (Matt. 10:16). Otherwise we can be caught in the snare that they lay for us. May the Lord expose all these intentions and uncover all the plans of the wicked. May we be filled with wisdom to know and recognize what others with impure motives will do. May the Lord Himself judge this and avenge and punish those who would work such things against the righteous. We have a right to call for these judgments from the Courts of Heaven.

> *Lord, as we approach Your Courts, we ask that every deceitful*
> *motive and intent would be uncovered. May it be judged as*
> *unrighteous before You as You avenge Yourself upon those who*
> *would do such things. In Jesus's name, amen.*

JUDGMENT AGAINST IMMORALITY

*"They were like well-fed lusty stallions; every one neighed after
his neighbor's wife. Shall I not punish them for these things?"
says the Lord. "And shall I not avenge Myself on such a nation
as this?"* —Jeremiah 5:8–9

The Lord vows to punish and avenge Himself upon the lust and sexual immorality that is operating within a culture. There is a sexual perversion operating where men are pursuing and lusting after women who are the wives of others. Any form of sexual sin is destructive. However, it appears that when someone goes after the spouse of another, this is especially offensive to the Lord. The Lord vows to punish those who do these things. This is true in the Word of God. Both First Thessalonians 4:6 and Hebrews 13:4 speak of the judgment of God that will come on those who defraud and seek another in sexual activity that is forbidden by the Lord. We must repent for any of this activity in actuality but also within our heart. Jesus was clear that if anyone lusted after another in his heart, this was as serious as having committed the actual sin (Matt. 5:28). The devil can claim a legal right to visit destruction on our lives should we be guilty of this. May the purity and holiness of the Lord move us to new levels of devotion to the Lord. May we be free and not involved in any form of sexual activity that would provoke the judgment of God upon us or our lineage.

*Lord, as we come before Your Courts, we allow the examining
nature of the Holy Spirit to announce to us any place of offense to
You. We ask that any place of sexual uncleanness will be removed
and washed away by the blood of Jesus. In Jesus's name, amen.*

THE SURE PROTECTION OF GOD

*A thousand may fall at your side, and ten thousand at your
right hand; but it shall not come near you. Only with your eyes
shall you look, and see the reward of the wicked.*
—Psalm 91:7–8

We do not have to fear becoming a statistic. What is meant by this is that we don't live by the law of averages. In other words, we don't have to worry that we or our families will suffer tragedy based on the fact that so many people do. Our safety is not a result of *luck* or of *good fortune*. Our safety comes from the Lord. There is a divine shield of favor that we can live under in the spirit world so that nothing evil can touch us. When we walk in covenant with the Lord, there is a place that will not allow the powers of darkness to come and seek to hurt, harm, or destroy us. We are told that only with our eyes will we behold the effects of evil in the world. We will not suffer the touch of any of it. The key to living a peace-filled life is to not allow what we see with our eyes to cause fear in our hearts. We can live in a divine place of peace that God is watching over us, that His Word is true, and what touches others, for whatever reason, will not come near us or what we love. We can live in this place as we operate in the Courts of Heaven and undo any legal right satan might claim against us. We should be proactive in this process.

> *As we approach Your Courts, Lord, we ask for Your divine
> protection and safety. We ask that the blood of Jesus would speak
> for us and silence any claim the enemy would assert. We ask that
> though thousands would fall on either side of us, it will not come
> near us or what we love. In Jesus's name, amen.*

THE SURROUNDING CARE OF GOD

Those who trust in the Lord are like Mount Zion, which cannot be moved, but abides forever. As the mountains surround Jerusalem, so the Lord surrounds His people from this time forth and forever. —Psalm 125:1–2

When our confidence is in the Lord to keep us and guard us, we become like that which cannot be moved. Mountains would seem immovable. However, God even sustains Mount Zion, the place of His presence and power. It will not be moved but will abide forever. This is who we are like when our trust is in the Lord. The Lord is surrounding us as the people of God, setting His divine protection and presence over us. We are told this is perpetual. This is because God is a covenant-keeping God that can be trusted. When everything else might be shaking and being moved, we as the people of God are those which can be immovable. The protecting, sustaining hand of God is with us because it is recorded in the Courts of Heaven that our confidence is in the Lord and not in the flesh. Our strength comes from the Lord who neither slumbers nor sleeps and is always watching over us (Ps. 121:4).

> *As we approach Your Courts, may it be recorded that our confidence is in You, O God. May this testify before the Courts and grant You the right to protect, guard, and cause us to be immovable. Let nothing come against us that would harm us in any way, In Jesus's name, amen.*

SHIELD OF FAVOR

For You, O Lord, will bless the righteous; with favor You will surround him as with a shield. —Psalm 5:12

God's favor is a shield that protects and guards us. It is that which we live under and behind to find protection for our lives. Notice that it is the *righteous* or those who are in *right standing* with the Lord. *Right standing* is a legal status that we have with the Lord. God places His favor or delight upon the righteous. This delight and favor actually creates a protective force around our lives that the enemy cannot penetrate. When the Lord delights in someone, He is jealous to protect and guard them. The cruel intentions of satan cannot prosper against this person because of the love with which they have been loved. May God's favor rest on us and create an impenetrable shield. The loving kindness and mercy of the Lord will not allow satan and his forces to prosper against us. On every side we will be protected and sustained because of the goodness of the Lord toward us and our families.

> As we approach Your Courts, Lord, we request that Your favor might surround us. May we be esteemed as the righteous of the Lord, set a part unto You. Allow, Lord, this favor to be an impenetrable shield that causes Your care to be sure over us. In Jesus's name, amen.

SAFETY IN HIS NAME

The name of the Lord is a strong tower; the righteous
run to it and are safe. —Proverbs 18:10

The *name of the Lord* is a place of safety and protection. It is not just a normal name; because of the authority in this *name* demon forces have no power to interfere or harm. When we live *in the name* of the Lord, we garner His protection and care over our life. The word *safe* actually in the Hebrew is *sagab*. It means "to be inaccessible." So when we are in the name of the Lord, we are in a place where we are untouchable. Satan has no right or power to come close to us or to interfere with us or what we love. Notice that the righteous, or those who are in legal right standing, *run* to this name. This means to *rush* in. In other words, it depicts an awareness of where we are to run to. Running or rushing into the name says that in our need, desperation, and longing for protection, we know where to go. It is into who the Lord Jesus Christ is. We know that in Him we are guarded, protected, and kept. The enemy cannot breech this place and touch us. We are inaccessible to him. The covering and protection of the Lord is our portion.

> Lord, as we come before Your Courts, I thank You that I enter Your name. I come close to who You are. I know that there is safety and protection in this place. May I be inaccessible to all the powers of darkness and nothing shall by any means hurt me. In Jesus's name, amen.

UNDER HIS SHADOW

He who dwells in the secret place of the Most High shall abide
under the shadow of the Almighty. —Psalm 91:1

The shadow of the Most High is in His secret place. The *shadow* of the Most High provides His *shade.* The word *shade* is *tsel* in the Hebrew. It means "a shade" but also "to hover over." Isaiah 4:6 tells us that God and His presence will cover us from the sun's heat and from the power of the storm. When we learn to live in the shadow or shade of the Almighty, we know His divine protection and keeping power. He will hover over us and protect us from storms of life but also the pressures of life, which is what the heat of the sun speaks about. This place of His shadow and shade is in the secret place. This is a place in the spirit world of intimacy with the Lord. Through His Word, prayer, worship, and other spiritual activities, we can enter this secret place. In this place is security, safety, calm, and tranquility. He will keep those in perfect peace, whose mind is stayed on Him (Isa. 26:3). The more we exercise our spiritual rights by the blood of Jesus, the more we can step into this secret place where His shadow and shade are. We are kept and preserved in this place.

> *As I approach Your Courts, Lord, I thank You for Your secret*
> *place and the place of Your shadow, shade, and covering. In this*
> *place I am protected and shielded from storms and the pressures*
> *of life. Thank You for allowing me entrance into this realm*
> *through the blood of Jesus. In Jesus's name, amen.*

UNDER HIS FEATHERS

He shall cover you with His feathers, and under His wings you
shall take refuge; His truth shall be your shield and buckler.
—Psalm 91:4

Here we see the guarding and protecting presence of the Lord being pictured as a bird's wing. We are told we are covered by His feathers. Speaking over Jerusalem, Jesus declared how He longed to gather them to Himself as a mother hen would gather her chicks under her wing (Luke 13:34). A hen gathers her little ones close to her heart and under her wing to protect them from enemies and adverse conditions. So the Lord will do for us. We can come close to Him and hear His heartbeat concerning us. However, Jesus said Jerusalem *would not*. They forfeited the protection and care of the Lord because of stubbornness. They chose to be obstinate rather than to accept the loving mercy and kindness of the Lord. The Lord is beckoning us to come under His wings. May we not reject the closeness of who He is, where His protection is manifested over us. We will be covered by His wings and under His feathers find safety and strength.

> *Lord, as we approach Your Courts, we declare we do not reject*
> *Your offer of coming under Your wings and the safety of Your*
> *feathers. May we surrender ourselves to You and find the closeness*
> *of Your presence as our protection and place of security. In Jesus's*
> *name, amen.*

THE LORD OUR DWELLING

Because you have made the Lord, who is my refuge, even the
Most High, your dwelling place, no evil shall befall you, nor
shall any plague come near your dwelling.
—Psalm 91:9–10

When we make the Lord our dwelling place and not just a place we visit sporadically or periodically, He becomes our place of safety. In other words, dwelling in His presence is our lifestyle. It's not just something we do occasionally; we *practice the presence of the Lord.* We are promised that when we do this, no evil can befall us or any plague come near us. The Lord has become my place of habitation. We have learned how to walk before Him and enjoy Him and His closeness. This requires a lifestyle of worship, prayer, and meditation on His Word. We become intentional in our spiritual disciplines. When we do this, He surrounds us and is near to us. That which is evil cannot penetrate this presence of the Lord that has become our portion. We can come before the Courts of Heaven and request that this would be that which would possess our lives. May we desire Him as much or more than we desire what He does. When this is our passion, nothing can attack or harass us. The Lord is our dwelling and our place of habitation.

> *As we come before Your Courts, we want it known that we*
> *desire You, Lord, as much as we desire what You do. You are*
> *our passion. May we live in You as our place of dwelling and*
> *habitation. As we do, may no evil thing touch us or come near us.*
> *In Jesus's name, amen.*

WALKING WITH GOD

And Enoch walked with God; and he was not,
for God took him. —Genesis 5:24

Enoch was a man that did not die. He was translated into the heavenly realm because of the closeness of His walk with God. The statement made here is quite phenomenal: *"He was not, for God took him."* It would seem that Enoch progressively walked so closely with the Lord that he moved from the earthly realm to the heavenly one. His walk was so intimate with the Lord that their union allowed Enoch to translate into the heavenly dimension without physically dying. This can be the *power of our walk* with the Lord. We quite often don't know what is really available to us. We think there are some things we can only experience once we are in Heaven. However, it would seem that for those who would pay the price, we can *walk* with the Lord in a union today that would bring us into heavenly places perhaps few experience. May we be willing to leave this earthly dimension and separate ourselves to the Lord in a walk that would usher us into a place of joining to the Lord. Deliver us, Lord, from the love of this life so much that we might find our passions in You.

> *Lord, as we come before Your Courts, would You allow it to be recorded that our passion is to walk with You as Enoch walked. That we might move into such a union with You that we are separate from the things of this world. In this place, Lord, let us be protected and guarded as those who have found mercy in Your sight. In Jesus's name.*

THE REVELATION OF GOD

*...(as it is written, "I have made you a father of many nations")
in the presence of Him whom he believed—God, who gives life
to the dead and calls those things which do not
exist as though they did. —Romans 4:17*

Abraham was a man who knew God. He is called the *"friend of God"* (James 2:23). In this verse we see two ideas that Abraham had and knew about God. God is One who brings dead things to life and brings into existence things that don't exist. This revelation of God that Abraham had was what made him the *father of the faith.* As a result of Abraham's awareness of this about God, he was able to believe God when others would have given up. Even when things seemed *dead,* Abraham knew God could resurrect them. Even when things didn't *exist,* Abraham knew God could call them into being. This was the God of Abraham. Who is God to you? What kind of God do You have? The revelation of who we see God to be will create the faith dimension we are able to walk in. We must ask the Holy Spirit to bring revelation to us of the God of Abraham that we might have the same faith that Abraham walked in. As we do, we can see the same level of miracles that Abraham saw. Nothing will be impossible to us.

> *Lord, as I come before Your Courts, may I walk in a revelation of who You are that will bring me into a big faith. I desire to know You as the God of resurrection life and the One who calls nonexistent things into existence. Thank You for this, in Jesus's name, amen.*

LOOKING FOR FAITH

*I tell you that He will avenge them speedily. Nevertheless, when
the Son of Man comes, will He really find faith on the earth?*
—Luke 18:8

We are told that when the Lord returns, He will be looking for faith. In speaking the parable about the widow who got a verdict from the unjust judge, Jesus finished it with this declaration. He is proclaiming that God's faithfulness as the Judge of all the earth will birth real faith in His people. Or will we be hard-hearted and not allow the faithfulness of God to create faith in us? When the Lord will avenge us speedily from His position as Judge, will it birth a deep faith to believe Him? It is possible for the Lord to be true and faithful, yet we still not choose to believe Him. Real faith is not an emotion; it is a choice. Thomas said that unless he saw the print of the nails and the hole in Jesus's side he *would not believe.* He didn't say he *couldn't believe,* he said he *wouldn't believe* (John 20:24–25). As we operate in the Courts of Heaven, the faithfulness of God we encounter must birth faith in us. This is what Jesus is looking for. Has His faithfulness developed a faith in us that is precious and unshakable? Or are we fearful and yet unbelieving and uncertain whether the Lord can be trusted. As we operate in the Courts of Heaven and see God move in our behalf, may real genuine faith develop in us and be released through us.

> *Lord, as I stand before Your Courts, may faith rise in my heart.
> Forgive me for choosing not to believe. Make me courageous
> to believe You and be found faith filled in the midst of Your
> faithfulness. In Jesus's name, amen.*

NOVEMBER 14

GENUINE FAITH

Now the purpose of the commandment is love from a pure heart, from a good conscience, and from sincere faith.
—1 Timothy 1:5

The Lord desires these three things. It is what everything is for. Love from a pure heart, a good conscience absent of shame, and sincere, genuine faith. As the Lord works in us on a daily basis, He is seeking to fashion in us these three. Genuine faith is one of them. We really don't know if we have a *genuine faith* until it is tested. Will what has been formed in us through the Word of God and the ministry of the Holy Spirit hold up under scrutiny and pressure? Real faith that can pass the test is a precious thing. Peter called his faith, *a like precious faith that had been obtained by the righteousness of Jesus* (2 Pet. 1:1). Remember that satan through sifting wanted to destroy Peter's faith (Luke 22:31). Satan sought to turn Peter into a skeptic, cynic, and pessimist. Jesus, however, in the Courts of Heaven contended for Peter's faith (v. 32). Faith is of utmost importance. Without it we cannot please God or win victories (Heb. 11:6; 1 John 5:4). If satan can destroy genuine faith in us, he disempowers us from the purpose for which we were created. Jesus has contended for us in the Courts of Heaven so that genuine faith will be ours.

> *Lord, as I approach Your Courts, I agree with Your intercession that my faith might be strong and genuine. I pray I would have a precious faith that has passed the test. Thank You for finishing my faith that You have authored in me. In Jesus's name, amen.*

UNFINISHED FAITH

And to whom did He swear that they would not enter His rest,
but to those who did not obey? So we see that they could not
enter in because of unbelief. —Hebrews 3:18–19

In spite of all that God did for the children of Israel on their journey through the wilderness, they still rebelled in unbelief. When they came to the border of Canaan and it was time to pass over into their inheritance, they chose unbelief over faith. This was even though God had faithfully manifested Himself time after time as the One who would keep them, sustain them, and empower them. They still chose not to overcome the slave mentality that would not allow them to believe. Every test they went through in the wilderness was designed to show them God's faithfulness to His word and promises. Yet they did not allow this to cause faith to be born in their hearts. Therefore, they rebelled again when the spies returned with the report of how good the land was, *but* there were giants, walled cities, and iron chariots. They allowed the adversities to outweigh the goodness of what God had planned for them. As a result, the Lord *swore* they would not enter the land, rest, and promises He had made for them. They missed what God had.

> *Lord, as we approach Your Courts, we request that this spirit*
> *of unbelief would not be in us. We ask that all You have done*
> *will instead birth faith that will move forward to conquer in this*
> *season. May we not miss out on what You have for us because of*
> *unbelief. In Jesus's name, amen.*

THROUGH FAITH SUBDUED KINGDOMS

...who through faith subdued kingdoms, worked righteousness,
obtained promises, stopped the mouths of lions.
—Hebrews 11:33

Everything the people of God accomplished they did through faith. Their belief in God and what He had said was the empowering force of their feats and might. We are told these normal people accomplished supernatural things through faith. They are celebrated because of what they did through simple faith. One of the things listed is the *"subdued kingdoms."* They were able to bring kingdoms under the authority of the then expression of the Kingdom of God. This is what God told Adam and Eve to do before the fall. They were to subdue, take dominion, and rule over the earth (Gen. 1:28). The Garden of Eden was the expression of the Kingdom of God. Their job was to take what was in the Garden and transplant it into the rest of the earth, until the earth looked like Heaven. This is still our call today. We are here as God's people to subdue kingdoms. We are here to bring under the authority of God the different spheres in the earth. We do this by faith. In the natural it looks impossible. However, just like in the days of old, we by faith are able to see the rule of God, and that which opposes God becomes a part of the Kingdom of God. We are to be God's people of faith!

> *Lord, as we approach Your Courts, we ask that all that would claim a legal right to rule over portions of this earth be revoked. Let it be known that the earth is the Lord's and the fullness thereof (Ps. 24:1). Have for Yourself a Kingdom people full of faith who will subdue kingdoms in Your name. In Jesus's name, amen.*

THE SUBSTANCE
AND EVIDENCE OF FAITH

Now faith is the substance of things hoped for, the
evidence of things not seen. —Hebrews 11:1

Real faith is that which we possess in the spirit realm before we see something manifest in the natural. We by faith possess a substance in our spirit. This has come out of what we have *hoped for.* Hope is not faith, but hope is the breeding ground for faith. When we move from hope to faith, it is because we possess this substance in our inner man. We simply wait for that which we now possess in the inner parts to manifest in the outward realm. Faith is also us having an evidence of what isn't yet seen. Even though we may not see it yet, we have the evidence in our spirit that it is ours. This can occur through us hearing a word from the Lord. Romans 10:17 tells us that faith is the result of the living word of God having erupted and ignited in our spirit. When this happens, this substance and this evidence is placed in our spirit. From these we can contend until what we are holding inside is manifested in the natural. This is the way that mortal, normal, natural people accomplished such great things in God. May we too tap into this realm of faith, believe God, and see the glory of the Lord.

> *Lord, as we approach Your Court, we ask that we could function*
> *in real faith. Allow, we ask, Lord, that we would possess the*
> *substance and evidence of faith. Let what we hold in the inner*
> *places cause things to manifest in the natural. In Jesus's name,*
> *amen.*

FAITH AND THE SPOKEN WORD

...who, contrary to hope, in hope believed, so that he became the father of many nations, according to what was spoken, "So shall your descendants be." —Romans 4:18

The power of Abraham to walk in faith to apprehend the promises God made Him was based on what Abraham had heard from the Lord. Faith always has at its core and foundation a *word* from the Lord. This is why Romans 10:17 declares that faith comes through hearing the word of God and from God. Abraham had heard God say his descendants would be as the stars of the sky and the sand by the seashore. This word resonated in Abraham for decades, keeping him in faith. When we hear a word from God, we can believe with real biblical faith. We move from hoping to faith that possesses. Hope is something that anticipates the future. Faith, however, is present tense. It has an aggression about it that reaches into what might otherwise be in the future and pulls it into the now. This is why Hebrews 11:1 speaks of *"now faith."* As the word of the Lord creates real faith in us for supernatural things to occur, we move into agreement with that faith which is in our hearts. The result is the manifestation of God in our lives and in the earth today!

> *Lord, as I approach Your Courts, I request that I might hear a word from You that will birth faith in my heart. As this faith rises, allow me to move in agreement with it until there is a true manifestation in the earth of You and Your will. In Jesus's name, amen.*

FAITH AND AUTHORITY

And these signs will follow those who believe: In My name they
will cast out demons; they will speak with new tongues.
—Mark 16:17

Notice that the signs that follow *believing* is casting out demons. Demons respond only to authority. Real authority in the spirit realm is a result of biblical faith. When we function in faith, we produce in and through us an authority that requires demons to adhere to. This is why when dealing with devilish powers they seek to intimidate to pull us out of faith. If they can get us to question the Lord's power and ourselves and who we are in the Lord, then they can *sap* our authority. Authority too often is connected to *believing* the right things about God and about ourselves. If we doubt either, we lose the ability to function in the authority of God in the earth. Instead of ruling over we can be ruled over. The more we can be saturated in right believing, the more authority we can carry. This is why Jesus said in Mark 9:23 *if* we could believe all things are possible to those who believe. The more we operate in the faith realm, the more authority we can exercise. This will result in great breakthroughs and victories.

> *Lord, as I stand in Your Courts, I ask that I might believe. Help*
> *my unbelief, I pray. Let me increase in real spiritual authority in*
> *Your Courts and from Your throne. Allow my faith to move me*
> *into these new places of power and authority in You. In Jesus's*
> *name, amen.*

MUSTARD SEED FAITH

Then the disciples came to Jesus privately and said, "Why could we not cast it out?" So Jesus said to them, "Because of your unbelief; for assuredly, I say to you, if you have faith as a mustard seed, you will say to this mountain, 'Move from here to there,' and it will move; and nothing will be impossible for you."
—Matthew 17:19–20

Jesus said the reason for the disciples ineffectiveness was their unbelief. Their inability to remove a demon was because of lack of faith. Jesus explained the nature of faith. If they had faith as a mustard seed, which is the smallest of seeds, nothing would be impossible to them. When Jesus spoke of faith as a mustard seed, He wasn't just speaking of the size, but rather the potential. A seed has potential in it. Locked up in a seed is a harvest. Locked up in a seed is the ability to feed multitudes. Locked up in a seed is wealth when crops are sold. Jesus was speaking of the potential of the faith that was in them. The faith that was in them had earth-shaking ability. They needed to just unlock the potential by using the faith that was resident in them. Not only would demons be removed, but any other impossible thing could be done. Mountains that would stand in the way of God's purposes and their success would be picked up and displaced. This was the power of the faith that was in them, and it is also in us.

Lord, as we come before Your Courts, we repent for our unbelief. Forgive us for not using the faith You have given us and graciously deposited in us. Break us of spiritual laziness and teach us, we pray, how to unlock this powerful seed that resides in our spirit. In Jesus's name, amen.

STANDING IN FAITH

Therefore take up the whole armor of God, that you may be able to withstand in the evil day, and having done all, to stand.
—Ephesians 6:13

There is a place and a time when we have done everything we know to do. We have taken care of all responsibilities. We have been faithful with all circumstances as best we know how. We have sought the Lord and cried out to Him with all our hearts. We are told that in these times, we must *stand*. This implies in the midst of our waiting, we are staying in faith. We are not wavering but being strong, trusting that what we have heard from the Lord will transpire. This is what was reported of Abraham. In Romans 4:20 we are told that Abraham *did not stagger at God's promise but was strong in faith, giving glory to God.* This means he was *standing,* having done all. So as we wait on the fullness of God's promises to materialize, we must stand, not stagger because of passing time, and give glory to God. Worshipping the Lord is a critical piece to *"having done all, to stand."* As we worship the Lord and set our face to Him, we keep our faith in what He has promised. We are reminded of His greatness and how faithful He is. This empowers us to stand as we await on the fulfillment of the promises of God that has birthed faith for now and the future.

> *Lord, as I approach Your Courts, I ask that I might stand in faith. Even when it might appear that it is foolish to yet believe, Lord, let it be recorded that I take You at Your word and believe with a believing heart. Allow the fulfillment of all You have said to come. In Jesus's name, amen.*

THE FIGHT OF FAITH

Fight the good fight of faith, lay hold on eternal life, to which you were also called and have confessed the good confession in the presence of many witnesses. —1 Timothy 6:12

Faith is a fight. We use our faith to fight in the spirit world and possess all that has been given to us through the death, burial, resurrection, and ascension of Jesus Christ. Everything we need for life and godliness is already ours and has been granted (2 Pet. 1:3). However, we must fight the good fight of faith to possess what has been granted to us. This is what Joshua and Israel had to do. God had *given* them the land (Josh. 18:3). They, however, had to aggressively march through the land and combat and contend for it until every parcel became theirs. There were enemies to take down and remove. As they moved in agreement with the word of the Lord and through the grace and empowerment of the Lord, they possessed their inheritance. We too must use our faith and fight for what is rightfully ours. We must contend for all that Jesus's sacrifice provided for. Healings, salvation, prosperity, harmony, peace, long life, and other realms are rightfully ours. Learn to use your faith and fight for that which the Lord has given. With our faith we possess all that belongs to us.

I am asking You, Lord, as I stand before Your Courts, that I might fight with my faith for what it rightfully mine. I don't want to neglect or give away any part. I arise in faith and seek to possess all that You have already graciously given me. Let it be recorded and testified before Your Courts that this is my heart and desire. In Jesus's name, amen.

SEEN FAITH

And in Lystra a certain man without strength in his feet was sitting, a cripple from his mother's womb, who had never walked. This man heard Paul speaking. Paul, observing him intently and seeing that he had faith to be healed.
—Acts 14:8–9

As this lame man heard Paul speaking, teaching, and preaching, Paul *saw* his faith. Perhaps Paul discerned it in the spirit world. Or maybe there was something about the man's *body language* that caused Paul to know faith to be healed was in his heart. Perhaps it was a combination of the two. Regardless, there was an awareness that this man was now in a place where he was ready to believe God for something that had never happened before. He was a cripple from his mother's womb. He had never walked. Yet there was a rising of faith in his heart and Paul saw it. The Bible says that when the four let the lame man down through the roof Jesus *saw* their faith (Mark 2:5). Because He saw their faith, Jesus declared the word, forgave the man, and spoke healing into his life. Real faith can be seen. Is there a faith in us that can be seen? Is our faith apparent? This means that faith is not just an inward attitude or even thought process. Faith has action attached to it. If we really believe, there will be a corresponding action attached to our faith. When this occurs, our faith is then connecting to the power of God. May we have *seen faith,* a real biblical faith that trusts God and alters our activities for others to witness.

Lord, I approach Your Courts. May it be recorded before You that I have faith that can be seen. My faith has been taken out of the unseen realm and is being manifest in the natural. Let it be known that I believe the Lord and my confidence is in You. In Jesus's name, amen.

FAITH AND WORKS

But someone will say, "You have faith, and I have works."
Show me your faith without your works, and I will show
you my faith by my works. —James 2:18

James is making the case that faith requires works. So often in this New Testament era works are frowned on. If we are *working* to obtain righteousness, this can never be done. The Apostle Paul clearly said no one will be justified by their works (Gal. 2:16). However, biblical faith has works attached to it. These are not works seeking to be justified but works flowing from a heart of faith that is believing God. These works are demonstrations of a faith in God that from a loving relationship cannot be thwarted or averted. It would be literally impossible to stop these activities that flow out of this heart that delights in believing the Lord. The new nature that we have received from the Lord at our new birth will produce in us and from us works consistent with this nature (1 John 3:9). We will progressively by *nature* do the works of God. This is a manifestation of faith that is working in us and through us. Faith and works begin to work together as inseparable manifestations of the nature of God that is working deeply in us.

> *Lord, as I come before Your Courts, would you allow the nature*
> *of God to be in me to produce works in me that manifest my faith.*
> *Let there be a connection between what I believe and how I live*
> *my life. May I demonstrate who You are in the life I live by faith.*
> *In Jesus's name, amen.*

THE SPIRIT OF FAITH

And since we have the same spirit of faith, according to what is written, "I believed and therefore I spoke," we also believe and therefore speak. —2 Corinthians 4:13

Faith is a spirit. This spirit of faith creates a voice. When the spirit of faith is in us, we believe and therefore speak. You can always tell when a person is of faith because of their speech. They are full of hope; they are positive; they are looking forward to the future. This is because of the spirit of faith in them. On the other hand, when this spirit of faith is not present, people can be negative, judgmental, and critical. The key is not necessarily to try and control our mouth, as important as this is. The key is to have within us this spirit of faith that changes the way we view life and the world. When we see life through this spirit of faith, we will speak in agreement with this. The result will be words flowing from us that are full of life. We will actually be able to speak into being the life that we desire, even as God Himself did (Heb. 11:3). We are told that the worlds were framed and created by the words that came from the mouth of God. God Himself spoke in faith. His words carried the creative force that shaped the world. We too can speak the words that frame our world from the spirit of faith. We will see the kind of world we desire to have fashioned as we operate in this spirit of faith.

> *Lord, as I approach Your Courts, I ask that the spirit of faith might rise in my heart. May my words be in agreement with faith even as Your words from faith created the worlds. I thank You that I speak in agreement with the spirit of faith and not the spirit of this world. In Jesus's name, amen.*

AUTHOR AND FINISHER OF FAITH

...looking unto Jesus, the author and finisher of our faith, who for the joy that was set before Him endured the cross, despising the shame, and has sat down at the right hand of the throne of God. —Hebrews 12:2

We are told that it is the Lord Jesus who began our faith and will also finish it. Our faith is His own personal project. He is committed to bringing us to a place of mature faith throughout the duration of our lives. The Scripture mentions no faith, little faith, and even great faith. We should desire to see the Lord walk us through the process of developing great faith that He can use to birth His intent in the earth. Only by faith is God's will done. Unless He can find a person of faith to work through, He cannot accomplish what He desires. The passion, will, and intent of the Lord can be frustrated. Therefore, He is committed to increasing and developing our faith. We must cooperate, but it is the working of the Lord that causes our faith to grow. Through the Word of God, the person of the Holy Spirit, and even the testing of our faith, the Lord increases our faith to believe Him and walk in agreement with His purposes. As we move through life, one of the main things that should occur is the increasing of our faith. All of us will go through places of testing, trials, and having the Lord invest in our lives through the Holy Spirit and His Word. The question is will we allow Him to mature our faith and bring us to the place of gaining a full harvest in us and through us? He is the author and the finisher and will complete what He started as we agree and cooperate with Him.

Lord, as I stand before Your Courts, I ask that You might mature my faith. Would You as the author and finisher perfect that which concerns me, that I might be of ultimate use to You. I yield my heart to You and say yes to You always. In Jesus's name, amen.

NO FAITH

But He said to them, "Why are you so fearful?
How is it that you have no faith?" —Mark 4:40

The disciples were on a boat in a storm and were afraid. In their fear they cried to Jesus, who was asleep in the boat during the storm. They thought they were going to drown and perish. When Jesus awoke, He rebuked the wind, spoke to the waves, and silenced the storm. He then asked them, *"How is it you have no faith?"* Jesus said their fear was a sign that they had *no faith.* Despite having walked with Jesus for a while, having seen His miracles and heard His words, when they went through the storm, they were sure they were perishing. Yet Jesus was in the same storm in perfect peace, at rest and sleeping. All of us know what it is to be afraid. The issue is, do we allow our fear to overcome us? Does it move us from an awareness of a dangerous situation to a place of panic? The disciples were not just aware of how dangerous things were; they were having a *panic attack.* Jesus, however, knew the authority He carried. He understood this storm was under His rulership. Many times the reason we have *no faith* is because we forget the authority we have. If we can simply believe not only who the Lord is in us, but who we are in the Lord as well, then panic will not set in. We will be able to survive and even thrive in dangerous situations without panic taking hold. We will not allow ourselves to have no faith. We will believe to the saving of our souls.

> *Lord, as we approach Your Courts, we repent for having no faith. Forgive us for allowing fear and panic to rule our lives. We ask that it might be recorded before Your Courts that we are pressing in to faith and believing You rather than being ruled by fear. In Jesus's name, amen.*

LITTLE FAITH

But when he saw that the wind was boisterous, he was afraid;
and beginning to sink he cried out, saying, "Lord, save me!"
And immediately Jesus stretched out His hand and caught him,
and said to him, "O you of little faith, why did you doubt?"
—Matthew 14:30–31

Peter has stepped out on the water to walk to Jesus. He has done the impossible. However, as he is standing on the water, he becomes aware of the wind and how strong it is. This causes him to move from faith and to begin to sink. He cries out to Jesus to save him, and of course He does. The Lord, however, asks Peter why he doubted. He also tells him he is of *"little faith."* Little faith staggers and shakes when the test comes. Any of us can have some faith when things are good. However, when the storms come, it will manifest the level our faith has grown to presently. Peter has faith, it is just little faith. This is revealed by the storm. The Lord will allow storms to come at times to unveil for us where we have grown to in our faith. Peter later considers his faith stronger than it was. He boldly declares that he would die with and for the Lord, only to discover that when tested he denies Him to his shame (Mark 14:29–31). Even though these times of revelation about ourselves can be painful, they are necessary to move us to the next places of faith. It is never pleasant to come to the realization that we are not what we thought; we haven't arrived to where we thought we had come to. The Lord, out of His love and goodness toward us, allows this for our maturity process. He grows our faith from little to great as we wrestle through these times and moments.

> *Lord, as I approach Your Courts, I thank You that You are*
> *faithful as the author and finisher of my faith. Thank You that*

in teaching me how to walk in the supernatural with You, You help me keep my eyes on You that I might go from faith to faith in my growth and experience. In Jesus's name, amen.

NOVEMBER 29

GREAT FAITH

Then Jesus answered and said to her, "O woman, great is your faith! Let it be to you as you desire." And her daughter was healed from that very hour. —Matthew 15:28

When the Gentile woman came to Jesus to heal her daughter, she was persistent and would not stop. Even though at first Jesus denied her because He was sent only to the lost sheep of Israel, her unrelenting request caused Him to respond to her. Her consistent seeking of Him moved Jesus to declare her daughter healed and to proclaim this woman to have *great faith*. One of the characteristics of great faith is persistent seeking of the Lord and a heart that will not be detoured or denied. Hebrews 11:6 tells us that God is a rewarder of those who *diligently* seek Him. Great faith will drive us to keep pursuing when others quit. Our revelation of the goodness of God and our faith in His kindness will motivate us to not stop until we see the breakthrough we know only He can bring. This was one of the things that created great faith in this woman. She understood Jesus was her last and only option. If He didn't intervene, only heartache, pain, and sorrow would be hers and her daughter's. These things combined drove her to not stop even when others would seem to push her away and to discourage her efforts. Jesus was moved by her great faith that would not be denied. Do we have this kind of faith that births this realm of persistence? It clearly is of great value and worth to the Lord. My desire is that I would have this level of faith that would drive me forward in the face of all adversity. We will see God's glory revealed.

> *Lord, as we come before Your Courts, I ask that great faith might be formed in me. Would You allow a persistent heart that will not stop believing You to be in me? As it is, would You allow it to speak before Your Courts in my behalf and cause victory to come? In Jesus's name, amen.*

INCREASE OUR FAITH

And the apostles said to the Lord, "Increase our faith." So the
Lord said, "If you have faith as a mustard seed, you can say to
this mulberry tree, 'Be pulled up by the roots and be planted in
the sea,' and it would obey you." —Luke 17:5–6

The apostles came to the awareness that they were insufficient in their faith. They did not have what was necessary for the job they had and were being commissioned to do. Therefore, they requested that Jesus "increase our faith." Perhaps they were asking Jesus to just magically and with supernatural power cause them to have a new level of faith. However, in response to their request Jesus spoke to them about a mustard seed. A *seed's* potential is only unlocked if it is *planted.* Jesus was letting them know that the increase of faith would be a result of taking what they had and using it. They had to be willing to plant their seed of faith and allow it to grow. As they faithfully handled the seed of faith they possessed, they would grow in the authority and power of the Spirit to speak to rooted things and see them dislodged and removed. Jesus promised that what seemed immovable would obey them as they learned to use the faith they had been entrusted with. Increase of faith comes on purpose. In other words, we must intentionally use our faith if we are to see it grow. This requires that we take risks and step into the unknown of the supernatural realm. It is much easier, convenient, and safe to stay in the natural. However, our faith will not grow and increase there. We must move in faith and take risks that will unlock supernatural powers in our behalf. As we listen for the voice of God and move at its beckoning, we step into a journey of faith that will produce excitement and awesome results. Our faith will increase as we witness the faithfulness of God.

As I approach Your Courts, Lord, I ask that my faith might increase. Would You allow it to be known before Your Courts that I desire new levels of faith? I do not want to stagnate or stay the same. Move me into new places in You, I ask. In Jesus's name, amen.

FAITH TO FAITH

For in it the righteousness of God is revealed from faith to faith;
as it is written, "The just shall live by faith." —Romans 1:17

We see that we go from faith to faith. This means that the growth of our faith is a progressive and step-by-step experience. Notice that the *righteousness of God* is revealed through this process. We see and become acquainted with the faithfulness of God as He shows us His salvation as we grow in our faith. In other words, the more faith we operate in, the more the revelation of God's goodness, righteousness, and display of His power is seen. If we desire to see a progressive unveiling of God's works in our behalf, it will require that we learn how to live in and from the faith realm. *"The just shall live by faith."* Those who are justified and vindicated by the Lord in His eyes and the eyes of others, are those who have chosen to live by faith. They have placed their confidence in the Lord and are progressively growing in their ability to believe God. They become convinced that God is unable to fail them. This rock solid conviction causes them to live a life of faith that is even increasing and going from faith to faith. Therefore, they are also seeing the supernatural hand of God move for them with every increasing frequency and strength. Doubts, fears, and unbelief vanish as faith takes more and more of their heart. It becomes their immense pleasure to believe the Lord and move from faith to faith.

> *As I approach Your Courts, would You let it be testified that I am moving in faith? Would You let it be known that I believe You? May this speak before You and be verified in Your Courts. I ask that this record of my increasing faith be known as decisions are rendered in my behalf. In Jesus's name, amen.*

FAITH AND THE GLORY OF GOD

Jesus said to her, "Did I not say to you that if you would believe you would see the glory of God?" —John 11:40

As Jesus is standing at the tomb of Lazarus, Martha resists rolling the stone away from his grave. He has been dead four days and has begun to decay. Jesus, however, has promised that Lazarus will rise. Martha must decide if she is willing to believe. Her choice in this moment will determine whether the glory of God through the resurrection of her brother, Lazarus, will be revealed. Will she allow the stone on the mouth of the tomb to be rolled away? Her faith or the lack of it will determine if God's glory is seen or not. The manifestation of the glory of God is always connected to someone's faith. If we are to see God's glory in miracles, breakthroughs, and victories, we must be willing to believe. It is highly risky. If we believe and nothing happens, then the stench of that failure is known. If we believe and nothing happens, then the shame and ridicule of the failure is seen. If, however, we believe and God's glory manifests, then not only are we and others touched, generations can be empowered by the glory of God that is seen in these moments. This is what happened at this tomb. Jesus manifests the glory of God. Lazarus is brought out of the tomb. This miracle is still affecting people more than two thousand years later. All because Martha chose to believe in a moment of time. May we believe and see the glory of God also.

> *Lord, I ask that I have the faith to believe You in intense moments. May I choose faith over fear. Would You allow this to speak before Your Courts, that this one has chosen to believe You? As this is known, allow Your power to be known and Your glory to be seen. In Jesus's name, amen.*

UNLOCKING WEALTH FROM THE COURTS OF HEAVEN

For you know the grace of our Lord Jesus Christ, that though He was rich, yet for your sakes He became poor, that you through His poverty might become rich. —2 Corinthians 8:9

Many read this Scripture and immediately place it in a spiritual context. They consider that Paul was speaking of being spiritually rich. However, Second Corinthians 8 and 9 are explicitly about finances, and Paul urges them to give. Therefore, when Paul declares that what Jesus did for us on the cross can *make* us rich, he is speaking not just spiritually but naturally as well. It is God's will for us to prosper and even be rich. God declared in Deuteronomy 8:18 that He needs a wealthy people for His purposes to be done in the earth. The devil knows this as well. He, therefore, builds cases against us to prohibit us from gaining the benefit of what Jesus did for us on the cross. Part of that benefit is prosperity, wealth, and even being rich. We cannot see God's purposes in the earth accomplished without the wealth to do it. Whether it is the evangelism of nations, the reformation of culture, or us and our families being blessed and empowered with finances. We must know how to address these issues in the Courts of Heaven and see any legal right the devil is claiming be revoked and removed. The first thing, however, is *believing* that God wants us to be prosperous and undoing any poverty mindset that would say it's more spiritual to be poor. This is not true. We must repent for believing this is the heart of God.

> *Lord, as we approach Your Courts, we agree with Your Word and heart that it is Your will for us to prosper. We repent and ask that any agreement with the poverty spirit that might be in force would now be revoked. We desire to prosper, in Jesus's name, amen.*

DISOWNING THE POVERTY SPIRIT

A little sleep, a little slumber, a little folding of the hands to
sleep—so shall your poverty come on you like a prowler, and
your need like an armed man. —Proverbs 6:10–11

Notice this Scripture declares *your* poverty. In other words, poverty will try to claim you as its own. Also, we must be mindful that poverty is not a condition; it can be a demonic spirit that will not allow us to prosper. This is why it is referred to as a *"prowler"* or an *"armed man."* In other words, it is an entity with a mind and desire to control and possess you. It wants to fashion the future you have rather than allowing God to do this. If we are going to be free from this spirit of poverty and prosper, we must renounce its rights to own us and control us. This can be done by repenting for any attitude, action, or agreement we have entered into with this spirit. Also, we should deal with any iniquitous activity from our bloodline that would be granting this demonic thing the right to function against us. Once this is done, we must repent of every mindset we have that would allow this spirit of poverty to possess us and our destinies, and we must change our thinking. Once we have set things legally in place to disown this spirit, we must with aggression in the spirit world revoke and rebuke this thing and declare its power against us null and void. We will then be freed from this spirit and allowed to prosper, accumulate wealth, and even become rich!

> *Lord, as I approach Your Courts, I ask that every claim of the*
> *spirit of poverty to own me be revoked. I repent of all activities,*
> *agreements, attitudes, thought processes, and any and all iniquity*
> *in my bloodline that would allow this thing to operate. Let every*
> *claim now be annulled. I also with great spiritual aggression*
> *declare the rights of this spirit revoked and that it must now*
> *leave me, in Jesus's name, amen.*

WEALTH TRANSFERRED

*For God gives wisdom and knowledge and joy to a man who
is good in His sight; but to the sinner He gives the work of
gathering and collecting, that he may give to him who is good
before God. This also is vanity and grasping for the wind.*
—Ecclesiastes 2:26

The Lord is said to use the sinner to gather and collect so that God can then give it to the one who is good before God. We see this happening several places in Scripture where there was a transference of wealth. One of those places is when Israel, as a band of slaves with no material wealth, left Egypt with all its riches. The Scripture says that because they asked the Egyptians for their wealth, they gave it to them, and they plundered the whole nation (Exod. 12:35–36). The Lord gave them favor in the eyes of the Egyptians so that they did the unthinkable: they gave them their gold, silver, and their precious things. The result was a great transfer of wealth from Egypt to the nation of Israel. Israel would now have what they needed to build God a house in the wilderness. Why else would a group of former slaves need such wealth. There were no stores or shops in the wilderness. They had what God would require to build His dwelling place among them. We must realize that a transference of wealth is not just so we can be blessed. It is so we can fulfill the mandate of God in the earth. As we allow Him to work in our hearts this desire, we can then be trusted with prosperity, wealth, and riches. May the great wealth transfer come into the hands of us the people of God. As it does, may we be abundantly blessed but also empowered to fulfill God's desire.

*As we approach Your Courts, Lord, would You allow our passion
to see Your will done in the earth? May we be trusted with wealth
not just so we can be blessed, but also so Your pleasure might be
done. In Jesus's name, amen.*

WEALTH AND GOOD MEN

A good man leaves an inheritance to his children's children, but the wealth of the sinner is stored up for the righteous.
—Proverbs 13:22

The righteous will be trusted with the wealth of this world. Many believe it is unbiblical and unspiritual to care about wealth. Nothing could be further from the truth. Without wealth God's agenda cannot and will not be accomplished. The Lord declares that a *good man* doesn't just bless his children but will have enough to bless even his grandchildren. God declares the righteous are His appointees to steward any wealth the sinners have accumulated. When the Bible calls someone *good*, it is speaking of a deep heart of kindness, wholesomeness, and integrity. It speaks of an inability to do evil. This is why Jesus said there is only One who is good—God (Matt.19:17). God is the only One who carries the qualities that would correspond with being good. However, as we are transformed and renewed in our salvation, we can begin to exude at least some of those qualities. This will enable us to be the good and righteous of the Lord that God might trust us with the wealth the sinners have stored up. As we are evaluated by the Lord, may we be those He can entrust with His wealth. After all, all the silver and gold belong to Him (Hag. 2:8). He will trust it to those who from His goodness and righteousness will steward it for His desires and longings.

> As we approach Your Courts, we ask that we might be found acceptable before You. May we be good before You and may we be righteous. We humbly ask that we might be considered as ones who You allow to steward the wealth that ultimately belongs to You. In Jesus's name, amen.

MEETING URGENT NEEDS

And let our people also learn to maintain good works, to meet
urgent needs, that they may not be unfruitful. —Titus 3:14

Understanding the purpose of a thing is very important. Otherwise we misuse it. This is true for wealth and riches. If we don't understand what it is for, we will assign it a purpose contrary to why God created it. One of the purposes of wealth is to meet urgent needs and to not be unfruitful. Paul is admonishing those who are connected to him to be gainfully employed. This is so they can meet these urgent needs. The word *urgent* in the Greek is *anagkaios*. It means *close, near, necessity.* It comes from the word *anagkē,* which means *constraint, distress.* So *urgent needs* place constraints and distress on our lives when they are unmet. There is no pressure like financial pressure. Many people live their entire lives under this pressure. Their constant need to war against just *getting by,* causes them to become unfruitful. Paul admonished his company and people to work and have prosperous businesses so their needs would not distract from their Kingdom assignment. Some think they need to be in *full-time* ministry, yet the supply is not there. They try to make it work, but they and their families suffer. They think that if they worked in the business realm, they would be distracted from ministry. The financial need they and their families suffer is more of a distraction than if they had a job. God desires us to prosper and not live under the distress of financial lack. He has a plan for your success and blessing.

> *Lord, as I stand before Your Courts, I ask that every constraint*
> *and distress I am living under because of the lack of finances*
> *would be lifted. Help me, Lord, to listen to You and abide in*
> *Your wisdom for me. You, Lord, have a strategy for my financial*
> *future. In Jesus's name, amen.*

WEALTH AND INFLUENCE

There was a little city with few men in it; and a great king came
against it, besieged it, and built great snares around it. Now
there was found in it a poor wise man, and he by his wisdom
delivered the city. Yet no one remembered that same poor man.
—Ecclesiastes 9:14–15

Even though the poor man in his wisdom delivered the city from the attack, his poverty caused him not to be remembered. This demonstrates that even though we have wisdom that can bless society, without money we are denied the influence to do so. It is amazing that through his wisdom the city was saved, yet his poverty denied him a consistent place of influence in the city even though he had much to offer. The principle is that wealth affords us influence. Wealth is not just about having money. Wealth is about having influence as a result of the money. This is why the riches of the wicked are to be transferred into the hands of the righteous (Prov. 13:22). It is not just so we can finance our agenda and what the Lord desires. It is so we can be granted influence for ongoing change in cities, states, territories, provinces, nations, and continents. This is the only way our cultures and societies will become expressions of the Kingdom of God. When those who have the money are righteous and can wield their influence for God's Kingdom agenda, change will come into our world. This is why the devil resists the godly from having wealth. We must contend in the Courts for any and all legal right satan would use to stop this transference of wealth. Then the righteous will gain the influence necessary for change.

As we approach Your Courts, O Lord, we ask for wealth. Not just
so we can be blessed and comfortable, but so that we can have the
influence to alter society into a Kingdom expression. Let every
legal thing the devil would use to resist this transference of wealth
be annulled and revoked. In Jesus's name, amen.

ENJOYING WEALTH

*Command those who are rich in this present age not to be
haughty, nor to trust in uncertain riches but in the living God,
who gives us richly all things to enjoy.* —1 Timothy 6:17

Those who are wealthy in this life must never place their confidence in their wealth. Proverbs 23:5 says that riches can suddenly make wings and fly away. In other words, it can go as fast as it came, or faster. Our confidence must always be in the Lord. However, we are told that riches are to be enjoyed. It actually declares that God gives us *things* to enjoy. These things are the result of the riches that we have. No one should ever feel guilty about enjoying what God has blessed them with. If He has trusted you with wealth, then one of the purposes of it is to enjoy it. The Lord is not a miser who does not want us to enjoy this life. Our ultimate reward is to be in the next age. However, God loves to bless us as His people. As a good Father, He loves to see His children enjoying themselves. As we steward the wealth and blessings we are entrusted with, we must always remember the Lord. In fact, Deuteronomy 8:11–14 exhorts us to never forget the Lord in the midst of what He has blessed us with. We must always remember that He is our source. Developing and maintaining a thankful heart before Him concerning any wealth we have is paramount. This will keep us from forgetting God, the source of our blessings, and also allow us to enjoy the wealth and riches entrusted to our care.

> *As we approach Your Courts, Lord, we ask that we might enjoy
> the things You have richly blessed us with. Thank You, Lord, that
> You are our source. All good things come from You. Therefore,
> as we enjoy Your wealth poured into our life, we do not forget
> You. May it be recorded in Heaven before Your Courts that we
> acknowledge You in this. Let this speak before You. In Jesus's
> name, amen.*

REVOKING THE SPIRIT OF RELIGION

*The thief does not come except to steal, and to kill, and to
destroy. I have come that they may have life, and that they may
have it more abundantly. —John 10:10*

Jesus promised abundant life. This doesn't just mean financially, but it is included. Abundant life is difficult to have if there is no financial blessing and we are in need. The thief, which is the devil, wants to steal, kill, and destroy. One of the ways he does this is through the religious spirit. In regard to prosperity, the religious spirit makes people think that to be poor is noble and spiritual. Nothing could be further from the truth. Money doesn't determine whether we are spiritual. However, the religious spirit would criticize prosperity, and make people judge anything that would declare God wants His people financially blessed. Without the blessing of the Lord financially, we will not be able to accomplish the commission the Lord left us. We will not be able to evangelize the world, disciple nations, or reform cities. All of this requires money. We must break any and all agreements with the religious spirit that would think otherwise and believe God's desire is to prosper us. Otherwise this spirit will have a legal right to make a claim before the Courts of Heaven to keep us stymied in our accumulation of wealth. We must ask that our minds might be freed from this religious spirit. Then we should ask that our minds might be renewed with the true principles of the Word of God concerning His heart to bless and prosper us. If we can be freed from this religious spirit, we can then believe God for the prosperity that He has promised us in His Word.

> *As I approach Your Courts, Lord, I ask that any and all agreements
> with the spirit of religion would be annulled and revoked. Let my
> mind go free from this spirit's influence and its fashioning of my
> future. I believe Your promise of abundant life. I believe this includes
> financial blessing. Let it be mine, I pray, in Jesus's name, amen.*

REVOKING UNFAITHFUL STEWARDSHIP

"Is it time for you yourselves to dwell in your paneled houses,
and this temple to lie in ruins?" Now therefore, thus says the
Lord of hosts: "Consider your ways! You have sown much, and
bring in little; you eat, but do not have enough; you drink, but
you are not filled with drink; you clothe yourselves, but no one is
warm; and he who earns wages, earns wages to put into
a bag with holes." —Haggai 1:4–6

The people of Israel had been sent back to rebuild the temple, the city of Jerusalem, and the nation. However, they had instead taken the provision of the Lord appointed for this and used it to build their own houses. They had in fact set their houses ahead of and instead of the house of God. This lack of properly stewarding what they had access to caused a lack of prosperity. They had little instead of much, not enough, unmet dreams and aspirations, and a devouring of finances. This was all because they had not properly stewarded what God had set in their control. They had misappropriated funds designated for the house of God. It wasn't that God was against them having nice houses. The problem was they had put their own houses ahead of the house of the Lord. They had violated the principle of seeking first the Kingdom of God (Matt. 6:33). If there are places in our lives, history, or bloodlines where we have mishandled finances, satan can use this to build a case against us. We must repent of this, change anything we need to, and ask for the blood of the Lamb to speak in our behalf (Heb. 12:24). Once this silences the accusation of improper stewardship, these claims of the devil will have no more power against us. The result will be a blessing of the Lord that can overtake us and bring us to new realms of accumulating wealth.

> *As we approach Your Courts, O Lord, we ask that every place we have not stewarded properly what You trusted us with, may be forgiven. We ask that the blood of Jesus might speak for us. We also ask that if we have misused that which You designated for Your house, please, Lord, forgive us. Revoke satan's claims against us, we pray. In Jesus's name, amen.*

DEMONIC COVENANTS

Because you have said, "We have made a covenant with death,
and with Sheol we are in agreement. When the overflowing
scourge passes through, it will not come to us, for we have made
lies our refuge, and under falsehood we have hidden ourselves."
—Isaiah 28:15

The people of God had actually made a covenant with demonic powers and were trusting in them for protection and provision. If this has happened in our bloodlines, then these devilish entities will continue to claim us and our lineage. Should those who came before us, having made an agreement with the "other gods" for protection, provision, rain in season or other "benefits" to their lives, then these demons claim legal authority to rule over us and dominate certain aspects of our lives. This can include the financial realm, especially if we are believers in Jesus and have a heart to bless the Kingdom of God. These demon powers use this to stop people's favor, undo business deals, restrict creative ideas, and stop other means to prosperity. We must come before the Courts of Heaven and see the rights they claim be revoked and removed. When this is done, that which is restraining the breakthrough into prosperity, wealth, and riches can be removed. We will become free to increase. That which hasn't seemed to produce before can begin to produce now. This is because the legal rights satan claims as a result of a covenant in our bloodlines and history has now been annulled.

> *As I approach Your Courts, Lord, I ask that any covenant with*
> *the power of darkness made in my bloodline be revoked. I give*
> *back anything these powers would say I have gained from them.*
> *I ask and declare that I only want what Jesus has for me. I am*
> *His, bought by His blood. Let me now prosper and increase, in*
> *Jesus's name, amen.*

TRUST IN THE FLESH

Thus says the Lord: "Cursed is the man who trusts in man and
makes flesh his strength, whose heart departs from the Lord.
For he shall be like a shrub in the desert, and shall not see
when good comes, but shall inhabit the parched places in the
wilderness, in a salt land which is not inhabited."
—Jeremiah 17:5–6

If our confidence is in the flesh and its abilities and we do not factor in the
supernatural of God, we can make wrong decisions. We are actually told that
we will not see when good comes. This means we will miss opportunities that
would otherwise cause us to prosper. We will disregard them because we are
making decisions only from a natural perspective. We are not seeing as God
sees. The result will be us inhabiting the parched places of the wilderness. In
other words, we will vanquish in the place where there is no fruitfulness. This is
all connected to a curse on the one who trusts in the natural realm more than in
God and His ways. The enemy will use this to build a case against us and cause
us not to prosper. We must repent for the places we have trusted man and his
strength instead of believing in the Lord and His Word. Notice also that this
causes our heart to depart from the Lord. We leave a vital, loving relationship
with the Lord because of a misguided approach to life. May we get our eyes back
on the Lord and focus intently on Him. The result will be seeing what others are
missing and the gaining of prosperity it can bring.

> *Lord, as I approach Your Courts, I repent for any place I have*
> *trusted flesh and even my own strength rather than Yours.*
> *I ask that my attention might be focused again on You, that I*
> *might believe You, Your word, and Your ways. Let any claim*

against me by the devil now be revoked, as I set my heart fully toward You again. Open my eyes to see that I might not miss the opportunities You set before me. In Jesus's name, amen.

DECEMBER 14

OPERATING IN GRACE

Is it not lawful for me to do what I wish with my own things?
Or is your eye evil because I am good? —Matthew 20:15

Jesus tells the story of a vineyard owner who hires laborers at different times of day. Some are hired at the last hour and work only that time, yet they are paid the same amount as those who labored all day. Those who worked the longest are upset because they only get paid what they had *agreed* to. The last, however, are paid on the basis of *whatever was right.* In other words, they trusted in the goodness, kindness, and generosity of the owner of the vineyard. As a result of this they received much more than those who had a contract. The lesson is we must *work* out of His grace and trust the reward to Him. When we serve Him from this place, He delights in rewarding us greatly. Even in the realm of prosperity in this life should we apply this principle. When we serve Him from grace, the renumeration is much greater. The Lord takes much delight and joy in seeing His servants prosper (Ps. 35:27). He is actually looking for those who will serve Him from grace. When these are found, He uses them to manifest His goodness for others to see. The blessing and increase He bestows on our lives are used to challenge the perspective so many have of God. He removes ideas that He is a hard and even cruel God and replaces it with the correct concept that He is liberally generous toward us.

> *As I approach Your Courts, Lord, I serve You from grace. I ask that I would not serve You from law but from the goodness of who You are. As I do, Lord, use me to challenge the idea others have of You. Let them see in me the goodness of God manifested as Your prosperity overtakes and overruns me. In Jesus's name, amen.*

THE GIFT OF GOD

As for every man to whom God has given riches and wealth,
and given him power to eat of it, to receive his heritage and
rejoice in his labor—this is the gift of God. —Ecclesiastes 5:19

Not everyone enjoys the blessing of having wealth. The wealth some have actually causes them heartache and pain. However, we are told that when we have wealth, experience prosperity, and get to enjoy it, this is God's gift to us. The key to enjoying the wealth God might have trusted us with is to possess it and not allow it to possess us. In other words, no matter how much we might have, it must always be viewed in a proper perspective. We must never see it as our source, but rather the Lord. When this is true, we are free to enjoy the goodness of the Lord in what He has blessed and trusted us with. Notice in this Scripture that we are told *God has given* us this wealth. We understand that our own power and might did not produce it. We may have worked and sought to be faithful, but it was the blessing of the Lord that made us rich with no sorrow added to it (Prov. 10:22). Many people work hard, but not all prosper. Prosperity is the result of the blessing of God on someone's life. When we know this, we are freed to realize it is the goodness of God that has trusted us with this. There are responsibilities that go with this, but I am also free to enjoy and eat of the goodness of the Lord that He has afforded me.

> *Lord, as I come before Your Courts, I thank You for the blessing*
> *that makes me rich and adds no sorrow with it. I recognize You*
> *as the giver all good gifts. Help me to enjoy the blessings You have*
> *and do bestow on Me. I worship You and magnify You for Your*
> *goodness to me. In Jesus's name, amen.*

GOD OF THE OPENED HAND

You open Your hand and satisfy the desire of every living thing.
—Psalm 145:16

The Lord is not the God of the closed hand or fist. He is the God of the opened hand, who loves to satisfy His creation with good things. We must recognize the Lord's heart and posture toward us. He is not seeking to keep things from us or to withhold what is good. He delights in blessing every living thing in His creation. Without this awareness we will have a wrong perspective of who God is. With this right idea, however, we can move in faith and confidence of who He is toward us. This is a basic issue that has to be settled. Many, because of religion, theology, experience, and formed belief systems, consider that God doesn't want us to prosper. At least they believe this is of no interest to Him one way or the other. Provision for life, however, is basic to the quality of life we can live. If we are certain that it is the passion of God to *open His hand* and satisfy us, we can believe He is a good God who delights in the prosperity of His servants (Ps. 35:27). The word *satisfy* in Hebrew is *saba`*. It means "to fill to satisfaction, have enough, be weary of." In other words, when God opens His hand, His provision is so abundant that we can even become *weary* of it. Wow! This is not a negative; it is just letting us know that when God provides, it is in superabundance and not just enough to get by. He *satisfies us!* In His hand is such blessing that we never want again.

> *Lord, as I approach Your Courts, let it be known that I believe You are the God of the opened hand. Your provision is so abundant that we as Your people will not want (Ps. 23:1). Thank You that from Your Courts there is a release of this, which I believe and trust You for. In Jesus's name, amen.*

HEALING FROM THE COURTS OF HEAVEN

Surely He has borne our griefs and carried our sorrows; yet we esteemed Him stricken, smitten by God, and afflicted.
—Isaiah 53:4

The word *griefs* is the Hebrew word *choliy*, which means *malady, disease, sickness*. The word *sorrows* is the Hebrew word *mak'ob*. It basically means *pain*. This can be physical, emotional, or mental. When Jesus died on the cross, it wasn't just to forgive us so we could go to Heaven. When Jesus died on the cross, He bore away our sicknesses and carried away pain on every level. This was all done in a legal dimension. The cross of Jesus legally accomplished everything necessary for our healing. The Person of the Holy Spirit is the One who functionally sets in place what Jesus legally did for us. He is the executor of the legal work of Jesus on the cross. When we by faith believe in who Jesus is and what He has done, the Holy Spirit has the right to functionally set in place in our life all Jesus has legally provided for us. We can take this reality and present it in the Courts of Heaven as evidence in behalf of our healing. Should it seem that something is resisting us from being healed, this is a good practice. We plead our case for healing based on the legal work of Jesus on the cross and the Person of the Holy Spirit's present-day function to administer this into our lives. We are now by faith accessing all that has judicially been provided for us. Should satan bring any case against us seeking to deny what is rightfully ours, the blood of Jesus agreed with, will silence that claim.

As I approach Your Courts, Lord, I declare I believe in what You have done on the cross. I present as evidence the work of Jesus in my behalf for my healing. I ask that any voice against me that would seek to deny what is rightfully mine be silenced. I now ask for the Holy Spirit to administer to me all Jesus died for. In Jesus's name, amen.

JESUS THE HEALER

God anointed Jesus of Nazareth with the Holy Spirit and with
power, who went about doing good and healing all who were
oppressed by the devil, for God was with Him. —Acts 10:38

To be healed, we must first be established in who is the healer and who is the one who afflicts with sickness. This verse clearly defines the two separate parties and their functions. Jesus has come to do good and heal, while the devil is the one who oppresses with sickness. If we have questions about who the author of sickness is, then this can hinder us in our endeavors in the Courts of Heaven to be healed. There are portions of Christianity that would believe God *uses* sickness to discipline and work in His people. Nothing could be further from the truth. Sickness is from the devil, and its torments come from him. Only good and perfect gifts come from God (James 1:17). We must be able to stand before the Courts of Heaven and make these statements without hesitation or dispute in our minds. This requires an awareness of God's Word and a revelation in our heart of His goodness. People are only sick for one reason: satan is taking advantage of something and using it to work against a person. If that sickness is a result of a legal case against us, we must undo that before God can heal, even though all that is necessary for our healing has already been provided (2 Pet. 1:3). We should come before His Courts and establish that Jesus is the Healer, anointed by God. The result can be that what we know Him to be will manifest in our lives.

> *As we stand before Your Courts, O Lord, we decree that Jesus*
> *is our Healer. Satan is the one who afflicts with sickness. We*
> *therefore come out of agreement with him through any belief*
> *that God would use sickness. We ask from the Court that who*
> *Jesus is as Healer would now manifest in our lives. In Jesus's*
> *name, amen.*

HEALED BY HIS STRIPES

*...who Himself bore our sins in His own body on the tree, that
we, having died to sins, might live for righteousness—by whose
stripes you were healed.* —1 Peter 2:24

We *were* healed. Not that we are going to be healed or are even now being healed. We are told we *were healed*. This is the legal status we have before God. When Jesus took the stripes on His back, He was legally purchasing our healing. This is why the verse speaks in the past tense. We were healed when Jesus suffered the agony, beating, and stripes that were laid on Him. This means that everything necessary for us to be healed has already been accomplished. If we can believe in what has legally been done, then we can see the Holy Spirit, the anointing of God come and minister that healing present tense into our lives. It is very much like coming to a realization my father bought and purchased a piece of land. The deed and title are still clearly in his name. There is also a will betrothing to me everything pertaining to his estate. It is all legally mine. I, however, must aggressively approach a court to have a judge render a decision that concludes that it is mine. There would be a settling of any argument from another that it belonged to someone else. This is what we do in the Courts of Heaven when contending for healing. We can present before the Courts that Jesus purchased healing for us through the beating He took in our place. He has *willed* this to us through His blood and body. As we present this before the Courts, every argument to question the legitimacy of our healing is silenced. We are healed!

> *As I stand before the Courts of Heaven, I remind the Courts that
> when Jesus died and was beaten, my healing was purchased. I
> remind the Courts that this has been willed to me through the
> body and blood of the Lamb Himself. I, therefore, ask the Courts*

of Heaven to render a decision that I receive and am healed through the work of Jesus and the power of the Holy Spirit. In Jesus's name, amen.

HEALED THEM ALL

When evening had come, they brought to Him many who were demon-possessed. And He cast out the spirits with a word, and healed all who were sick, that it might be fulfilled which was spoken by Isaiah the prophet, saying: "He Himself took our infirmities and bore our sicknesses." —Matthew 8:16–17

Jesus healed all who were sick. This was done as a demonstration and fulfillment of Isaiah 53:4, which declared Jesus's sacrifice would be sufficient for complete and total healing. Jesus had not yet died on the cross in the natural. However, He had already been *"slain from the foundation of the world"* (Rev. 13:8). This was adequate for God to release healing to all who came to Him. God was absolutely confident that His Son would go to the cross. It was already agreed upon and prepared that this would occur. Based on Jesus's future complete obedience, the manifestation of God's healing power was seen in an unrestricted way. Those who were brought or came to Jesus were healed. When the Bible says He *"healed all who were sick,"* clearly this doesn't mean everyone on the planet got healed. No! This means all who came and were brought to Him were healed. To apprehend the promises of God and the provision of God from the cross, we must come to Him. None were denied. All were healed that came believing in Jesus and His power to deliver. Even Jesus's future work on the cross was sufficient to heal all who came believing. If this was true before Jesus's died, how much so now after He has died. Regardless of the condition, may we believe who Jesus is and what He has done legally for us. We can be healed.

Thank You, Lord, that all were healed. I thank You that Your cross was a legal transaction that purchased complete healing. Even before You died, people were healed. Thank You that Your cross and sacrifice are speaking now in the Courts for my healing. In Jesus's name, amen.

LOOSED!

And behold, there was a woman who had a spirit of infirmity eighteen years, and was bent over and could in no way raise herself up. But when Jesus saw her, He called her to Him and said to her, "Woman, you are loosed from your infirmity." And He laid His hands on her, and immediately she was made straight, and glorified God. —Luke 13:11–13

Jesus did two things to bring healing to this woman. He *loosed* her from the infirmity that was claiming her. The word *loosed* is the Greek word *apolyō*. This word can have legal connotations. It means "to free fully, pardon, divorce," among other things. When Jesus spoke to the woman, He undid what was legally claiming a right to own her and therefore hold her. This had been happening for eighteen years. In a moment, because Jesus dealt with a legal issue, she was freed. He *cancelled* her debt. He *dissolved* the devil's contract with her that let him hold her in this condition. He also *decreed* a divorce from satanic powers. This is what this word can imply. When Jesus said, *"you are loosed,"* He broke and dismissed the demonic powers that had claimed the legal right to torment her with this condition. The other thing Jesus did was He *touched* her. The *touch* of Jesus was now free to bring healing because the legal right of satan was revoked. Without the revoking of the right satan was claiming, the *touch* would not have worked or brought healing. Jesus understood how to remove the claims of satan so the power of the anointing on His life could bring healing.

> *Lord, as we approach Your Courts, we ask that any and all legal rights satan might be claiming to hold us in bondage would now be revoked. Because of who You are and what You have done, allow me to be loosed that Your touch might bring life and healing. In Jesus's name, amen.*

FORGIVEN AND HEALED

"But that you may know that the Son of Man has power on earth to forgive sins"—He said to the paralytic, "I say to you, arise, take up your bed, and go to your house." Immediately he arose, took up the bed, and went out in the presence of them all, so that all were amazed and glorified God, saying, "We never saw anything like this!" —Mark 2:10–12

After Jesus had forgiven the man's sins, He then released healing to him. It was this man's sins that had him in this paralytic state. Not all sickness is a result of personal sin, but some are. If this is the case, then only when the legal right the enemy is claiming based on the sin is dealt with, can someone get healed and stay healed. So many *lost* healings can be traced to this. If someone gets healed but then *loses* their healing, it can be because there is something legal that is causing the problem. The anointing and faith allowed healing to come, however, the devil claimed a legal right to revisit it again. If sickness is a result of a legal attack against someone, then only when they deal with that issue can healing be received and maintained. When Jesus spoke forgiveness to this man, the legal right satan was working against him was removed. Jesus could then proclaim, *"Arise, take up your bed, and go to your house."* What a powerful miracle that caused people to stand in absolute wonder and amazement. As legal rights against us are revoked, everything Jesus died for us to have can be ours, including healing!

As I approach Your Courts, Lord, I ask that any legal claim against me that would hinder healing now be removed. I ask that I might be forgiven by Your blood for any and all trespasses. Allow then Your voice and Word to release healing that will be maintained and sustained. In Jesus's name, amen.

THE PRAYER OF FAITH

*Is anyone among you sick? Let him call for the elders of the
church, and let them pray over him, anointing him with oil in
the name of the Lord. And the prayer of faith will save the sick,
and the Lord will raise him up. And if he has committed
sins, he will be forgiven.* —James 5:14–15

The prayer of faith from the leaders of the church, we are told, will cause God's healing flow to minister to any that are sick. They are to symbolically anoint with natural oil that the real spiritual anointing of God will touch the afflicted person. As they pray, they are to pray in faith. We are told that if we ask anything without doubting, we can have what we ask (Mark 11:23). Elders and leaders in the church are those who should be keeping themselves in a place of faith. When they do, they are able to pray strong prayers of faith that will release the healing life of God. Notice that in this process, if sin is the reason for the sickness, it will be forgiven. This is necessary if the sickness is connected to a legal right the devil is claiming. As the sick person is prayed for, it is appropriate to help discern any legal complaint the devil has. When this is repented of, forgiven, and cleansed, healing is free to flow. This person is not only healed physically but is freed spiritually to walk in the newness of life that belongs to us as believers. It is true that so often sickness is connected to a legal claim of the devil against us. Once this is renounced and removed, healing can and will be our portion.

*As we come before Your Courts, O Lord, we humble ourselves
before those whom You have set. We ask that You use them to
minister Your healing life to us. Also, we ask that any sin satan
would use to afflict us would be forgiven and dismissed from our
lives. Thank You, Lord, for Your healing touch, in Jesus's name,
amen.*

SIN NO MORE

Afterward Jesus found him in the temple, and said to him,
"See, you have been made well. Sin no more, lest a worse
*thing come upon you." —*John 5:14

After Jesus healed the man who had been sick for thirty-eight years and had been waiting on the stirring of the waters at the Pool of Bethesda, He found him in the temple. This was a good thing. This means the man was bringing an offering and worshipping the Lord for his healing. He was acknowledging God and thanking Him for his healing even though he didn't know who Jesus was (John 5:10–13). Jesus found him in the temple and spoke this word to him. He told him to not sin anymore. His sin was the reason why the sickness had come on him. Jesus was letting him know that if he was to maintain his healing, he had to make sure he didn't grant the devil anymore legal rights. We can see clearly from Scripture that many times sickness is connected to us having given satan a legal right to visit us with these diseases. The only way to be healed if this is the reason is to repent and stay free from these sins. We don't know what the man's sin was. All we know is it had led to thirty-eight years of suffering and incapacitation. Jesus warned him that should he enter that sin again, even something worse than the last thirty-eight years would come upon him. When we understand the Courts of Heaven, we will press into new levels of holiness. Not just because we want to please the Lord, but also so we can stay free from satan's devices against us. When we walk holy, we keep ourselves separated from the cruelties of the devil. Jesus's healing life is free to flow into us.

> *Lord, as we approach Your Courts, allow new realms of holiness*
> *to overtake us. May we walk free from sin, that satan would have*
> *no rights to visit us with sickness and disease. Thank You, Lord,*
> *for Your forgiveness, but also for Your power to walk in freedom*
> *and liberty from sin. In Jesus's name, amen.*

LIVE AGAIN

Then they took away the stone from the place where the dead man was lying. And Jesus lifted up His eyes and said, "Father, I thank You that You have heard Me. And I know that You always hear Me, but because of the people who are standing by I said this, that they may believe that You sent Me." Now when He had said these things, He cried with a loud voice, "Lazarus, come forth!" —John 11:41–43

Clearly on the way to the tomb of Lazarus Jesus had been praying. He actually says that the prayer He prayed at the tomb wasn't for Him or even Lazarus. It was for the people who were there listening and watching. He said that the Father had *already heard* Him. He wanted the people to know that what was about to happen was a result of the business Jesus had already conducted in the spirit world with and through the Father. Lazarus died prematurely and before his appointed time. The devil had to have discovered a legal right to do this. Jesus through His prayers, before He stood at the tomb, had dealt with the legal rights satan had claimed. He had stood before the Father and seen the devil's claims dismissed. Now all Jesus did was utter the proclamation of *"Lazarus, come forth"* (John 11:43). The result was the one who had been dead for four days came to life, out of the tomb and back to the life of his family. What a powerful miracle. It, however, was a result of Jesus having revoked the legal claims of satan to hold Lazarus in death. He then could simply speak the word and see him brought back to life. As we undo every judicial issue that satan would bring, the resurrection life of God can flow to bring healing to our bodies. We can be restored because of our judicial activity and the release of the power of God.

As we approach Your Courts, Lord, we ask that any claim of the devil to bring any form of death against us would be dismissed. We repent for any and all agreements that would allow his cruelties to operate. Thank You that as these are removed, the declaration of Your life will cause Your healing to flow. In Jesus's name, amen.

LEGAL OR ILLEGAL

*Most assuredly, I say to you, he who does not enter the sheepfold
by the door, but climbs up some other way, the same is a thief
and a robber.* —John 10:1

When contending for healing in the Courts of Heaven, we must discern if satan is doing something legally or illegally. He actually works from both places. We are told in First Peter 5:8 that satan devours as our *adversary*, or in the Greek *antidikos*. This word means "one who brings a lawsuit." In other words, satan is our *legal opponent*. Satan, however, is also a thief and a robber. This is illegal. Satan will seek to operate from both places. If satan is operating as a thief and a robber, or a bully who is just seeing what he can get away with, we simply need to take our authority, operate in faith, and release the anointing for healing to flow. If we do this but see no change, then we should conclude that the sickness is a result of a legal issue. We then need to examine things by the Spirit of God and see what claim the enemy might be making that would cause this sickness to land against us. Many times the devil is operating from an illegal place. He is simply trying to hinder, handicap, and even bring destruction and death to us. His hatred for us is perfect. We don't have to suffer though. Quite often all we need to do is pray the prayer of faith to see Jesus's provision of healing flow (James 5:15). If we give our best efforts to this, but healing seems to allude us, then we should ask the Lord for His wisdom in regard to what satan might be claiming against us. As we do, God will show us how to approach the Courts and see these rights revoked. Healing will be revealed and manifest.

> *As we approach Your Court, O Lord, I ask that we might discern
> the source of any sickness and disease. Help us, Lord, to know if
> satan is operating legally or illegally. As we do, help us to know
> how to administer Your healing life and see health and wholeness
> restored. In Jesus's name, amen.*

THE ANOINTING OIL

*It shall come to pass in that day that his burden will be taken
away from your shoulder, and his yoke from your neck, and the
yoke will be destroyed because of the anointing oil.*
—Isaiah 10:27

When we contend for any breakthrough from the Lord, we need His anointing. This is also true in the realm of healing. It is the anointing of God that brings healing to our lives and bodies. Sickness and disease can be a yoke of bondage that satan uses to control and dominate us. We need the anointing of God to destroy that yoke. The word *oil* is the Hebrew word *shemen*. It means *grease, fat*. Of course this is where grease comes from, the fat attached to meat. However, the only way we get grease from fat is to cook something or heat it up. This would mean that the anointing that destroys the yoke comes from the heated places we walk through. In other words, as we walk in the pressures and stresses of life, it pulls from us the anointing oil that has the power to destroy the yoke of bondage. This included sickness and disease. All of us walk through hard places. The issue is do we allow these places to activate and pull out of us the anointing that is in us? When we received the Holy Spirit, we received the anointing that comes from Him. The difficult places we walk in can be used by God to teach us to use this anointing to overcome. As we do this, *grease/oil* that destroys every yoke is brought forth in power.

> *As we stand before Your Courts, Lord, we ask that the hard places
> we walk in would allow us to have Your grease brought out of our
> lives. May we be used to carry an anointing that breaks every
> bondage, including sickness. May we choose to use that which is
> in us, and may it be recorded before Your Courts that this has
> been done. In Jesus's name, amen.*

GRACE FOR GRACE

And of His fullness we have all received, and grace for grace.
—John 1:16

We are told that we have received grace that we might be able to embrace grace! What a wonderful thought. God even helps us with His grace to be able to not miss the grace He would pour into our lives. Grace isn't just something we get saved by. Grace is the empowerment of God in our lives on every level. Through His grace, we are saved, gifted, empowered, and even ushered into the next life. His grace is truly amazing. However, we can be denied His grace if we are arrogant and proud. We are told in James 4:6 that *"God resists the proud, but gives grace to the humble."* This means that the Courts of Heaven must consider us humble before the wonderful grace that is necessary for this life and the one to come can be ours. We must humbly approach the Lord and ask that *more grace* be ours. We should ask that we could be judged and esteemed as those who walk humbly with their God and with others in our life. When we do this, the abundant grace of God will come over us. However, if we become prideful and resistant, we can cut ourselves off from the wonderful kindness of who God is. May we approach His Courts and ask for this abundant grace to be ours.

> *Lord, as we come before Your Courts, we request the abundance of Your grace. We would humbly declare that we need Your grace. Without Your grace we are incapable of maneuvering our life. We ask that we might be found yielded and humble before You and others. In Jesus's name, amen.*

DEATH AND GRACE

But we see Jesus, who was made a little lower than the angels,
for the suffering of death crowned with glory and honor, that
He, by the grace of God, might taste death for everyone.
—Hebrews 2:9

Even Jesus needed grace to accomplish His assignment from God. His ability to die was empowered by the grace of God. His transition from this natural life to the afterlife was a result of the grace of God bestowed on Him. Jesus only *tasted* death. This is because He did not die forever. He died, rose again, and is alive for evermore. However, His ability to walk through the death experience was a result of the grace of God on His life. So it is with us. Unless Jesus's second coming prevents it, we will all die. The good news is that those who belong to Jesus do not die absent of the influence of God. In the time of death there will be grace to transition from this life to the next. It will not be a time of sorrow and dread but rather a time of expectation. Ecclesiastes 7:1 declares that the day of our death can be better than the day of our birth. For those who have faithfully served the Lord, this time will be filled with the grace of God. We have a picture of one dying and being escorted by the angels into the presence of the Lord. The poor beggar in the story that Jesus told was carried by the angels into God's presence (Luke 16:22). This is a depiction of the grace of God. Just like Jesus, we are preordained to live forever. Anything we have to do with death will involve the grace of God. Don't dread that which is to come. Believe that God's grace is sufficient in all things.

Lord, as I stand in Your Courts, I beseech You for the grace of God
to increase and operate in my life. May I live my life empowered
by Your grace, and at the time of my death, may I walk through
it with Your grace as my companion. Thank You so much for this
confidence and assurance. In Jesus's name, amen.

SUFFICIENT GRACE

*Concerning this thing I pleaded with the Lord three times
that it might depart from me. And He said to me, "My grace is
sufficient for you, for My strength is made perfect in weakness."
Therefore most gladly I will rather boast in my infirmities, that
the power of Christ may rest upon me.*
—2 Corinthians 12:8–9

Grace is essential to our overcoming life. Paul sought the Lord three times to deliver him from an unpleasant and even harassing thing. However, the Lord refused to do that, instead giving Paul grace to endure the hardship associated with this affliction. God allowed the suffering of Paul that he might be inundated with the grace of God he received during this trouble. This is a marvelous truth. When we walk through things that we don't see deliverance from for a season, we are being impregnated with new levels of grace. When God chooses not to deliver us in the moment, He instead releases levels of grace that let us deal with the situation we are in. We are therefore able to endure while being saturated in increasing realms of grace. So in fact, sometimes the suffering we experience is that which God is entrusting us with that we might carry great dimensions of His grace. After the place we have walked in is over, this grace will still be a part of our life and the breakthrough it brings to us and others. We must learn to be thankful in all things, even unpleasant places. God is working in us a far greater weight of His glory (2 Cor. 4:17).

*As we approach Your Court, Lord, we thank You for the places
You allow us to walk through. In these places, O God, would You
work into our lives a great grace that will reside after the trial is
over. Thank You for this grace from Your graciousness. In Jesus's
name, amen.*

ABOUNDING GRACE

Moreover the law entered that the offense might abound. But where sin abounded, grace abounded much more.
—Romans 5:20

The grace of God is always greater than the need it is sent to meet. There is no sin that grace can't forgive. There is no destruction that grace can't restore. There is no death that grace can't promise life and deliver it. The law magnified the offense. Grace on the other hand is the answer to how big the offense or sin would seem. This is why Paul declared that he was the chief of sinners (1 Tim. 1:15). He declared God saved him so he could be an example. If the Lord's grace was able to redeem Paul, then anyone is redeemable. There is nothing or no one unreachable through the grace of God. What a glorious, liberating truth and reality. This means that no matter what someone has done, there is grace for that person. If we could only realize the great love that God has for us. He is not looking for a reason to judge and annihilate us. He has a reason to redeem us. The reason is the grace and truth that came through Jesus Christ (John 1:17). Simply believe in who He is and what He has done. Let this belief work deeply in your life until the grace of God fashions the nature of God in you. This is the wonderful truth and marvels of His grace.

> *As we approach Your Courts, Lord, we celebrate Your grace. Thank You that where sin abounds in all its ugliness, grace does much more abound in all its beauty. May this grace work deeply in our lives from the very Courts of Heaven. You are not looking for a reason to judge us, Lord. Your grace has given You the reason to redeem us. Thanks so much. In Jesus's name, amen.*

About Robert Henderson

Robert Henderson is a global apostolic leader who operates in revelation and impartation. His teaching empowers the Body of Christ to see the hidden truths of Scripture clearly and apply them for breakthrough results. Driven by a mandate to disciple nations through writing and speaking, Robert travels extensively around the globe, teaching on the apostolic, the Kingdom of God, the "Seven Mountains" and most notably, the Courts of Heaven. He has been married to Mary for 40 years. They have six children and five grandchildren. Together they are enjoying life in beautiful Waco, TX.